WHICH SIDE ARE YOU ON?

Ken Loach and His Films

ANTHONY HAYWARD

BLOOMSBURY

First published 2004
This paperback edition published 2005

Copyright © 2004 by Anthony Hayward/Profiles International Media

The moral right of the author has been asserted

Bloomsbury Publishing Plc, 38 Soho Square, London W1D 3HB

A CIP catalogue record for this book is available from the British Library

ISBN 0 7475 7412 X

10 9 8 7 6 5 4 3 2 1

All papers used by Bloomsbury Publishing are natural,
recyclable products made from wood grown in
well-managed forests. The manufacturing processes
conform to the environmental regulations of the
country of origin.

Typeset by Hewer Text Ltd, Edinburgh
Printed by Clays Ltd, St Ives plc
www.bloomsbury.com/anthonyhayward

ACKNOWLEDGEMENTS

For their memories of working with Ken Loach, quoted and unquoted, I wish to thank Barry Ackroyd, Dean Andrews, Bernard Archard, Antony Audenshaw, Geoffrey Banks, Ray Beckett, Terry Bird, Ellis Birk, Eva Birthistle, Paul Bonner, Richard Booth, David Bradley, Melvyn Bragg, Charlie Brown, Julie Brown, Packie Byrne, Ken Campbell, Robert Carlyle, Dave Chatterley, Don Christopher, Jimmy Coleman, Martin Compston, Paul Copley, Deirdre Costello, Tom Craig, Richard Creasey, Ali De Souza, Charles Denton, Justin Dukes, Joe Duttine, Glynn Edwards, Elaine Mackenzie Ellis, Peter Eyre, Lucy Fleming, Liz Forgan, Jane Freeman, Tony Garnett, Debra Gillett, Sean Glenn, Louise Goodall, John Halstead, Gabrielle Hamilton, Nicholas Harrison, Karen Henthorn, Sally Hibbin, Tom Hickey, Lorraine Hilton, Barry Hines, Richard Hines, Sir Gordon Hobday, Gordon Honeycombe, Nerys Hughes, Steve Huison, Tony Imi, Jeremy Isaacs, Barry Jackson, John Jackson, Roger James, Arbel Jones, Tom Keller, Ruth Kettlewell, Paul Laverty, Colin Leventhal, Patricia Leventon, Gary Lewis, Christopher Logue, Stephen Lord, Simon Macallum, Paul Madden, Suzanne Maddock, Geoffrey Maitland Smith, Doreen Mantle, Kika Markham, Eoin McCarthy, Emer McCourt, Chris Menges, Ann Mitchell, Lee Montague, Jonathan Morris, Billy Murray, Linda Myles, Philip Newman, Rebecca O'Brien, Geoffrey Palmer, Bob Pegg, Ann Penfold, Bob Phillis, Tony Pitts, Stewart Preston, David Puttnam, Mollie Randle, Sandy Ratcliff, Stephen Rea, Jill Richards, Stan Richards, Yvonne Riley, Crissy Rock, Maurice Roëves, Lewis Rudd, George Sewell, Ned Sherrin, Jackie Shinn, Roger Smith, Max Stafford-Clark, Ivan Strasburg, Irving Teitelbaum, Malcolm Tierney, Ricky Tomlinson, Venn Tracey, Vladimir Vega, Doremy Vernon, Chris Webb, Stephen Webber, Colin Welland, Geoffrey Whitehead, Frank Williams, Kate Williams, Anna Wing, Gilbert Wynne and Atta Yaqub. Several of those interviewed for the 'Questions of Censorship' chapter did so off the record and must therefore remain anonymous.

I would also like to express my appreciation to Tom Bower, Steve Bowyer, Bob Clay, Bob Cole, Margaret Crosfield, Rita Cumiskey, Trevor Dolby, Philippa Finnis, Barbara Gatford, Sarah Gristwood, Derek Jeary, Bill Leader, Fred Loach, Lesley Loach, Sue Longfils, Derek Malcolm, Kneale Pearce, Gwendoline Render and John Todd, as well as to Liz Calder, Katherine Greenwood, Holly Roberts and Mary Tomlinson at Bloomsbury Publishing, and staff at the British Film Institute National Library, London, the British Library Newspaper Library, London, Coventry Central Library, Birmingham Central Library, Sutton Coldfield Library, Cardiff Central Library, Leicester Central Reference Library and Northamptonshire Central Library.

Most of all, though, I wish to thank Ken Loach for giving so much of his time for interviews and access to his personal archive. Special thanks are due to Leigh Pickford and all at Sixteen Films, Richard Jeffs and, as always, my wife, Deborah.

Anthony Hayward

CONTENTS

Part IV The Lean Years and Censorship

Part V Renaissance and International Acclaim

Born 1936 in Nuneaton, Warwickshire. Started work as probably the worst actor in Britain. Directed murder plays in repertory theatres before joining the BBC as a trainee in 1963. Since then, due to good fortune and many good working relationships, has managed to survive in cinema and television. A recurring theme in work with writers – e.g. Jim Allen, Barry Hines and Paul Laverty – has been to explore the two curses of the labour movement: Stalinism and Social Democracy, the latter exemplified by the Blairite project of trying to give a radical gloss to hard-line capitalist politics.

Ken Loach's self-written mini-biography, requested, then rejected, by the Foreign Office in 1997 for its Planet Britain CD-Rom and website promoting British culture.

INTRODUCTION

MY FIRST DAY IN THE company of Ken Loach was an experience that I shall not forget. After a morning spent chatting at his North London home, where he quietly acknowledged my muttering of congratulations on his latest picture taking top honour at the previous night's British Independent Film Awards ceremony, we hop on to a bus to go to his production company's West End offices.

As we pass through Camden, a crowd of people is gathered outside Mornington Crescent Tube station. 'Ooh! I'm supposed to be there,' Ken suddenly tells me. 'I said I would speak. Do you mind?' Moving swiftly from the top deck of the bus, we jump off at the next stop and run to the meeting. It is part of a day of action by the Stop the War Coalition pressure group, protesting against the United States' threat – backed by the British government – to attack Iraq as part of its so-called war on terrorism. Labour MP Jeremy Corbyn stretches his hand out to Ken, who shakes it before taking the microphone, as I look after his bag.

Soon, we are on our way again and sharing our thoughts about a television documentary screened a few nights earlier. It revealed that actor and former trade unionist Ricky Tomlinson, who appeared in two of Ken's films, was among many 'subversives' to have been investigated by Special Branch officers and included in MI5 files thirty years earlier. The same programme reported that the late former miners' leader, Joe Gormley, had colluded with the government – echoing the theme of betrayal by the Left frequently seen in Ken's politically charged films over the years, and ironic considering the censorship of his 1980s documentaries about some trade union bosses selling out their members. Polite, mild-mannered and self-effacing as always, Ken does not take the opportunity to blow his own trumpet, however.

Once at the offices of Sixteen Films, good news arrives. Ken's latest picture, *Sweet Sixteen*, released a few weeks earlier with an 18 certificate slapped on it by the British Board of Film Classification, has been reclassified with a 15 rating in the area where the story is set. The very strong language, truthfully reflecting the underbelly of this Clydeside former shipbuilding community, is not too much to take for the good citizens presided over by Inverclyde Council. Ken and producer Rebecca O'Brien clearly scent a small victory but are keen not to appear smug in the way they put out this news to the media.

Over the coming weeks and months, I saw examples of Ken's gentle, courteous character time and again, and it was not surprising that these qualities were invariably spoken of by those who had worked with him. Indeed, the response from actors, collaborators and others involved in his films and television plays was phenomenal. They were not only very willing to speak, but talked of him in such hallowed tones that I often wondered whether I was writing about a saint. However, some revelations about the trickery that Ken uses to elicit such remarkable realism from his performers persuaded me that he might not *quite* qualify for that status. Nevertheless, it was clear that they were happy to do absolutely anything for Ken and many regarded working with him as their most treasured experience.

This is a facet of Ken Loach that makes him one of British cinema's most cherished assets, although he has often been un-appreciated in his own country. It also makes him unusual as a director, as does a background that provided him with no special enthusiasm for watching or making films. Theatre was his first love, and a switch from acting to directing led him into television when work dried up. Arriving at the BBC at the dawn of a new era, when fresh ideas were allowed to flourish under the director-generalship of Hugh Greene, he fell in with a crowd determined to seize the opportunity to shake up British television. Working with producer Tony Garnett and story editor Roger Smith, he became an avid listener and absorbed their left-wing politics. This led him to embrace the social realism of Joan Littlewood's Theatre Workshop.

The gritty depictions of working-class life that he brought to 'The Wednesday Play' were also influenced by stage productions written by the Angry Young Men of the Royal Court Theatre and by the new trend of British 'kitchen sink' films. When that fashion was dumped by the cinema, Loach continued to tread his own path of giving voices to those who were usually denied them in the media and he refused to sentimentalise their plight. With *Up the Junction* and *Cathy Come Home*, he cast no judgment on characters who were at the bottom of the heap, with few choices, and in television he found a medium that could have an unparalleled effect. His documentary style of film-making, using real-life locations, caused a furore among television critics and moral guardians such as Mary Whitehouse: those on screen appeared so real that the truth Loach was telling through drama was a genuine threat to the established order. *Cathy Come Home*, with its revelations about homelessness in Britain, proved that television could trigger a response to a social issue, but its failure to address the politics set Loach and producer Garnett on a new path.

As one of television's brightest young talents, it was inevitable that Loach would be given the chance to make feature films. But the film industry's conventions that he was forced to accept while making *Poor Cow* with another producer served for him as a lesson in how not to direct for the cinema. So, with *Kes*, he established an observational style in which the camera was kept as far away as possible from the performers, who were allowed the space to live the story as if it were real. As part of this aim, Loach established his tradition of casting non-professional actors and those who had similar experiences to their characters', not letting them see complete scripts and throwing in surprises aimed at eliciting 'natural' reactions. The combination of careful casting and creating an atmosphere in which his performers often revealed their feelings and emotions in the most raw and naked way was, ironically, in sharp contradiction to Loach's own reserved manner. For him, the desire to depict reality on screen overrode almost anything, but, when these 'surprises' included the genuine caning of schoolchildren, just as toddlers had been prised away from Carol White as their mother in *Cathy Come Home*, some voiced disquiet about whether such a loyalty to 'realism' could be justified.

Many battles were fought to get *Kes* screened in cinemas at the turn of the 1960s and, despite its success, Loach found it hard to find funding for feature films over the next decade. He made just two and returned to television to direct writer Jim Allen's four-part epic *Days of Hope*, which traced the betrayal of the working class by the trade union and Labour Party leaderships in the years leading up to the General Strike of 1926. This theme of betrayal was a recurring one in Loach and Allen's on-off collaborations over thirty years. The director's work with another writer, Barry Hines, which started with *Kes*, featured scripts containing more implicit messages about working-class life. So he had the benefit of rich and varied material, but his own input was essential to the results: the collaborations were exactly that, with Loach contributing to a shared vision, picking through the words and themes with the writers, and guiding them through rewrites. In the 1990s, he found another such professional partner in writer Paul Laverty.

In between, he suffered a miserable decade of wandering around Wardour Street, home to the British film industry, with a briefcase in his hand, looking for a desk and a sympathetic backer. With Tony Garnett having left for the United States, ending a fifteen-year professional partnership, Loach seemed rudderless. For a while, he turned back to television and found a temporary home at ATV, which became Central Independent Television in an ITV franchise reshuffle. But a switch to making documentaries proved disastrous when the subjects he chose became hot potatoes and the victims of censorship. The notions of impartiality and balance adopted by the Independent Broadcasting Authority, which then regulated commercial television, were based on the fallacy that one view or interpretation could be offset against another to provide truth, whereas the real result was confusion and the safeguarding of Establishment-approved truths.

In *Questions of Leadership*, a series made by Central for screening on Channel Four, Loach sought to give a voice to those trade unionists who were unhappy with their own leaders. The IBA deemed this to be 'one-sided', even though the 'other side' was frequently heard in the media without any such balance, so Channel Four ordered Central to edit down the films and make follow-up programmes to answer the allegations. Although Central's programme-makers did this, its conservative board, under pressure from Robert Maxwell, performed the most effective act of television censorship ever in Britain – behind the smokescreen that the films were potentially defamatory – by deciding that *Questions of Leadership* should not be sent back to Channel Four, and it was never broadcast. Further frustration came with the Royal Court Theatre's decision to ban *Perdition*, a Jim Allen play that marked Loach's return to the theatre after a quarter of a century.

As everything he touched turned sour, Loach began to look unemployable. Hitting rock bottom, he realised he could no longer afford to stick to his anti-capitalist principles, swallowed hard and started directing commercials. It was his lowest point and a humbling one after such great predictions had been made for him twenty years earlier. The making of *Hidden Agenda*, about the Royal Ulster Constabulary's shoot-to-kill policy in Northern Ireland, signposted a return to the cinema that was both prolific and remarkable for its uninterrupted run of successes. With *Riff-Raff*, *Raining Stones* and *Ladybird Ladybird*, which might be seen as big-screen versions of his 'Wednesday Plays', Loach found his way again, charting with humanity – and often humour – the misery and squalor of life as lived by so many in Britain. Year after year, he walked away from European film festivals with top awards and became a darling of cinemagoers across the continent while struggling at home to get widespread distribution of his pictures.

Loach's Spanish Civil War epic, *Land and Freedom*, truly internationalised his work; not only did he depict on screen a landmark in modern European history, but the multinational financing established a framework that continued with future projects and guaranteed him the independence he demanded as a director, without interference from above. Producers Sally Hibbin and Rebecca O'Brien were crucial to this 1990s revival, giving Loach the support that he had lost after the parting of ways with Tony Garnett. With *Bread and Roses*, Loach took up the challenge of filming in the United States, on Hollywood's doorstep, and he furthered his portfolio of British social dramas with the acclaimed *My Name Is Joe* and *Sweet Sixteen*, both set in Scotland and written by Paul Laverty.

Social realism has been the constant thread through all these films and it makes Loach almost impossible to compare with any other director. John Schlesinger could, at the time of his death in 2003, match Loach's film output and longevity, but he chose a different route, which included Hollywood, after being one of the 'kitchen sink' pioneers of the early 1960s. Another British film-maker who found long-term success in Hollywood was Alan Parker, who credited *Cathy Come Home* with inspiring him to direct, but he also followed a populist path. When some compare Mike Leigh to Loach, they do so because of each director's reputation for allowing actors to ad-lib. But the difference is that Leigh's performers start with a blank canvas, whereas Loach's have a well-mapped-out story to follow. Comparisons have also been drawn with a relative newcomer, Michael Winterbottom, who similarly makes low-budget films, sometimes casts unknowns in lead roles and allows them to improvise, and enjoys more attention from cinemagoers on the European mainland than those in Britain. The simple reality is that, regardless of trends, Loach has carved out his own niche, fuelled by the politics of social justice.

A year after my first meeting with Ken Loach, I travelled to Glasgow to watch him directing *Ae Fond Kiss. . .* In a busy day that packed in four locations, his love of film-making was clearly on display and his happy nature rubbed off on everyone around him. In his late sixties, he still clearly relished his chosen job – even lived for it, said one of his crew. Another uttered the oft-repeated remark that this director would prefer making a film without any camera or technicians, a reference to the way in which he guards his performers' space ferociously. Suddenly, as the camera is about to roll, he turns towards me and, with a smile, points to my left. I'm not in the shot – but in his lead actress's eye-line. The filming continues, without any shouts of 'Action!' or 'Cut!' He is known for having the quietest sets anywhere, encouraging his cast to 'live' the experience rather than act it. He later tells me that the priority is to find truth in the performances. Over forty years, it seemed that his devotion to this was undimmed.

PART I

THE EARLY YEARS

I

'AN EAGLE FOR AN EMPEROR
. . . A KESTREL FOR A KNAVE'

DAVID BRADLEY WAS THE Barnsley schoolboy saved from a pre-destined future down the local pit when he was chosen to play Billy Casper in *Kes*, who had no such opportunity. There was no way out either for the miners who died in a pit explosion in the television drama *The Price of Coal*. But, after beginning his working life in the north Warwickshire coalfields where his father and brothers toiled, John Loach – always called Jack – managed to find an escape route and a path that took him to a responsible position on the shop floor in a machine-tool factory. It was, perhaps, as far as he could go in those days, without the benefit of a grammar-school education.

Although he passed the scholarship exam to give him this privilege, his parents would not let him take it up. They could not afford the uniform, and Jack's destiny was to leave school at fourteen and provide a much needed wage for his family. He always remembered that those who went to grammar schools were pre-sented with the unique chance of further education and a place in life, rather than being consigned to the scrapheap of labour fodder for the mines and factories. That was the reality of the system and, later, he reflected bitterly on another boy at his junior school who was able to seize the opportunity and went on to become a head-master. 'I used to come above him in maths,' he complained.[1]

The Loaches were a Warwickshire family of farm labourers who switched to mining when they moved from Exhall to the small market town of Bedworth, called 'Bed'th' by the locals and working class through and through. Its only claims to fame were a group of almshouses built in the eighteenth century, after a local priest left a wad of cash and land to the town, and the fact that the female novelist who wrote under the pseudonym George Eliot was born at nearby Arbury. Light industry was growing up alongside mining, but it was overshadowed by the giant car factories of Jaguar and Rover in Coventry, five miles to the south.

Jack's parents, Walter and Jane, lived in a small terraced house at 17 Newtown Road, where they kept pigs in the back garden and sides of bacon were hung up in the scullery. Born in 1905, one of ten children, Jack started down the mines as an apprentice electrician in the pits between Bedworth and the neighbouring market town of Nuneaton, three miles to the north. This had become the area's major source of employment over the previous 200 years. By the end of the twentieth century, the coalfields would disappear and the heavy industry be replaced by Bermuda Leisure Park, boasting a multiplex cinema, superbowl and four restaurants. But Jack had no intention of hanging around to see even the beginnings of this demise.

Learning a trade gave him the means to break out. He took his new-found skills to the Herbert Machine Tools factory in Coventry, the world's largest business of its type. Run by Alfred Herbert, the son of a wealthy landowner, it was built on the success of its drills and hand lathes, and was to machine tools what Rolls-Royce was to cars. Jack was employed on the plant maintenance as an electrician, before becoming a foreman and then assuming full responsibility for that division. He worked Saturday and Sunday mornings on top of five full days a week, with just two weeks' holiday each year.

In 1933, he married Vivien Hamlin, a hairdresser whose lower-middle-class background put her a short rung above him on the social ladder. Her grandfather had been a baker in the Gloucestershire spa town of Cheltenham and her father, Charles, owned a tailor's shop in Nuneaton and lived there in a semi-detached Edwardian house with his second wife, Kate. On marrying, Jack and Vivien bought a small 1920s semi in the town, at 103 Manor Court Road, an achievement of great pride for the former pit worker. Their only child, Kenneth Charles Loach, was born at nearby Manor Hospital on 17 June 1936. It was the year when the BBC opened the world's first regular television service and the Spanish Civil War started. It was also the tenth anniversary of Britain's bitter General Strike, and the country was now in the depths of economic depression.

When his son was born, Jack was on a short working week, like many others in industry, but was proud that he was never laid off. Vivien gave up hairdressing to bring up her son, as mothers always did then. 'It was certainly what my father wanted,' explained Ken Loach, 'because it would have reflected badly on him if his wife had had to go out to work.'[2]

Despite the uncertainties of the time, Jack clung on to what he knew. 'Once he became a foreman, they wanted him to go "on the staff",' Loach recalled of his father. 'The labour force got their money in cash in their wage packet weekly, whereas the staff were paid monthly by cheque and had benefits such as pension schemes. But he didn't want to give up getting his money weekly and there were questions like whether he would be paid for overtime, so he felt he was better off just as a wage earner. I think he was shrewd and a very bright man, actually.'[3] Later, though, Jack capitulated.

When the young Loach was three, war broke out. As a major manufacturing city, nearby Coventry became one of the Luftwaffe's main targets and, in November 1940, much of the centre was levelled by 400 tons of bombs, which destroyed twenty-one factories, reduced the cathedral to rubble, with only its spire left intact, and killed more than 500 civilians. The Loach family found refuge in the nearest Anderson shelter while the German bombs rained down just miles away. A plan to escape danger by sending Loach and his mother to her sister Irene in the Devon town of Exeter was thwarted when that became the Germans' next target. So close were mother and son to the action that the street in which they were staying was hit and several people killed. The windows of Aunt Irene's were blown in and the Loaches quickly headed back to Nuneaton.

War or no war, Ken had to go to school, and Jack Loach was determined that his son would have every opportunity after seeing his own education hopes dashed. 'That rankled with him all his life,' said Loach. 'Because he hadn't gone to the grammar school, he was fanatical about education.'[4] As a result, from the age of four, Loach attended a co-educational primary school attached to the all-girls' Nuneaton High School.

The big event of the Loach family's year after the war was a one-week holiday in Blackpool, where the source of Loach's practice of using stand-up comedians in straight acting roles can be found. 'We always stayed at the north end,' he recalled, 'because that was seen as slightly more refined than the Pleasure Beach and the goings-on in the centre. There were three piers – the Grand, the Winter Gardens and the Palace – and we used to see a different variety show every night. All the great comics were there: Frank Randle, George Formby, Albert Modley, Jewel and Warriss, Nat Jackley and the female double-act of Ethel Revnell and Gracie West.' These performers left an indelible impression on the young Loach. 'I remember the audience just rocking and rocking, completely hysterical with laughter, and the old fellow laughing until the tears ran down his cheeks,' he recalled. 'It was an extraordinary, collective mirth. That was the place I got the bug for the theatre.'[5]

Another source of amusement for Loach was his father's meticulously laid plans to get to Blackpool on time and in a state of tidy dress. 'My father had two suits,' he explained. 'He travelled in his best suit because he didn't want to get it creased in the case. We would get to the station an hour early and stand around waiting for a steam train, which was belching smoke and smut when it arrived, and he'd be trying to keep his suit clean! Then, when we sat on the beach, he would roll up his trousers to about two inches above his ankles, but that was as far as it went!'[6]

Loach's passion for the theatre was reinforced by visits to pantomimes in Coventry and occasional productions at the Nuneaton Hippodrome. The family lived close to Nuneaton Borough Football Club's ground and his father had a season ticket. Sometimes, he would take his son along but, by his early teens, Loach was more interested in the stage – his enthusiasm for soccer would reappear in his adult life.

In the meantime, the major event of Loach's childhood was taking the scholarship exam that would determine whether he went to Nuneaton's all-boys' King Edward VI Grammar School. Passing it meant that he fulfilled his father's ambition. 'That was a huge thing in our house,' said Loach. 'There was a feeling of "Thank God!". The wicked thing about it was that, from the age of eleven, if you went to a secondary modern or technical school, you were not on a course that would take you to higher education or even to do A-levels – university was out of the question. From a town with a population of sixty to seventy thousand, there were only sixty boys each year who went to the grammar school and had the possibility of going on to university. Everybody knew what it meant. You "passed" or you "failed", and it was talked about in those terms. For the lucky ones who got through, it was a nice way to go, but not at the cost of putting everybody else down as "failures". '[7]

The privilege afforded to Loach as a 'success' was evident to all. 'It had a very distinctive uniform and the ethos of a small public school,' he recalled of King Edward VI. 'There were houses, like a public school, and we played rugby. I'm sure all the kids were bright, although, surprisingly, most of them in my year left at sixteen. There were then two sixth forms – the science and arts ones – and I went into the arts one with only one or two other boys. A dozen did science and the rest left, out of an intake of sixty.'[8]

With six O-levels to his credit, Loach studied English, history and French at A-level. His interest in history was fuelled by a teacher at the grammar school. 'There were some good teachers and, as in every school, some very indifferent ones,' Loach reflected. 'We sent some of them up rotten and I used to make terrible puns, which is a deeply unattractive characteristic. I remember being sat in the wastepaper basket by a maths teacher for one very bad joke.

'The person who really made the difference was a history teacher called Sidney Reed Brett. He wasn't inspirational and not particularly popular, but he was a brilliant teacher and absolutely analytic and rigorous in disentangling the different strands of any topic. He showed you how to make notes and, whatever the topic, you would have root causes, immediate causes, events and results, and a main heading, a sub-heading and, beneath that, "1, 2, 3" and, alongside each of those, "a, b, c". If you had to sub-divide the "a", there would be a little Roman numeral "i". Woe betide you if you got an event mixed up with an immediate cause or an immediate cause somehow slipped into root causes! That was a disciplined way of learning that enables you to see an event with clarity. For people who weren't self-motivated, that teacher might not have had much impact, but four or five of us were keen.

'He gave me books such as Churchill's biography of Marlborough, which was a huge tome! He would say: "Here, read this." It took me about a term to plough through each one, but it was magic stuff. He was a Methodist and wrote a book on John Pym [leader of the Long Parliament during the English Civil War]. He was minded to support the parliamentary cause – he wasn't a royalist – but he wasn't in any way politically radical or, if he was, he never showed it. He was very much a disciplinarian and would have been horrified at the 1960s idea of child-centred learning; he believed you had to be taught how to learn and how to deal with information.'[9]

However, throughout his secondary education, Loach's interest in theatre was becoming all-consuming. For three nights once every three weeks, the touring Midland Theatre Company performed at Nuneaton's Co-Op Hall and the teenager sold programmes there. This enabled him to see the works of late-nineteenth- and early-twentieth-century playwrights such as George Bernard Shaw, Oscar Wilde, Noël Coward and Terence Rattigan, interspersed with the company's occasional versions of London West End hits, which included the farce *Rookery Nook*.

Just thirty miles away was the Bard's home of Stratford-upon-Avon. Often, Loach would undertake a marathon cycle ride there on Saturdays to watch theatrical greats such as John Gielgud, Laurence Olivier, Michael Redgrave, Anthony Quayle and Peggy Ashcroft in matinée performances of Shakespeare classics.

Shakespeare was also the usual diet at Loach's school, where the big event of the year for him was the annual play. 'Of course, the language was difficult,' he recalled, 'but you had to grapple with it. Being forced to learn it was an extraordinarily educative process. The idea that school plays are now about "contemporary" ideas, that they are improvised and the kids tell their own story is not helpful. You can only do the one because you've done the other. That's what it grows out of, that real regard for language and analysis of the play and the role and the conflict and the development; that should be the bedrock. The idea that you just go and spill out yourself on the stage is the opposite of what it should be.'[10] (With this, Loach gives an insight into his approach to drama, which has only ever allowed improvisation that follows the narrative of a script or plot.)

Being part of the spectacle of school plays was the crowning glory for Loach. 'It was just fantastically enjoyable, great fun,' he explained. 'Somebody would be responsible for the make-up and they would put on the old Leichner an inch thick so that these orange schoolboys were striding across the stage with their wooden swords! It had a kind of comic, coarse aspect, but an underlying seriousness to it as well. It was stirring stuff.'[11]

During his sixth-form years, the school performed *Richard II*, with Loach playing Bolingbroke. With his school days running out, an English teacher, Stanley Gibb, suggested that he apply to take a degree at Gibb's former Oxford University college, St Peter's Hall. This meant staying on an extra year at school to retake his failed Latin O-level, which was essential, and to study for the Oxbridge entrance examination, which he passed.

Loach decided to study law, influenced by his father being an avid reader of biographies of QCs, his own knowledge of the legal world not stretching beyond the little he had come across in books, in the cinema and on radio. Re-enactments of famous trials had left an impression on him, mainly through their theatricality.

But there was one more obstacle to be overcome before he could take up his place at Oxford: national service. Thinking it the soft option, Loach chose to join the RAF. He started with a week at Cardington, in Bedfordshire, where uniforms were handed out, before travelling to Padgate, in the Cheshire countryside near Warrington, for a six-week course that included the ritual of square-bashing. 'The sergeant and corporals really gave us a hard time,' he recalled. 'They tried to build it up as a terrible experience, make you scared about it and instil a certain amount of apprehension, which they did. We were all quaking in our uncomfortable boots at the prospect. The psychology was to make you into a unit that did what you were told without question. The only way they could do that was to put you through it, make you feel there was no way out. And there literally *was* no way out – you couldn't leave camp, except on Sundays. If you were religious, you could go to a service if there wasn't one on the camp. I suddenly became religious and went to a Methodist church, where they gave me tea and thought they had a convert, but it didn't last! It was a way of getting out and meeting people, but they probably knew I was there as an escape.'[12]

Although joining the RAF proved not to be so cushy, Loach later reflected that he had not suffered from the experience. 'It was a wholly inflated, artificial harshness, but I don't think it was very harmful in the long term,' he said. 'We did all the stupid things, like painting coal black, digging the garden with an eating fork and cutting the grass with nail scissors. Of course it's stupid, but there's a humorous side to it. Some people got very depressed, though, and the NCOs would always tell you that somebody from the previous lot had committed suicide, but I think that was a myth put about in order to scare you!'[13]

After six weeks of 'short, sharp shock', all recruits had to learn a trade. So, in the late autumn of 1955, Loach was sent to Credenhill, near Hereford, to train as a typist. This was deemed a skill for the more studious types who were due to go on to university. Over the next few months, the nineteen-year-old from Nuneaton sat among the rows and rows of young airmen behind old-fashioned type-writers learning to touch-type. (Memories of typing 'The quick brown fox' lingered, but the skill was allowed to die as the years went by.) Long hours of laborious typing were occasionally re-lieved by lessons in office organisation.

A greater relief for Loach was the opportunity to pursue his interest in theatre. 'We put on a play with the officers' wives, who were hugely desirable but out of reach,' he said. 'We did *While the Sun Shines*, a Terence Rattigan comedy, and the whole camp came to watch. Unfortunately, it was in an aircraft hangar that had an echo like St Paul's Cathedral. We had a little stage in the middle and our voices just boomed out and I don't think anybody heard a word!'[14]

With a skill under his belt, Loach was sent to RAF Syerston, in the Nottinghamshire countryside, six miles south-west of Newark. It had opened in 1940 as a bomber station and, since the war, was used to train pilots. For the next eighteen months, Loach worked as a typist in the equipment section's office, sharing a barracks with twenty-one other young men from all over the country. 'It was uniquely boring, typing equipment schedules and letters from offi-cers in charge of the section,' he recalled. 'In the barracks, I slept in a bed next to a lad from Middlesbrough who was an avid smoker. He would smoke last thing at night and first thing in the morning. When you did guard duty and patrolled the camp at night – to keep the enemy away! – you would go in and wake up those on an early call, at about five-thirty, and they reeked of humanity and stale smoke. For all of us, it was very savage after such a sheltered life at home with our parents. The old phrase was that it would knock the corners off you and it certainly did. It changed you, and its effect on individuals, by and large, was very good. You did have to put yourself second and realise you weren't the most important person in the world and just get on with it. Otherwise, your life was hell.'[15]

For Loach, coming to terms with national service was a necessity and the prospect of studying at Oxford University seemed a long way off. But respite came once more through amateur dramatics after he discovered Nottingham's Co-Op Arts Centre (since re-named Nottingham Arts Theatre). Just as he had previously 'found religion', Loach hit on another way to get time away from the camp. Those RAF men who intended to continue their education could get passes allowing them to attend evening classes. He enrolled for an acting course in Nottingham and travelled the ten miles each way by bus twice a week. His teacher, John Wills, produced plays for the Co-Op Arts Centre's junior section and asked Loach if he would like to take part. Michael Jayston was another involved in the group (under his real name, Michael James), and John Bird had just left. Throughout many productions, Loach was usually cast as old men.

Loach in *The Guinea Pig* at the Co-Op Arts Centre, Nottingham, 1957

When one of the other aspiring actors, Roy Harris, decided to leave home and rent a flat, Loach agreed to share with him. 'It was part of a cow shed and incredibly damp,' he recalled. 'The sheets were like blotting paper and there were spiders as big as your fist. We rented it for a pound a week and I lived out of camp illegally for three months. It meant I didn't have to go back at night, but I had to get the first bus of the morning, at about half-past five, from Nottingham to Syerston.'[16] Loach slipped back into the base by mingling with outside contractors who arrived early each day, but he was eventually rumbled and suffered a loss of privileges.

A more successful ruse was Loach's excuse for missing the weekly parade. 'That was the real bugbear and, to my great joy, I discovered a Latin class in Nottingham on Saturday mornings,' he explained. 'I was going to do law at Oxford, so Latin was important. I managed to get a chitty to allow me to attend, which meant that I didn't have to take part in the parade. I went to the first one, practically no one else turned up and the further-education organisation putting on the class cancelled it. But I already had my chitty, so every Saturday morning I went home to my parents in Nuneaton or, more often, met up in Nottingham with my friends from the theatre, these budding thespians.'[17]

In the autumn of 1957, with his national service completed, Loach headed for Oxford and his law degree. Getting the chance to study among the dreaming spires of one of Britain's two leading university cities was an achievement for a young man of his humble origins in the late 1950s. 'It was unbelievable for me, a lad from Nuneaton, to go to Oxford,' said Loach, 'and the town itself was stunningly beautiful, not at all touristy, like it is now.'[18]

His ambitions were lofty, too. 'I thought I would go to the Bar, but it was a fantasy,' he explained. 'I didn't really know what was involved when I started to study law and I really found it difficult to get interested. I hadn't written an essay or done academic work for two years, so I had completely lost the hang of it. I really worked at the first essay I did and it received a good response from the tutor but, after that, it was knackering. There were other, more exciting things to do.'[19]

There was no incentive for Loach to get back into the practice of academic work when there was a ready-made distraction – student theatre. There were two organisations: the Oxford University Dramatic Society (OUDS), which performed major classical works, and the Experimental Theatre Club, which put on contemporary plays, as well as a musical or revue in the summer term.

On seeing audition notices for an ETC production of Tennessee Williams's *Summer and Smoke* go up during the first week, Loach secured a one-line part in a tea-party scene with Dudley Moore, who was studying at Magdalen College. 'He stole the scene completely,' recalled Loach. 'He was just brilliant and funny.' Moore was to go on to great heights as a comedy actor, and Loach himself realised that they were in a privileged position. 'If you were ambitious, and I was embarrassingly ambitious, the big thing was to break out of the college circle and make a mark at university level,' he said. 'Entirely by good fortune, I was in a university production, as opposed to a college production, so it was taken far too seriously by national critics. They would come along and review it in the *Telegraph* or *The Times*. Suddenly, in my first term, I was in a play that was getting national reviews. I thought: "This beats typing equipment letters and certainly beats law." I was hooked!'[20]

With growing enthusiasm came bigger roles. During the second term, Loach was cast as the king's companion, Kent, in *King Lear*, a marathon, four-hour OUDS production directed by an American post-graduate, Stephen Aaron. Others who appeared in the play and went on to find success included Vernon Dobtcheff (Lear), who became a prolific screen character actor, Michael Simpson (Gloucester), who was to run Birmingham Repertory Theatre and direct television programmes such as *Rumpole of the Bailey*, Charles Lewsen (The Fool), who had a long stage, film and television career, Patrick Garland (Edmund), who became a leading West End theatre producer, and David Webster (Edgar), who played police cadet Jamie MacPherson in *Dixon of Dock Green*, before switching careers to work as a barrister, then a judge.

The influence of Stephen Aaron on Loach was significant. 'He got us to write out scenes in our own words, to understand what the content was, and then to improvise the scenes in rehearsal so that we understood what we were saying,' he explained. 'That's something that stuck in my mind. It was much more influential than I ever thought it would be.'[21] After grappling with the language of Shakespeare at school, this was a progression that Loach would adopt in his later work as a director, enabling actors to stick to a story but deliver the lines with realism, without their sounding rehearsed.

With Dudley Moore and others, Loach peformed in a revue, *All for Money* – the title being a parody of the seventeenth-century John Dryden play *All for Love* – at the Edinburgh Festival during the summer of 1958. He was becoming immersed in student theatre, to the exclusion of everything else. 'It took over my life,' he admitted. 'I became secretary of the Experimental Theatre Club and president of OUDS.'[22] He also directed productions during his last eighteen months at university, including plays by Shakespeare and Tennessee Williams.

It was a dangerous path that spelled near-disaster in his second year at Oxford, when he was threatened with having his grant withdrawn after failing to attend a single lecture. An attempt to switch courses, to history, was thwarted when the lecturer refused to take him. Sticking with law, Loach rescued himself by ensuring that he completed the compulsory weekly essay, often copied from Harold Burnett, an undergraduate in the senior year. 'He was very diligent and saved my bacon on many occasions,' said Loach. 'Fortunately, the tutor set students the same subjects each year!'[23]

Continuing his 'fantasy' of going to the Bar, Loach joined Gray's Inn, one of the four Inns of Court in London, and started eating dinners there, which would eventually allow him to take the Bar exams. 'It was a wholly bizarre, ludicrous thing,' he reflected, 'because you went along just to eat the dinner. It was so rigidly formal. You sat at long refectory tables and, at the top, right-hand corner were some senior barristers who happened to be eating in that night as senior members of the Inn. Each group of four people at a table was called a mess, with a junior member in the bottom, right-hand corner. The most junior member of the most junior mess, who was the last person to arrive, had to stand up at some point after the meal and ask the most senior person of the most senior mess for permission to smoke. The joke, which had gone on from time immemorial, was that Mr Senior from the senior mess pretended not to hear Mr Junior from the junior mess. It was a most archaic ritual. Until he got heard, nobody was allowed to leave. It could take half-an-hour and we would miss trains back to Oxford because this old fart at the top pretended not to hear the other man. The ironic twist was that most of the students were black kids from the Commonwealth and, invariably, there would be a young black man trying to make himself heard by a pompous judge or barrister.'[24]

Loach never took his Bar exams: theatre continued to consume him. 'He was very good in the title role of Strindberg's *The Father*, which established him as an actor,' recalled Roger Smith, who was reading English at New College, Oxford, edited the university magazine, *Isis*, acted alongside Loach in productions and later played an important part in his career. 'Ken wasn't at all political then. He was just interested in being an actor and liked a good laugh. He was much more involved in theatre than I was. I saw him as another one doomed for the acting profession.'[25] Smith mixed with a much more politically heavyweight crowd, sharing digs in Oxford's car-making suburb of Cowley with Dennis Potter and Kenith Trodd. 'We were the left-wing radicals,' he said. They even staged a production on the early Aldermaston marches, which established the Campaign for Nuclear Disarmament, but Loach did not take part. 'I liked him,' said Smith, 'but politics seemed a long way away from him then.'[26]

Politics had been no part of Loach's experience during his childhood in Nuneaton; it was never discussed. 'My father wasn't very political,' explained Loach. 'He took the *Daily Express*, which was a Tory newspaper, and probably voted Conservative. My mother would have done what he did. When I was fifteen, they had a mock election at school and I stood as a Young Conservative, just because I read the newspaper that came into our house. Later, I think my father became disillusioned with the management in his own factory, who he saw run it into the ground, so I think his respect for the ruling class diminished. He wasn't a strong union man, though. Considering where he began, he had done rather well for himself and thought that, if he could do it, anyone could. It's a very flawed argument.'[27]

During his final term at Oxford, Loach played Angelo in a production of *Measure for Measure* – recalled by fellow student actor Gordon Honeycombe, two years his junior, as 'thin and nervy'[28] – but he swotted hard for six weeks to prepare for his exams, 'cramming' facts in the hope of salvaging something from three years spent in one of Britain's elite education establishments. 'I did want to get a degree, for my father's sake,' he said. Although he passed, he left Oxford with only a third, to the despair of Jack Loach. 'I think the old man was very upset, really,' said Loach. 'To have a son reading law at Oxford was a big thing and he knew I could have done better. I'd obviously blown it.' Acting was the young Loach's ambition. He recalled, 'My father said to me: "It's your life and you have to lead it as you wish, but you'll never have two pennies to rub together." He couldn't understand that I'd had a chance and thrown it away.'[29]

2

LIVING THEATRE

BY THE SUMMER OF 1960, Oxford University was consigned to an entry in Ken Loach's CV, but the associations he made there were not over. Shortly after taking his exams, he and David Webster returned to the Edinburgh Festival to perform the German playwright Schiller's *Wallenstein* trilogy, which they edited down to one play, and *From Jacqueline with Love*, a musical based on a French drama, with songs written by another former Oxford student, Herbert Chappell.

However, the reality of stepping into the big, wide world beyond Oxford could not be delayed much longer. When another university peer, Richard Booth – whose mother's family founded the Yardley perfume organisation – offered to finance a new theatre company, Loach's acting ambitions received a boost. He and a friend from Nuneaton, Bill Hays, who had attended art school and designed the sets for his latest productions at the Edinburgh Festival, scoured England during the autumn of 1960 in search of a suitable venue. 'It was complete madness, totally unrealistic,' recalled Loach. 'We found the Royal County Theatre, in Bedford, which had shut, and started to negotiate with the owners. After a while, Richard, quite rightly, got cold feet and backed out because we had ideas way beyond our station.'[1] Booth returned to his family roots around Hay-on-Wye, just across the Welsh border in Herefordshire, and the following year opened the bookshop there that led it to flourish as Britain's first 'book town', with a world-famous festival of literature and arts.

Loach and Hays were left licking their wounds in Bedford. 'Bill and I were stuck because we had taken a flat above a shop and were committed to it,' said Loach. 'So we started teaching. I became a supply teacher in a junior school in Bedford for the autumn term and put on a production of *Oliver Twist* there. Then I went home at Christmas, completely deflated.'[2]

Salvation came with a phone call from the office of theatre impresario Michael Codron, who had seen Loach in an Oxford University revue and asked him to join the company of a similar production – in London's West End. He was to understudy Lance Percival, who was the foil to Kenneth Williams, in *One Over the Eight*, with many sketches written by Peter Cook, the rising star later to form a double act with Loach's former fellow Oxford thespian Dudley Moore. Cook had been a luminary in Cambridge University's *Footlights* revues and teamed up in 1960 with other Oxbridge graduates, Moore, Jonathan Miller and Alan Bennett, in the biting satire *Beyond the Fringe*. *One Over the Eight*, which also starred Sheila Hancock and was staged at the Duke of York's Theatre, was a sequel to the West End revue *Pieces of Eight*, a success for Kenneth Williams two years earlier.

Loach was clearly in distinguished company as he arrived at the rehearsal room in January 1961. 'I felt like a charlatan, completely out of my depth,' he said. 'I sidled along and sat in the chair nearest to the door, trying to look as inconspicuous as I possibly could. Various people came up and asked who I was and I must have mentioned the word understudy. Sheila Hancock said: "Have they measured you for my frocks?" I said: "What do you mean?" "They're terribly mean," she replied. "They only have one understudy for all the parts." There was a moment when my eyes must have opened wide. When you know nothing, anything is possible!'[3] After a moment's panic, the realisation that he was being wound up registered.

Any thoughts that Loach might actually understudy all the male roles disappeared when the director, Paddy Stone, an American dancer-choreographer, discovered that the actor had two left feet. 'Boys from Nuneaton don't dance!'[4] Loach later explained. But that never excused him from some memorable weekly rehearsals with another understudy, Jill Gascoine, who had a background in singing and dancing. 'Jill would gallop across the stage at me and I was supposed to grab her round the waist, turn her 360 degrees and lift her into the air and put her down feet first in front of me,' recalled Loach. 'I had no chance of ever accomplishing this. Every Thursday morning, her head would end up on the floor, with her

legs flailing around in front of my face. It was a disaster. Fortunately, I never had to do it in front of an audience.'[5]

Although he never stood in for Percival on stage, Loach appeared
in a blackout sketch every night, which meant that his understudy's
pay rose from £15 to £20 a week because the principal dancer, Irving
Davies, did not want to take part in it. The sketch was about four
Welsh miners who begin to suspect that one of their number is an
Indian, with his Welsh accent transmuting to an Asian one and back
again. The problem is in distinguishing which, because they are all
covered in coal dust. For the shy Loach, this must have been the
perfect way to maintain a low profile and earn an extra £5 a week.

The thought of appearing alongside Kenneth Williams filled him
with trepidation. 'He would have made mincemeat of me,' said
Loach. 'He was a very mercurial character whose mood would
change in an instant. One minute he would be your best friend, the
next he would cut you dead; he was very strange. He was interested
in history and we would have friendly arguments about it. I had just
read a biography of King John, which I had enjoyed, and I gave him
a copy. But the next day he would humiliate you in front of
everybody and no one would know how to respond.'[6]

Most enjoyable of all for Loach was the pre-West End tour
undertaken by the production. For eight weeks, the cast performed
all over Britain, from Golders Green Hippodrome to Blackpool's
Grand Theatre. 'That was extraordinary,' recalled Loach, 'because
we travelled on steam trains and would meet other actors at railway
stations such as Crewe. It made you feel you were part of that long
theatrical tradition of touring companies, which was coming to an
end. It was really magical for me.'[7] Three months followed at the
Duke of York's, when Loach soaked up the West End atmosphere
after shows by retiring to a pub across the road and sharing stories
with other actors.

He started renting a flat in Notting Hill Gate, West London, with
Derrick Goodwin, a technician working on the production who
was later to find success as a television scripwriter and director.
Goodwin penned two short plays that Loach directed, with a young
James Bolam as the star, performed one Sunday morning in a room
off St Martin's Lane, in the heart of the West End. Most of those
watching were friends.

An audition with the touring Arena Theatre Company, based in

Sutton Coldfield, landed Loach three months' acting work during the summer of 1961. It gave performances in a large tent in Cannon Hill Park, Birmingham, as well as at the Prince of Wales Theatre, Cardiff. 'The standard wasn't great, but it was good fun,' recalled Loach,[8] who acted in Molière's *Le Bourgeois Gentilhomme*, under the English title *The Would-be Gentleman*, Thornton Wilder's *The Matchmaker*, Arnold Wesker's *Roots* and Hugh and Margaret Williams' *The Grass is Greener*; he also played Brer Fox in *Brer Rabbit*, specially written by the company's governing director, John English. One of his fellow performers was Jane Freeman, who much later found fame as café owner Ivy in *Last of the Summer Wine*. 'We used to send each other up quite disgracefully,' recalled Loach. 'My own performance, as Brer Fox, was appalling – not my greatest triumph.'[9]

More significantly, Loach met Lesley Ashton, who was the company's secretary and occasionally danced on stage. Born in Manchester and brought up in Birmingham, she was three years his junior. Her father, who managed a tyre factory and would not let her entertain ideas of dancing as a career, sent her to secretarial college. But, while subsequently working as a secretary, she heard that the amateur company at nearby Highbury Little Theatre was looking for dancers who were five feet two inches tall. She was taken on, performed in children's productions and then crossed over to Arena, its sister company of professional actors. Eventually, she was guaranteed permanent work by also becoming John English's secretary.

Then Loach arrived. 'We were all a bit awestruck by this young man who had been president of OUDS, appeared with Kenneth Williams on stage and wore a jacket and tie,' she recalled. 'I swear he wore ties in those days and had a rolled umbrella, although he denies it. I do remember thinking he wasn't a very good actor! He was the sort of actor he now wouldn't even look at or audition because his performance was all very thoughtful and worked out and detailed, and we were not that sort of a company. I quite fancied him but thought he was well out of my league because he was an actor and had been to university. We just started vaguely going out when we were in Cardiff, but not very often. I went out with all the boys – we were all so young. When we got to Birmingham, we started going out a bit more seriously.'[10]

Once the summer season was over, Loach was on his way.

Starting a theatre company was still his ambition and, with Bill Hays and Derrick Goodwin, he found an old schoolroom in Great Central Street, Leicester, and launched the Living Theatre. The trio intended to alternate as directors, with Jill Gascoine and Peter Blythe among their company, but Loach left before the first production (He returned later, briefly, to direct *Candida*.). He was able to gain from the experience of working at an established theatre after applying for a place on a scheme organised by ABC, one of the early ITV companies, whose 'Armchair Theatre' series featured both stage classics and new works. Television drama was still produced in the manner of stage plays, and ABC paid for six assistant directors to gain a year's experience with repertory companies around the country. The hope was to create the television directors of the future.

This led the budding director to the Theatre Royal, Northampton, which mixed West End successes with classics by writers such as Oscar Wilde and George Bernard Shaw. In the traditional manner of fortnightly rep, a new play was put on every two weeks. The highlight of the year was the Christmas pantomime, when the artistic director, Lionel Hamilton, acted the dame. 'I went on stage occasionally as an extra,' Loach recalled, 'but Lionel didn't rate my acting talents at all.'[11]

Although Hamilton directed most productions, he disliked murder mysteries and handed over to Loach for Agatha Christie's *Murder at the Vicarage* and Simon Amberley's *Murder at Quay Cottage*. 'Sometimes, they would hire a well-known actor to play the main part in a play,' recalled Loach, 'but we didn't with *Murder at the Vicarage* and used those in the company who normally played character parts. So Vera Lennox, a most beautiful, dainty old lady who had been in musical theatre as one of Charles Cochran's young ladies, played Miss Marple, but she couldn't remember her lines and did like a glass of gin. So, when we got to the end of the play, the gin and the lack of memory combined to make the mystery that Miss Marple had to unravel rather more than she could stand. Night after night, the audience would go home blissfully unaware of who had committed the murder.'[12] Loach also directed a farce, *Hot and Cold in All Rooms*, during his year at Northampton Rep. 'It was crude and dreadful, but we all did our best,' recalled actress Patricia Leventon. 'We just fell about laughing.'[13]

This useful experience on stage was accompanied by a significant event off stage: Lesley Ashton joined Loach in Northampton, where they lived together. The couple decided to marry and, after their wedding in Sutton Coldfield in July 1962, and the completion of his year as an assistant director, they moved into a flat in Shepherd's Bush, West London, and Lesley found a job as a secretary in Holborn. Meanwhile, Loach and Bill Hays – who moved in with them – tried to start a theatre company once more. 'One appalling night, we went to Southampton, in the coldest winter for years,' he said. 'We stayed in a boarding-house that wasn't much more than a doss-house and froze to death.'[14] The pair's long-held ambition was doomed to failure, which was no disappointment to Lesley Loach. 'I didn't like the idea of us all going to live down there,' she admitted.[15]

Ken Loach married Lesley Ashton in Sutton Coldfield, July 1962

Loach found some recompense with one-line parts in BBC television's satirical series *That Was the Week That Was*, his revue experience in *One Over the Eight* and at Oxford University landing him some much needed work. In one sketch, he played a Young Conservative. 'I said the line very badly,' recalled Loach, 'and the direction from Ned Sherrin, the producer, came down from the gallery: "Can you be more like a Young Conservative?" I had no idea what that meant! So I just put on a funny voice. I wasn't really interested in television at all. I wanted to work in theatre.'[16]

In July 1963, the Loaches' first child, Stephen, was born in the middle of another Arena Theatre Company summer season. 'We lived with my mother and father when we were in Birmingham,' said Lesley Loach. 'We were visiting Ken's parents in Nuneaton when my waters broke and his mother put me in the car and raced me back to my mother; she didn't want to be too involved! Ken came with me to the hospital, along with my mother and father. I gave birth that night and Ken came the next morning; in those days, fathers weren't at the birth.'[17]

Back on stage in *Poor Richard*, a new children's play by John English in which the actors were presented as a team of strolling players, Loach was seen not only as the Miller and the Grand Vizier, but also a cat. This might have convinced him that his fate lay elsewhere. Out of work and having already been turned down by BBC television as an assistant floor manager, he applied for a place on a directors' course and was accepted. This came in late 1963, in preparation for the launch of BBC2 the following year, and was intended to provide fresh talent for the new channel. Ironically, Loach would make programmes almost exclusively for BBC1. (Bill Hays was also taken on as a director by the BBC.)

The six-week course was intended to shape those with some directing experience into the BBC mould, with talks on form-filling and the corporation's ethos. The skill itself was restricted to one lecture titled 'What to Do with Your Cameras', given by John Jacobs, who had been responsible for productions in 'The Sunday Night Play' series and later became head of drama at rival ITV company Anglia. Loach, the theatre nut, was set for a baptism of fire in television.

3

ANGRY YOUNG MEN

IT WAS 1963, THE YEAR that marked the real beginning of the Swinging Sixties in Britain. The Beatles had their first three number one singles, the Pill became available on prescription, young people's voices were beginning to be heard, and a pillar of the Establishment fell when War Minister John Profumo resigned over his relationship with a call-girl who had also slept with a Russian diplomat.

A generation of Tory rule was in its death throes and the hardships of post-war austerity had melted into an apparent new prosperity. The 'green and pleasant land' view of England, with its middle-class values and accents to match, no longer had a monopoly. The new mood sweeping across the nation was reflected in the literature, stage plays and cinema films that had slowly emerged since the mid-1950s. At last, the stuffy old voices associated with a dwindling empire and middle-class 'respectability' were being replaced by Angry Young Men such as John Osborne, Lindsay Anderson and Tony Richardson. All three found in the new Royal Court Theatre, in London, a showcase for their messages, with Osborne's *Look Back in Anger* becoming one of its early successes.

Another significant outlet for working-class and left-of-centre voices was Theatre Workshop, which actress and director Joan Littlewood had established as a people's theatre with a home in East London, after years on tour. The German playwright Bertolt Brecht had entrusted Littlewood with the first British production of *Mother Courage and Her Children*. It tells the story of a resilient woman struggling to scrape a living for her family during the Thirty Years' War and being forced to make decisions that are ultimately political, despite her insistence that she is not interested in politics. As it unfolds, the play shows that Mother Courage is at the mercy of other events and the system in which she is forced to live.

This would become a theme of Ken Loach's work as a director, which drew on the influences of Brecht and Littlewood. From them, he borrowed the practice of making drama in the everyday language of the working classes and allowing the performers to utter the dialogue in their own words. Of Littlewood, he explained, 'I admired and enjoyed her work enormously and tried to emulate it – the way you often emulate someone when you're starting out. I was trying to get the same randomness that she got in live theatre. It was a way of telling a story where the images appeared arbitrary but none the less a story emerged . . . it suggests the richness of everything that's going on.'[1]

But film and television had never held any great fascination for Loach. He had occasionally visited the cinema in Nuneaton and Oxford, eschewing mainstream Hollywood productions for X-rated pictures from mainland Europe, by directors such as Italy's Michelangelo Antonioni and the pioneers of the French New Wave. This cinematic revolution in France at the turn of the 1950s, led by François Truffaut, Jean-Luc Godard and Claude Chabrol, was a movement against the studio-bound style that had developed in that country. At the same time, it acknowledged French film-makers of the 1930s, such as Jean Renoir and Jean Vigo, and the Italian neo-realists, led by Roberto Rossellini and Vittorio De Sica, as well as Hollywood directors who carved their own distinctive imprint on the pictures they made, notably Alfred Hitchcock, Nicholas Ray and Howard Hawks. Aligning itself with the post-war philosophy of existentialism, the French New Wave depicted anti-authoritarian characters who acted as free spirits, sometimes immorally; directors employed lightweight, hand-held cameras developed for documentary-making to film action on real locations and made as much use as possible of natural light and sound. Often, the performers' lines would be improvised and their dialogue would overlap, as in real life. One stylistic invention was the jump-cut, of which Godard was the master, going straight from one shot to another of the same person, with a noticeable space in time.

These stage and film influences might explain how Loach was able to approach directing for the screen in his own country with a fresh eye, unhindered by the conventions of the Hollywood and British studio systems. He joined the BBC at the time of an influx of new talent into Britain's publicly financed television service. Aligned with the liberal regime of director-general Hugh Greene, this heralded one of the small screen's most creative periods. Already, the satire of *That Was the Week That Was* had awoken politicians to the realisation that they were not immune to criticism. A new generation of writers and directors also sought to move television drama away from its theatrical, 'proscenium arch' approach and develop it in a form exclusive to the medium. As well as trying to break away from the stage-like presentation, this new form used various techniques to reduce dialogue and move stories along quicker.

One of those who helped to get this process under way, through adapting modern stage plays and novels for the anthology series 'Storyboard' and 'Studio 4', was Roger Smith, who had acted with Loach at Oxford University. 'We began to establish a looser form, using voice-overs, music, stills and long tracking shots, and reflected what was going on at the Royal Court Theatre,' explained Smith. 'We were considered very much the rebels, young men in leather jackets, but the BBC allowed it to happen. It certainly shook up television drama.'[2]

This shift continued with another anthology series, 'Teletale', featuring new plays for the screen. These half-hour productions were used to break in some of the graduates of the BBC directors' course. Loach was assigned to *Catherine*, Roger Smith's first original script for television, a very personal tale born out of the experience of the writer's own divorce. 'It was terrifying,' recalled Loach. 'I didn't do much directing. I was just trying to get through.'[3]

At least the fledgling director was spared the horror of *Catherine* being broadcast live, as most programmes still were in the early 1960s. After rehearsals in London, it was recorded in one day, using conventional television cameras at a BBC Manchester studio converted from a church, then the videotape was edited in London, which was an arduous task in those days. 'I had gone out on a limb to write the play in a narrative, edited form,' explained Smith. 'On stopping the fat, three-inch tape, you couldn't actually see the picture – there was no freeze-frame – and the editor was literally cutting with scissors and gluing it together. But I felt we were doing something to push back the boundaries.'[4] Producer James Mac-Taggart promoted the approach by describing *Catherine* as 'a very unusual script, breaking most of the accepted rules of television drama'.[5]

The story follows the title character, played by Kika Markham, as she comes to terms with living alone after the break-up of her marriage. She is seen going to the cinema by herself and being approached in a bar by a singer (actor Tony Selby) who asks her, 'Do you charver?' (meaning 'Do you fuck?' explained Smith).[6] The narrative is literally held together by a narrator, actor Geoffrey Whitehead, who performed his task in a corner of the studio, which was bare, had no conventional sets and relied on lighting to indicate scene changes. The play began with Markham sitting in a pool of light on the studio floor and Whitehead saying, 'This is Catherine. She is twenty-five. This is her room. Sometimes it tells her she is independent and free, and then she is happy. Sometimes it tells her she is alone . . . so much of her past is haunted.'

Whitehead recalled, 'Ken didn't want it like a lot of narrations can be – there's always the temptation to put on a bit of a voice. But it had to be as realistic and as natural as possible. Ken's note to me was: "I want it simple." Even then, you could see a kernel of how he developed, with this utter realism, but it wasn't easy to make it realistic because the play was slightly surreal.'[7] With that observation, Whitehead touched on the opposing forces that would do battle with each other in Loach's early BBC productions before he struck out firmly to become a social-realist film-maker.

Catherine, which was screened in January 1964, included two actors with whom Loach had worked in his repertory days – Peter Blythe, from Leicester's Living Theatre, and Patricia Leventon, from the Theatre Royal, Northampton. It also proved an important meeting place with Roger Smith, Tony Selby, who would take a string of lead roles for Loach, and Tony Garnett, who acted the title character's estranged husband, Richard, and was set to play an important part in the director's career, first as story editor, then as producer. 'Ken and I didn't speak much then,' recalled Garnett. 'He was too concerned with the technical problems, the cables and the cameras.'[8]

After making *Catherine*, Loach – who was working for the BBC as a contract director – was plunged into live television studio drama when he was assigned to make three episodes of *Z Cars*, the series that had revolutionised the way in which the police were depicted on screen. The homely image of *Dixon of Dock Green* was replaced by a warts-and-all portrayal in which the guardians of the law were seen as not infallible – and no angels. *Z Cars*, created by Troy Kennedy Martin and John McGrath and launched in 1962, was set in the fictional Liverpool suburb of Newtown, a symbol of the housing estates that had sprung up across Britain in the post-war years. Tough Detective Inspector Charlie Barlow (played by Stratford Johns) and the gentler Detective Sergeant John Watt (Frank Windsor) had set up a new crime division with mobile police officers in patrol cars nicknamed Z Victor One and Z Victor Two. As well as Johns and Windsor, the programme made stars of Brian Blessed, James Ellis, Jeremy Kemp, Colin Welland and Joseph Brady. A small amount of location filming was done and inserted into each live production, but almost all the action took place in a BBC studio. This included scenes of policemen in the patrol cars, with footage of streets and roads projected on to a screen behind them – the ultimate disaster occurring when it came to the end of a spool too early!

For a director, the challenge of making a live programme was compounded by the studio logistics. 'In a single episode, there could be ten or fifteen sets,' explained Troy Kennedy Martin. 'You would have actors leaping over half-frames of cars and rushing to get to the interior of the police station. It was a real adrenaline rush.'[9]

Loach also encountered the added stress of having to deal with a strong-willed actor in Stratford Johns (although called Alan Johns, he used his middle name for professional purposes). As Barlow, he had created a new breed of television policeman who bullied both suspects and inferior colleagues. He prided himself on moulding the character as bad-tempered, drawing on an unseen wife with whom he had constant rows and a whisky-drinking means of solace.

'I'll never forget the first episode that Ken directed with him,' recalled Colin Welland. 'It opened with James Ellis and me standing at the station counter, talking to the sergeant. Stratford Johns, who, of course, was the star, came in as Barlow and snapped at us, in that curt way of his: "Lynch, Graham – my office!" Ken said: "Stop a moment! Alan, why are you angry? I'm sorry. Is there something in the script I missed? Nobody is angry for nothing." Alan then said it was because of his family and home life. Ken said: "No, no, just come in at the beginning of the day – nothing has happened to make you angry – and say, 'Lynch, Graham – my office!'" You can imagine the relationship from that point on! That is Ken – he wants motivation for everything. Later, Sheila Fearn, who was playing one of the criminals' girlfriends, was being questioned by Barlow and he was coming the hard man again, leaning into her. In rehearsal, Sheila looked at Alan's face and said: "Shut up, fat face!" Alan replied: "Watch it!" Ken said: "No, no, it's wonderful, Alan. You've got her going. Smile at her." But, when it came to the live performance, he wouldn't take the direction and again replied: "Watch it!" Ken didn't get angry, but the man went down in his estimation.'[10]

In casting one episode of Z Cars, Loach sought to include another actor from his repertory theatre days – John Lowe. However, Lowe shared a flat with another young actor, George Layton, who returned home one day to find a written telephone message from their landlady: 'BBC Television Centre, White City, Ken Loach, 3pm.' Layton recalled, 'I phoned Ken, told him who I was and said I had a note but wasn't sure whether it was meant for me. He told me to go in and I got the part! Then I discovered that it was meant for John, who was given a smaller role. I just remember Ken as being so quiet, unobtrusive and shy. He had such a calm way of working, never raising his voice, and was very encouraging.'[11]

Some members of the regular cast were bemused at the use of inexperienced directors on the series, though. 'Ken was a totally unknown quantity at that point,' said Frank Windsor. 'The producer, David Rose, had one or two directors cutting their teeth on Z Cars and, when he said Ken had recently finished the BBC directors' course, I asked him why, as one of the top programmes on television, we had to have directors just off the course. He replied: "Look, we have enough confidence in the programme and the regular cast that, if we get somebody who we think is potentially good and they don't turn out well, we know we can carry them through." Ken turned out to be good but was, not surprisingly, in deference to the programme and the regulars. As for Stratford Johns, he was a law unto himself!'[12]

Loach, who found the task of directing Z Cars just as terrifying as he had with Catherine, recalled, 'The scripts, by John Hopkins and Robert Barr, had broken-up dialogue, full of interruptions, which made it quite difficult to direct. I was in awe of the whole programme, really, but the main cast were very good and helpful. Stratford Johns took himself rather seriously and was a bit impatient – if I was indecisive, he would show his disapproval.'[13] The experience of working live in a studio only reinforced Loach's ambitions to escape the traditional means of making programmes. 'The director was supposed to conduct the cuts at key moments,' he explained, 'but it was as much as I could do to keep my place in the script. I was a total failure in the gallery, but I don't remember any major catastrophes. The vision mixer worked off a marked-up script. She used to take her knitting into the control room and did it until just before we went on air. I was transfixed with horror!'[14]

The chance for Loach to direct a fresh television production and strike out in his own style came with Diary of a Young Man. The six-part tale of the trials and tribulations of two Northerners after arriving in London was written jointly by Z Cars creators Troy Kennedy Martin and John McGrath, who directed early episodes of the police series. (McGrath wrote extensively for television and the cinema during the 1960s but also, like Joan Littlewood, advanced the cause of popular theatre in the belief that changes would follow in society if the issues raised reached the widest possible audience.)

Diary of a Young Man came at a time when the ideas of the new breed of BBC writers and directors were being advanced as a means of 'saving' television drama. Unlikely as it might seem now, there was a feeling that the form was in danger of extinction, especially single plays. Influenced by Brecht, Kennedy Martin wrote an article in the theatre magazine Encore titled 'Nats Go Home', calling for 'new language, new punctuation and new style'. It was a rallying call to take television drama away from 'a theatre of dialogue, a theatre of performance . . . a writer's theatre', which he regarded as 'naturalism' and capable of being produced by the BBC's talks or outside-broadcast departments. He felt that television dramas were often just stage plays acted out in front of a camera, with concrete scenarios and dialogue. Instead, he called for a 'narrative form of drama', condensing scenes of dialogue through 'stream of consciousness and diary form', with editing being a critical component of the 'new grammar' and the director taking on a more creative role.[15]

This form had already been attempted by Roger Smith and others in the 'Teletale' series, but Kennedy Martin and McGrath had written *Diary of a Young Man* before that. Smith was an admirer of Brecht, as they were, and took on the role of story editor on the new production. Tony Garnett was another Brecht devotee who was set to make Loach more familiar with the playwright's ideas. 'Brecht's premise,' explained Kennedy Martin, 'was that in trying to get a message over, if the audience get swallowed up in the performance and think everything is natural and real, they are missing something. You have to show in a stage play that it is actually taking place in the theatre. With television, you have to use editing and cutting. In *Diary of a Young Man*, Ken caught on very quickly.'[16]

After McGrath changed his mind about directing the series, the six episodes were split alternately between Loach and Peter Duguid, another former actor who had graduated from the BBC directors' course at the same time as him and made a 'Teletale' adaptation of *The Black Madonna*. Studio scenes were recorded at BBC Television Centre in West London, but there was also some location shooting around the capital. Loach regarded *Diary of a Young Man* as 'a quirky, upbeat story about two comic characters'.[17]

Victor Henry and Richard Moore were cast in the roles of Joe and Ginger, who arrived in London from Hartlepool to face the problems of finding flats and jobs, and to discover women. Some of Joe's 'diary' entries were communicated in voice-over by Henry, who had grown up in Leeds and broke into acting after travelling to Canada at the age of sixteen. He occupied his 'resting' time with jobs in an iron foundry and as a salesman, and eventually worked with McGrath in the theatre. 'One way and another, I've had a lot of Joe's experiences,' said Henry. 'In different conditions, true, but then Joe is a modern-day Everyman.'[18]

The other star was Nerys Hughes, as Rose, who married Joe in an episode directed by Loach. She proved to be one of the first examples of his casting actors who looked like 'real people' from the streets. 'I had been at the beach in Brighton all day and my hair was full of sea-water,' she recalled. 'I arrived home and received a call from my agent saying that the BBC wanted to see me for a new series. I certainly looked pretty tousled and I suspect that's what

Ken liked.'[19] Her experience at the Royal Court Theatre also gave her an advantage. She regarded the casting of three unknowns in the starring roles as revolutionary. 'In those days, there was always glamour on the telly, but we were all so ordinary,' explained Hughes. 'This had a leading actor who was Northern, Victor Henry, and he was very exciting and dangerous. He always had a bit of a death wish and went hell for leather at whatever he was doing; it was a quite extraordinary performance he gave.'[20] Henry's hard-living reputation became legendary and it seemed ironic that, when he was tragically left in a coma after suffering severe head injuries in a road accident in 1972, he was perfectly sober; thirteen years later, he died.

Another Kennedy Martin–McGrath contribution to *Diary of a Young Man* was the casting of Ann Mitchell. She had worked as their secretary before training at the East 15 acting school, which opened in 1961 and based its methods, such as improvisation, on those of Joan Littlewood and Konstantin Stanislavski, the Russian who advocated that actors should totally immerse themselves in their roles. Mitchell spotted some of the qualities that were to endear Loach to actors over the coming decades. 'He had a wonderful energy and was very kind,' she explained. 'I got the feeling that he liked actors a lot.'[21]

Certainly, Loach drew on his own repertory theatre experience as an actor and director, as well as the influence of Joan Littlewood, when he gave Frank Williams and Wally Patch more than one role each in the series. (He also cast Jane Freeman, from his Arena Theatre Company days, as a nurse.) 'It was decided that I would play different characters, but always authority figures with whom Victor Henry came into contact,' explained Williams.[22] Loach confirmed, 'We thought Frank was really funny and couldn't find anybody better for the other parts. That was very much the spirit of the enterprise – throw anything in and make it work. It was an enjoyable haphazardness.'[23]

Although Glynn Edwards portrayed a police constable through-out the series, he reflected that 'he wasn't quite the same copper in each episode' and the actor detected 'shades of Joan Littlewood', with whom he had spent eight years. 'With Ken, it was like going back to Theatre Workshop,' he recalled. 'In some of the shows with Joan, we played four or five different characters.'[24] The director also encouraged some improvisation. 'Ken used to chuck ideas at us just before a take,' said Edwards.[25]

Loach recalled that putting the Kennedy Martin–McGrath ideas into action 'was very challenging' and added, 'By this time, I was watching the French New Wave cinema, and this was parallel to that, with its jump-cuts. There was a whole tangle of ideas coming into television because it was a relatively new medium. Having borrowed its drama from the theatre, it now had to strike out and find a new form, and define what television drama could be. The door was waiting to be pushed open.'[26] For Loach, like the New Wave directors, this new form also involved leaving the studio to film on real locations. One of those for this production was Box Hill, in the Surrey countryside. 'Suddenly, embarrassed courting couples in various stages of undress came shooting out of the bushes, wondering what was going on,' recalled Frank Williams.[27]

Diary of a Young Man certainly showed how individual and distinctive television could truly be. 'Vicar raps the BBC's "filthy" young man,' read a headline in the *Daily Herald*,[28] after a Nottinghamshire vicar complained to the Postmaster-General, who was then the government minister responsible for broadcasting. The Rev. Tom Richardson, of Radcliffe-on-Trent, wrote, 'Filth and depravity have no part in our family life. What right have the BBC to introduce them during an evening's entertainment?' The vicar further told the *Herald*, 'I found the carrying-on between the young man . . . and the woman particularly offensive. The language was also disgusting.'[29] Such reactions from the guardians of morals were a sign of what was to come when Loach's talents were given their full potential to evolve.

PART II

'THE WEDNESDAY PLAY' AND A CINEMA DÉBUT

4

'THE WEDNESDAY PLAY'

TELEVISION DRAMA'S RESPONSE to the cultural revolution taking place in Britain was 'The Wednesday Play'. The movement to present working-class voices had culminated in the cinema's 'kitchen sink' sagas, in which film-makers 'discovered' life north of Watford Gap and gave a mouthpiece to its people, and 'It's grim up North' became a phrase of mockery. Inevitably, by the mid-1960s, this novelty was growing thin. Over the decade, a more enduring theme was taken up by directors such as Tony Richardson, in *The Loneliness of the Long Distance Runner*, and Lindsay Anderson, in the public-school satire *If . . .*, with the idea that society could be changed through political upheaval.

In 'The Wednesday Play' and his subsequent work, Ken Loach showed that he knew it was not only 'grim up North', but in many backwaters of the English landscape (and, later, Scotland) too. Perhaps helped by his lack of British and Hollywood cinematic influences, Loach found his own way to portray everyday life on screen. He furthered the 'anti-naturalism' principles outlined by Troy Kennedy Martin and held on to some of the forms that he had used in *Diary of a Young Man*, such as voice-over, music and still photographs, in an attempt to achieve his own aim: social realism. In the British cinema's 'kitchen sink' dramas, this had been a euphemism for working-class realism: for the first time, the lives, language and sexuality of that class were depicted seriously, beyond the maids, taxi-drivers and comic characters traditionally portrayed in films written by, and featuring, the middle- and upper-classes.

As he became more confident in the role of director, Loach addressed his frustration with the limitations imposed by television studios and bulky cameras to develop a handheld style that blurred the distinctions between fact and fiction. Some scenes in the plays made by Loach could be mistaken for film from *World in Action*, ITV's hard-hitting current affairs series, which began in 1963. The BBC's other great young directing talent of the time, Peter Watkins, also showed the way: his production of *Culloden*, made as a 'drama-documentary' and screened in December 1964, was a re-enactment of the Jacobites' last stand against English rule in the eighteenth-century battle on Scottish soil, shot with lightweight, hand-held cameras that gave a real sense of immediacy and authenticity. Watkins cast an Anglo-French Mauritian in the role of Bonnie Prince Charlie, who was a Highlander with Polish and Italian blood, instructed his cast to wear their battle costumes through every minute of the three-week shoot, when they lived as a unit and talked constantly about the English massacre, and filmed current affairs-style interviews with the participants.

In his own search for authenticity, Loach adopted a similar style, but Watkins fell by the wayside after the BBC's banning of his 1965 television film *The War Game*, recreating the likely effects of an attack on Britain with a one-megaton nuclear bomb, with mostly local amateur actors from Kent taking part. At the time, the Corporation claimed it was 'too horrifying' to screen,[1] but subsequent research showed that the ban was a political decision, intended to prevent any questioning of the government's policy of building up nuclear weapons as part of the arms race. Lord Normanbrook, chairman of the BBC board of governors and formerly Secretary to the Cabinet, wrote to his Cabinet successor, Sir Burke Trend, '. . . the showing of the film on television might have a significant effect on public attitudes towards the policy of the nuclear deterrent,' and invited the government to share in the responsibility of deciding whether to screen it.[2] A subsequent private screening at Television Centre for Sir Burke Trend and senior Home Office, Ministry of Defence and Post Office officials led to this early case of political censorship in television. Watkins left the BBC and Britain to seek a new career in feature films and found a warmer reception to his documentary and drama themes in Scandinavian countries.

Of course, the fictions that Loach was telling had their roots in fact and similarly made his films a genuine threat to the established order in politics and broadcasting because they suggested there were real alternatives. For a government-appointed organisation such as the BBC, this might have seemed unacceptable but, while a liberal regime flourished there, Loach and his closest collaborators in the drama department found a freedom to make plays that presented issues that had previously been ignored or swept under the carpet.

'The aim was to make drama that was as much a part of contemporary life as the news and was seen in the same way,' explained Loach. 'We felt that, whatever happened in the news, we were a continuation of it – and "The Wednesday Play" usually followed it. We felt more like the news than we did classic drama and everything we did was about questioning the Establishment view of the world. That developed into a political analysis.'[3]

This was a consequence of the BBC's new head of drama, Sydney Newman, launching 'The Wednesday Play' with the team from *Diary of a Young Man* as its backbone. Newman, a Canadian, had been lured from ITV, where he made the publicly and critically acclaimed 'Armchair Theatre' series of classic and contemporary dramas. At the BBC, he restructured drama into three departments: series, serials and plays. His brief to producer James MacTaggart was to commission plays that would be popular with, and relevant to, a wide audience. MacTaggart appointed Roger Smith as story editor, charged with scouring the country for writing talent, and Smith asked Tony Garnett and Kenith Trodd – a friend from Oxford University – to be his assistants. He knew Garnett as an actor in his 'Teletale' play *Catherine*, directed by Loach, and from David Mercer's 'Generations' trilogy chronicling the rise and fall of socialist idealism over sixty years. At first, Garnett was reluctant to give up a successful acting career, but he was eventually 'worn down'.[4]

Loach's own politics reached maturity at about this time. Shortly before the Labour Party's re-election, under Prime Minister Harold Wilson, in 1964, after thirteen years in the wilderness, the director became a member of the Party and worked actively for it, attending meetings and distributing leaflets. 'We began to think that, after the Macmillan years, there would be some kind of change,' he explained. 'But, when Wilson assumed power, there was no structural change at all; they continued to operate the same system. [An economic slump led the Labour government to increase interest

rates within a month of coming to office, just as the previous
Conservative administration had done.] In retrospect, it was bound
to behave as a social democratic government and what Roger and
Tony were saying about the Labour Party was borne out: there was
an awareness that there was a political position to the left of the
Party. I sat through those discussions, listening, learning and
absorbing, and those radical socialist ideas were brought to
"The Wednesday Play".[5]

On screen, the new series had a brief to adopt varying styles,
although the revolution in contemporary television drama that it
helped to nurture rarely strayed outside the 'Wednesday Play'
banner. It proved a home to creative talents such as Dennis Potter,
David Mercer, John Hopkins, Robert Muller and Alan Plater, a
mix of new writers to television and some who were already
becoming established. On screen, it sat alongside other forms of
drama, including popular fantasy and espionage series such as *The
Avengers* and *The Saint*, the 'folk opera' of *Coronation Street* –
whose roots lay in the 'kitchen sink' revolution – the acutely
observed working-class situation comedies *Steptoe and Son* and
Till Death Us Do Part, the current affairs series *World in Action*,
This Week and *Panorama*, entertainment shows that included the
long-running *Sunday Night at the London Palladium* and *Top of
the Pops*, and the perennial quizzes *Take Your Pick* and *Double
Your Money*. BBC1 vied with its commercial rival, ITV, to win
viewers with these mainstream programmes and often lost the
ratings battle, but it maintained a belief that it was furthering
the lofty aims of its founding father, Lord Reith. In 1964, BBC2
was launched to cater for minority audiences and sought to do so
with the arts programme *Late Night Line-Up*, its own drama
outlet, 'Theatre 625', where John Hopkins found a home for his
acclaimed 'Talking To a Stranger' quartet, and *Match of the Day*,
which was broadcast on BBC2 until England's 1966 World Cup
victory designated soccer worthy of wider coverage.

In those days of three-channel television in Britain, 'The Wednesday Play' achieved notoriety by being given a shop window in the
peaktime BBC1 schedule, but perhaps was really a ghetto into
which the Corporation could channel drama that was prepared to
take risks and provoke moral indignation. ('Armchair Theatre',
which had given the BBC a lesson in how to move television drama

on from its theatrical roots and fostered such talents as writers Alun Owen and Harold Pinter and directors Philip Saville and Charles Jarrott, remained popular but rarely featured plays with the Swinging Sixties values and morals that were such an inherent part of its new rival's best productions.)

Loach was, without doubt, the one director who made his name through 'The Wednesday Play'. The only writer to become so firmly associated with it was Dennis Potter, who in its first year was responsible for *Vote, Vote, Vote for Nigel Barton* and *Stand Up, Nigel Barton*, autobiographical dramas about a miner's son who stands for Parliament. Potter's style was a non-naturalistic one that had sympathy with Troy Kennedy Martin's 'Nats Go Home' argument, but Loach and Tony Garnett travelled another route.

Birmingham-born Garnett, who as an actor had repertory theatre, television and film experience, had weighed into the debate about 'naturalism' in television drama. He contended that Troy Kennedy Martin's recipe for a new form was little different from that practised by the cinema for many years.[6] Shooting on film, away from the television studio, and editing later was his vision – and one that he shared with Loach. 'Ken was never very interested in multi-camera, television studio drama,' he explained.[7] If there was a weakness in Kennedy Martin's thesis, it was the assumption that television drama was studio-bound and therefore needed to find methods of overcoming the consequent logistical and time constraints, with rare chances to edit. He acknowledged that 'naturalism' did not equal 'realism' – 'Naturalism is when everything gets explained in dialogue, whereas realism is when images begin to take over from the dialogue,' he explained[8] – but Loach and Garnett sought to depict reality by taking drama out of the studio. As they pioneered the use of extensive location filming with lightweight cameras, it became clear that Kennedy Martin's 'anti-naturalism' argument had not been a blueprint for the future of television drama, but did contribute new ideas about how to portray realism.

Nothing could have been more realistic or gritty than Loach's first 'Wednesday Plays'. Three of them were written by James O'Connor, who gained a reprieve after being sentenced to death for a murder he maintained he never committed. He was due to be executed on his birthday, 20 May 1942, after eight weeks in the condemned cell. Just a day before his fate seemed sealed and after seeing his grave being dug, he was granted a 'respite'. He served ten years of a life sentence in Dartmoor Prison, then was released on licence but never won a pardon, despite attempts to clear his name.

O'Connor already knew Robert Barr, a leading writer on *Z Cars*, and arrived in Roger Smith's office with a play script, *Three Clear Sundays*. Based on his own experience, it was the story of a young man (eventually played by Tony Selby) who is not reprieved; shockingly, it ends with his gruesome hanging. He is dragged, sobbing, to the gallows, the rope is put round his neck and the trap released; the body is left swinging there. This was to have a huge impact on the television audience at a time when the abolition of capital punishment for murder was a current issue – it would finally happen in November 1965 – and Smith was instantly sold on the play. He also commissioned O'Connor to write another, *Tap on the Shoulder*, an amusing tale about a gang of four thieves on a bullion robbery and the rise of one of the villains to become a baronet, accepted by the Establishment and giving money to charity while conducting a criminal life. (A 'tap on the shoulder' is the phrase used to refer to the Queen bestowing a knighthood.)

'Jimmy introduced me, and drama, to a whole world we knew nothing about,' explained Smith, 'the world of the Sixties and of villains, looked at in a different way from usual. It was also the world of property tycoons, corruption and backhanders, all written with a great sense of humour.' Smith was keen that Loach should make O'Connor's plays. 'Ken was our major director,' he said. 'We spoke the same language and he was terrific with actors. Many of the ones we used came from Joan Littlewood, bringing London working-class authenticity to Jimmy's plays. They knew the scene; they weren't acting – they were "being".'[9]

Loach was attracted to the 'Damon Runyon, larger-than-life, *Guys and Dolls*-type characters' in O'Connor's writing and the way in which comedy would turn to farce and then, perhaps, to murder. 'The plays featured Jimmy's characters and stories,' explained Loach, 'but, without Roger's skill, they would have been almost unproduceable. When I was asked if I would like to make *Tap on the Shoulder*, I leapt at the chance.'[10]

James MacTaggart decided that this should be the first of the new team's work to be broadcast in the 'Wednesday Play' slot in

January 1965, although that series title had already been implemented the previous autumn for eight productions previously commissioned by the BBC drama department. Loach credited O'Connor and the Joan Littlewood actors in *Tap on the Shoulder* with teaching him much about 'what was true and what was not', particularly in listening to the writer's comments on whether actors at the auditions were 'real or phony'.[11] While shooting the first of the new breed, Loach relished his new-found freedom. At one point, he told Smith that a bridging scene was needed, O'Connor promptly wrote one in a bar and it was filmed the following day. Lee Montague, who starred as Archibald Cooper, recalled O'Connor being ever-present on the set. 'He was always smoking cigarettes,' he said. 'He would bring one out from the back of his hand and behind his back, as if he was smoking in the prison courtyard and not supposed to be. He drew in very strongly the breath of the smoke and then exhaled as if he wasn't doing it at all.'[12]

'The play created quite a stir,' recalled Loach. 'It had an anti-Establishment feel to it. We were saying the villains were in the Establishment and the Establishment were villains. Jimmy's great theme was that everyone is bent and the higher you go, the more bent they are.'[13] The battle to save the single play could have had no better start, with *Tap on the Shoulder* attracting ten million viewers. The BBC's programme journal, the *Radio Times*, had rather quaintly seen it necessary to educate them in advance with 'some slang phrases the villains use', such as '*to straighten* – to bribe', '*a kite* – a cheque', '*to graft* – to carry out villainy', '*to cop* – to get hold of' and '*porridge* – doing time'.[14]

Then, in *Three Clear Sundays*, a title that referred to the period between death sentence and execution, Loach found a like-minded collaborator in film cameraman Tony Imi. Location shooting was allocated to those working at the BBC film unit in Ealing, who used bulky, 35mm equipment. 'I was stuck in a rut after working on *Dr Finlay's Casebook* and *Maigret* – standard BBC productions,' Imi recalled. 'All of a sudden, with "The Wednesday Play" and Ken, there was a newness that fitted into the way I was thinking at the time.' BBC rules allowed only two or three days' location filming on any single production, with the rest recorded in a studio at BBC Television Centre, in White City. One day, while shooting outside in a street, Loach persuaded Imi to pick up the heavy film camera.

'We ended up with all sorts of shots that were not technically "acceptable" – much rougher than normal,' explained Imi. 'When it was screened, there were lots of askance looks from other cameramen who were classically trained, with a background in the cinema or newsreel.'[15]

For Loach, the primary reason for picking up the film camera was speed. 'With a television camera, you could track around and go up or down very easily because it was on a dolly that was very mobile, like a Dalek,' he said. 'So I was used to a camera moving about. To get the same effect with a film camera was a much more difficult job.'[16] Loach was also determined to get authentic dialogue from his cast. 'We spent a long time in the rehearsal room before shooting it,' recalled Glynn Edwards, who played a prison officer, having previously been cast by Loach as a policeman in *Diary of a Young Man*. 'It was full of improvisation. If you were doing a scene and thought of a line that fitted, he would approve of that.'[17]

Later in the year, Loach directed another O'Connor play, *The Coming Out Party*, set on the writer's home patch of Notting Hill, in West London, just before Christmas. The story followed a boy's search for his mother after discovering that she is in prison; his father is also in jail. With the boy clearly set to follow in their footsteps, this was one of Loach's early explorations of what drives people to crime, and his success in getting natural performances from actors was gradually being recognised. 'His careful casting gave the play an unrehearsed look,' wrote one critic.[18] Lyrics to songs featured in both *The Coming Out Party* and *Three Clear Sundays* were written by O'Connor's wife, Nemone Lethbridge, a barrister who later wrote television scripts herself.

George Sewell, a Joan Littlewood protégé who appeared in both *Three Clear Sundays* and *The Coming Out Party*, recalled of Loach's directing style, 'His way of working was comparable with Joan's and he would often allow us to improvise scenes. Just before working with Ken, I had been in a rehearsal room with another director. While doing a scene talking across a table, he said: "Don't lean too far forward over the table. Camera 4 will never get you there." Ken would never have done that. He made sure the camera got what you were doing.'[19]

During that first year of 'The Wednesday Play', a prolific Loach made six productions. One was the first television play to be written by Eric Coltart, a Liverpool toolmaker who had previously scripted two episodes of *Z Cars*. *Wear a Very Big Hat*, another gritty drama, was given regional authenticity by being set in the writer's home city. It was the tale of a woman (played by Sheila Fearn) who buys a stetson for an evening out with her Mod husband (Neville Smith) and is insulted by two men in a pub. The action revolves around the husband's fantasies of revenge, as he broods on the matter and is unable to let it rest.

Made before *Three Clear Sundays*, this was Loach's first 'Wednesday Play' to contain filmed inserts. His previous experience on *Z Cars* made him determined to make the exercise less cumbersome. 'In *Z Cars*, the filming was always done at night,' he explained, 'and it was a nightmare because the cameramen used big lights and it took ages to set up. At the time, I thought: "If this is filming, I never want to see it again." So, when we needed some film in *Wear a Very Big Hat*, I vowed not to do it in the same way. There wasn't the budget for a big film crew, so I went to Liverpool with the cameraman, Stanley Speel, and we did the exterior filming in front of shop windows, shooting with the handheld, 35mm camera wherever they were light enough.'[20] With this play, Loach also consolidated his style of using 'natural' speech and contemporary music to portray reality, although some found the combination difficult to take. *The Times*'s critic wrote, 'Mr Loach . . . allowed the opening dialogue to struggle unsuccessfully against the twang and jangle of electric guitars.'[21]

Music was an even more prominent element in *The End of Arthur's Marriage*, which was a far cry from the realism of O'Connor and Coltart. It was a collaboration between Stanley Myers, who composed the music for many 'Wednesday Plays' (as he had done for *Diary of a Young Man*), and poet Christopher Logue, who with Myers wrote songs for jazz singer Annie Ross and Peter Cook's satirical Establishment Club in London, as well as himself writing songs for *The Lily White Boys*, a Brechtian musical performed at the Royal Court Theatre. *The End of Arthur's Marriage*, a television musical, was an example of the wide variety of productions encouraged by Sydney Newman and James MacTaggart. Although based on a real-life news story, it was written as a surreal fantasy about Arthur (played by Ken Jones), who uses his father-in-law's life savings of £400, given to him as the deposit on a house, to go on a spending spree with his young daughter (Maureen Ampleford). Essentially a satire on the lower-middle-class desire for possessions and security, it follows Arthur as he sheds his acquisitions, including the purchase of an elephant and the scattering of bank notes in a canal. Among the singers heard on the soundtrack are Long John Baldry, a rhythm and blues performer who later found chart success by switching to easy-listening ballads. Loach found the girl, Maureen Ampleford, at a London school and, with no acting experience, she gave the unselfconscious performance he had sought.

Studio scenes recorded on six sets inside BBC Television Centre were interspersed with location shooting around London, at Fortnum & Mason, London Zoo, the Regent's Canal and a gas-works, on 16mm film – Loach's first move away from 35mm in an attempt to make the camera more mobile and flexible. As if to emphasise this, there was a location scene in which a television documentary team asks the girl whether she likes spending money while another camera crew, with director Loach, is in view. It appears to hark back to Troy Kennedy Martin's Brechtian call for television to acknowledge its presence in portraying the drama, although Loach would later redefine this approach in his search for realism.

The ever self-critical director did not regard this play as a personal success. 'It was very ambitious and involved an elephant on a barge,' he explained. 'I just wasn't experienced enough to know how to do it. I cocked it up, really, and didn't achieve what could have been achieved. The lesson I learned was that the director really needs to be inside the subject and know what the idea is – and I didn't.'[22] Christopher Logue also felt that he had learned a lesson. 'I was extremely inexperienced in the finances of television and film, and discovered that the facilities we had were inadequate for shooting the script,' he said. 'They had to drop the elephant on the barge. I should have worked much more closely with Roger Smith and Ken, and spent time with them discussing the resources and what we would be allowed to do.'[23]

Nevertheless, Loach continued to endear himself to his cast, which included Joanna Dunham and Edward de Souza as a young Chelsea couple looking for a flat near the canal, close to the actress's Islington home. 'Ken had wanted to cast me in *Catherine* more than eighteen months earlier, but my baby daughter, Abigail, was six months old and I had just finished breast-feeding, so I didn't want to be away from her,' she said. 'When Ken offered me *The End of Arthur's Marriage*, I was breast-feeding again – my three-month-old son, Benedict. Ken knew where I lived and realised I could keep on going home to fill Benedict up.'[24]

The End of Arthur's Marriage was made in the middle of 1965 but left on the shelf until November of that year. By then, Roger Smith had left the BBC and was soon to be followed by James MacTaggart. 'Roger was chafing under the rigours of script-editing a big series and longing to go off and write,' explained Tony Garnett, who took over Smith's job as story editor. 'Jim was chafing under the responsibility of producing all of these plays and wanted to go back to directing. So, within a short time, they both disappeared, leaving me to hold the baby.' Garnett seized the opportunity. 'I was very unhappy with having to do multi-camera drama in the studio and so was Ken,' he recalled. 'We were getting to know each other better and shared this ambition to leave the studio behind and go out with the new, lightweight cameras and shoot on real locations.'[25]

5

UP THE JUNCTION

TAKING LIGHTWEIGHT, 16mm film cameras out on to the streets of South London for their longest excursion to date brought 'The Wednesday Play' its greatest impact in *Up the Junction*. Scenes of uninhibited factory women and coarse language, as well as an illegal backstreet abortion, brought into viewers' living rooms an unsentimental, unidealised portrait of working-class lives, in grainy images reminiscent of a documentary. In doing so, this first collaboration between Ken Loach and Tony Garnett became a landmark in television history. Inevitably, the play elicited uproar from the self-appointed guardians of morality. Mary Whitehouse, who had just formed the National Viewers' and Listeners' Association to protest at increasing sex, bad language and violence on television, accused the BBC of presenting 'promiscuity as normal'.[1]

Certainly, the 1960s were seen as the decade of liberation in Britain, when the contraceptive Pill became available to women, and young people believed they could really change the world. The soundtrack of the Sixties was the pop music of the Beatles and the protest songs of Bob Dylan, playing along to the new freedoms and fashions on display in Swinging London and the chants of anti-Vietnam War demonstrators outside the American Embassy in Grosvenor Square. Behind this façade lay the reality that gross inequalities were opening up in society, despite the prime ministerial cries of 'You've never had it so good' from Harold Macmillan and Harold Wilson's 'pound in your pocket'.

Up the Junction set the tone for all of Loach's future work. In putting on screen people who normally had no representation – and few choices in their lives – he avoided being judgemental and moralistic. The play evolved from Nell Dunn's book of vignettes about 'factory girls' just south of the River Thames who worked in Battersea and went to the pubs and clubs 'up the Junction' – Clapham Junction. In the wake of Shelagh Delaney's play *A Taste of Honey*, about working-class women in the North of England, Dunn depicted the realities of everyday life for many of those in the South. It was a long way from wealthy heiress Dunn's own roots, as a descendant of Charles II, granddaughter of the Earl of Rosslyn and daughter of a beknighted millionaire stockbroker. But, in 1959, she established a reputation for being unconventional by moving across the river with her journalist husband, Jeremy Sandford, from their five-storey house in Chelsea's Cheyne Walk to a small, terraced cottage in the shadow of Battersea Power Station. There, she took a job wrapping chocolates in a factory alongside the women who would become the characters in *Up the Junction* and, later, *Poor Cow*. Their own lives were a patchwork of dead-end jobs, late shifts, dirty streets, crumbling houses, bawdy language and casual sex.

Vickery Turner (back), Carol White and Geraldine Sherman in *Up the Junction* [BBC]

Dunn's 1963 book of short stories, *Up the Junction*, grew out of several of her articles published in the *New Statesman*.[2] The characters, particularly Sylvie, Rube and Eileen, were so vivid and the dialogue so authentic that it needed little work to transform the book into a television play, although Tony Garnett probably never realised how prophetic his words would be in writing about it in *Radio Times* in November 1965. 'It is not a play, a documentary, or a musical,' he explained. 'It is all of these at once. It is something new – but, more important, it is something rare. If you watch it we can promise you something that will stay in your mind for a long time.'[3]

But making one of the seminal plays of the 1960s was, in fact, a result of Loach and Garnett's furtive plotting, from beginning to end. Story editor Roger Smith had already left 'The Wednesday Play' and, although producer James MacTaggart had not gone, he was on holiday. 'It was a case of "If the cat's away, the mice will play", ' explained Garnett. 'I set it in motion, knowing that, if we got quite a way down the line, we would have to be allowed to make it because it would be too late to stop it and, if they did so, there would be a hole in the schedule.'[4]

The production began with the need to fill such a hole in six weeks. 'It was all hands to the pump to find something to put on,' recalled Loach. 'I was talking to Stanley Myers after making *The End of Arthur's Marriage* and asked if he knew any good contemporary writers or was aware of books we could adapt. I had an idea in my mind for fragmented snapshots of everyday life and he mentioned Nell Dunn. So I got hold of her book and wrote a very simple adaptation of the stories – they read like little film scripts anyway. All I did was to reorder them and make some of the characters "through" characters, rather than different ones. I met Nell and spoke to her about it while I was doing that.

'For me, *Up the Junction* was a development of *Sparrers Can't Sing*, which Joan Littlewood's Theatre Workshop staged. It was in the same idiom, featuring street life, but I tried to push it just a bit further, capturing raw, fleeting moments of people caught off guard – something that tells the audience this is not a rehearsed piece of theatre – then assembling it into a mosaic. The aim was to create a sense of authenticity and find working-class voices in the drama and acknowledge that they were central to it; they weren't the peripheral figures of maids and taxi drivers.'[5]

For Garnett, the abortion issue was central to the play. 'It was very important to me, for personal reasons, and crucial that the story was told at that time,' he said.[6] Abortion was already back on the political agenda, in the wake of the thalidomide tragedy, when drugs prescribed to pregnant women caused serious malformations in unborn babies. In 1966, Liberal MP David Steel would sponsor an abortion reform bill, with its successful passage through Parliament the following year legalising terminations of pregnancies where they had not gone beyond twenty-eight weeks (this was later reduced to twenty-four). Garnett's GP, Dr Don Grant, who ran a progressive, left-wing practice in Kentish Town, North London, was used in voice-over in *Up the Junction*. 'Ken and I were influenced by Brecht,' explained Garnett, 'and we used my doctor to give the statistics about deaths from illegal abortions for the scene where Rube was having her backstreet kitchen abortion. The happy result was that he became the Loach family's GP and a great friend.'[7]

The story editor had no doubt that producer James MacTaggart would be unhappy with the play. 'We got well under way and committed quite a lot of money and resources to it before Jim arrived back from his holiday,' said Garnett. 'I knew that he would hate it, because of the controversial content, and would not have wanted to make it. For the BBC at that time, it was a bit close to the mark, with its language and general attitude to sex among these young women. Even more importantly, Jim would have hated it and vetoed it because there was no conventional narrative. Nell Dunn's book had picaresque little stories with loosely connected narratives of the lives of these girls. But, as far as Jim was concerned, there wasn't a script worth making with a number of loosely connected themes. When he arrived back from his holiday, he hit the roof. He and I had a huge, apoplectic, stand-up row in his office that went on for days. But, in the end, Jim – who was a very decent human being and a tolerant, liberal man – said we could do it if we felt that strongly about it. It was almost a *fait accompli* by then, really, because we had outmanoeuvred him. He even generously said to me: "I don't want the producer credit. You can have it." I told him: "You're the producer of this series. I'm not doing it to take the credit away from you." The play was then shot very quickly and turned into quite a triumph for Ken.'[8]

Getting a camera on to the shoulder of Tony Imi fulfilled Loach and Garnett's greatest ambition, partly inspired by the French New Wave directors. 'We had seen Jean-Luc Godard's *Breathless* and the work of his cameraman, Raoul Coutard, and were influenced by the realism of the films coming out of Eastern Europe and the Italian cinema,' explained Garnett. 'Ken and I had similar ambitions; aesthetically and politically, he and I became almost like one person.' The beginnings of this film-making partnership were built on two people from similar backgrounds, described by Garnett as 'working-class Labour aristocracy, from the Midlands', and became 'seamless, with our responsibilities overlapping but inextricably linked'.[9]

Loach managed to stretch the allotted time for location filming to four days – and, totally against BBC diktat, shot half of the play on the streets of South London. Director and cameraman clearly relished the opportunity to pioneer a new way of making television drama. 'We would set up a scene and Tony would shoot it from maybe two positions and perhaps walk in and get a close-up,' recalled Loach. 'We improvised large chunks of it, based on the situation in the story. Two hours later, we would do another scene.'[10]

With little location lighting allowed for in the BBC budget, Imi worked on the hoof. 'I just took a chance on some of the available lighting and shot it,' he explained. 'Ken said: "Try it. If it doesn't work, we'll do it again." I did quite a bit of shooting on the back of a motorbike, swinging the camera backwards and forwards. I was even in the water with a handheld camera when a group of kids busted into a swimming pool at night. Ken would tell the actors what a scene was about, then say: "Right, go ahead." He said to me: "Follow what you think is going on and it doesn't matter if the camera goes out of focus." So I zoomed and focused at the same time. Suddenly, someone would say something and I would whip-pan to whoever was talking. I thought: "What am I doing? I'll be out on my ear." '[11] But Garnett quickly saw his vision bearing fruit. 'By being liberated on location, Ken started to find himself,' he said. 'We saw the immediacy of the work and the bullshit meter he has built into him about what's honest and dishonest in a performance. It was just exciting.'[12]

Also exciting was the performance of Carol White as Sylvie, one of the featured trio of women, with Geraldine Sherman as Rube and Vickery Turner as Eileen. White had been a juvenile actress who appeared in British films such as *The Belles of St Trinian's*, *Doctor in the House*, *Around the World in 80 Days*, *The 39 Steps* and *Carry On Teacher*. By 1962, when she married Michael King, of the King Brothers singing group, she was tired of playing 'dull, very stupid blondes in skin-tight dresses and bouffant hairdos in awful, second-feature films'[13] and quit the business. But, after giving birth to two sons, Sean and Stephen, she yearned to act again and landed guest roles on television in established series such as *Emergency – Ward 10*, *Dixon of Dock Green* and *The Saint*. She had appeared along-side Tony Garnett in a 1962 film, the courtroom drama *The Boys*, and he remembered her when Loach was casting *Up the Junction* (she also appeared on screen weeks later in *The Coming Out Party*, the first Loach-directed play to be produced by Garnett).

By then, Loach had started his practice of auditioning actors by putting them into improvised scenarios. White vividly recalled, 'Ken gave me the script and said: "Just improvise. Pretend you've just come out of a public house drunk and you see your husband across the street and he calls you a slut and a whore." We ended up having a terrible fight and I screamed some dirty cockney words at him and he said: "That's it. You've got the part." '[14] Loach's method of casting and dedication to finding performers who could bring total authenticity to their roles became the bedrock of his aim to achieve realism on screen. Later, on more than one occasion, he would audition hundreds of people just to find one who could play the leading character in a feature film.

With *Up the Junction*, White proved to be an important find. 'What was ideal for Ken was that Carol, as an actor, had emotional availability,' recalled Garnett. 'It's the difference between being and doing. There is some acting where you see the wheels going round, which is "clever" and secondhand, and there's some where the person actually "is". Her emotions were available to the character, the piece, the director and the camera. She was also vulnerable, and rather *too* vulnerable for her own good in life. What was very good for the screen was not good for *her* because she did not have a defended or defensive personality, so she had an unhappy time.'[15]

Although making *Up the Junction* proved to be an exhilarating experience for those involved, something that did not go quite according to plan during location filming was Loach's casting of Anna Wing (later the matriarch Lou Beale in *EastEnders*) as a middle-aged woman at the scene of an accident. She recalled him as 'one of the first directors to really communicate with actors, a pioneer of removing barriers',[16] but it was only as they were about to shoot that he asked her, 'You do drive a car, don't you?' When he discovered she did not, he had to find her a chauffeur.[17]

Loach and Garnett's plotting and pushing back of barriers continued when they shot the other half of the seventy-two-minute play at BBC Television Centre, where ten sets were specially constructed. 'Quite expensively and stupidly, they had to be built to shoot a minimum quota on telecine,' explained Garnett. 'It was to be edited into the real film we had shot, which meant that nothing matched, so it was aesthetically unacceptable to us and expensive and crazy.'[18] In addition, Loach was unhappy that, while film could be edited exactly in line with the director's intentions, studio recordings on tape were at the mercy of a vision mixer, with a lack of precision in cutting from one shot to another.

Knowing that the BBC always 'backed up' electronically recorded studio material with 16mm film as a safety measure, Loach made sure that he would end up with 16mm throughout. 'I shot it in the studio in such a way that it had to be edited a lot,' he explained. 'We did lots of "takes" and let scenes run much longer than in the finished play, and I told the cameramen: "Instead of lining up shots, just find interesting ones in the course of the action." I remember ructions in the gallery. Cutting tape was very difficult in those days and would have taken too long, so we said we would cut the 16mm film. The technical experts said it would not be of transmittable quality and we had an argument, but eventually we won because to do anything else would have sent us over-budget. That devious route was the only way of achieving what we wanted and nobody could deny it was a success, despite an outrage in the *Daily Telegraph*!'[19]

Such press coverage of *Up the Junction* focused on the way that Loach blurred the distinction between fact and fiction, setting the tone for subsequent criticism of his 'Wednesday Plays'. However, the *Financial Times* dubbed it 'Experimental Slot', with T. C. Worsley conceding, 'The technical innovations, though they might be judged only 60 per cent successful by academic standards, undoubtedly succeeded in putting the piece across with an impact which no conventional methods could have achieved.'[20]

There was certainly an impact. 'The shit hit the fan,' recalled Garnett[21] of newspaper headlines such as ' "Working girl" play upsets viewers'[22] and 'This must be just about THE LIMIT'.[23] Hot on the trail of the programme-makers was Mary Whitehouse, who wrote to Health Minister Kenneth Robinson, 'The BBC are determined to do everything in their power to present promiscuity as normal . . . The parents of this country are not prepared to stand by and watch young people exploited for the indulgence of dirty minds. The continual denigration of womanhood is disastrous to our national life.'[24] As well as Whitehouse's complaint that the play featured titillation, her indictment of the abortion scene was widely reported by the press, with an insistence that the portrayal of 'clean living would obviate such a fearful thing'.[25]

Clearly, she did not consider for one moment that such lecturing and moralising only distanced her from reality and did nothing to tackle the issues faced by a modern, democratic society.

The conflicting arguments resurfaced when *Up the Junction* was repeated in both 1977 and 1993. Many critics recognised it as the play that revolutionised television drama, in its method of filming and for the subject matter it put on screen, while the moralising *Daily Mail* could only preach about 'the damage this play has wreaked' and ludicrously claim that Nell Dunn's story 'came from a perverse sense of middle-class guilt', leading to permissiveness and an increase in divorce and abortions, 'at the expense of family life'.[26] Little had changed from the days of the Spanish Civil War, when George Orwell cited the *Mail* as one of the biggest culprits as he observed 'history being written not in terms of what happened but of what ought to have happened according to various "party lines" '.[27]

Although the BBC took the flak at the time of the play's original screening, the regime of Hugh Greene and the attitude of head of drama Sydney Newman allowed programme-makers the freedom to court controversy. 'Sydney was an old hand,' explained Garnett. 'He tried to keep a straight face and discipline the "naughty boys at the back of the class", but really he was relishing it. We did have huge battles in those days and Mary Whitehouse was on the prowl, which was an added frisson, but it was actually very good free publicity and helped the ratings.'[28]

The other big fight, to make television plays on film, was set to be won, in the face of deeply entrenched opposition and an agreement between the BBC and the actors' union, Equity, stipulating that at least 10 per cent of any drama had to be shot in a television studio using the traditional multi-camera technique.

'After *Up the Junction*, I had a very bloody battle for months and months,' recalled Garnett, 'and Ken and I were on tenterhooks about it because this was the direction we wanted to go. We were straining to be allowed to go out and make films. But the BBC had two objections to our filming on location with 16mm cameras. It had just built the new Television Centre at White City, with huge, well-equipped studios designed mainly for big light-entertainment shows and drama. Just at that moment, one of their producers was saying: "I don't want to use them." I was having these arguments with Sydney Newman and the executives on the sixth floor. I told Sydney:

"Instead of doing these plays in the studio, give me the same amount of money and we will go out and shoot them on film."

'Ironically, the other objection to shooting on 16mm, with all the immediacy and flexibility of that camera, rather than the cumbersome 35mm one, came not from BBC management, but from the BBC film department in Ealing, who stood to gain most. They dug their heels in and refused on the basis that 16mm was for news, current affairs and documentaries, while 35mm was for drama, and they would not compromise their quality by allowing us to shoot on 16mm. Up until that time, drama on 35mm had been filmed inserts to electronic, studio-shot plays. For instance, a taxi draws up, somebody gets out, goes to the front door of the house, rings the bell and goes in, then you switch to the studio. For that, they insisted on 35mm to maintain the quality.

'Michael Peacock, BBC1's controller, said he wanted A-list drama, not B-movies, arguing that nothing of quality could be done with a small amount of location filming. Eventually, after months of fighting and shouting and screaming and blood over the floor, he relented and was very gracious about it. He said to Sydney: "Let him do one or two." We did, although even then we had to do 10 per cent in the studio for a while but, gradually, that died out.'[29] Loach recalled that Garnett was very good at 'the corridor politics', adding, 'They would give us an inch and we would try to take a mile.'[30]

As well as establishing the right to film with 16mm cameras, Loach, influenced by his experience in theatre and the ideas of Joan Littlewood, was beginning to build his own repertory company of actors. Those such as Tony Selby, Ken Jones and George Sewell took leading roles in more than one 'Wednesday Play', while others who appeared repeatedly among the supporting cast included Wally Patch, Will Stampe, George Tovey, Rita Webb, Hilda Barry, Gladys Dawson, Winifred Dennis, Doreen Herrington, Julie May and Alan Selwyn. A frantic first twelve months on 'The Wednesday Play' was crowned for Loach when he won the Guild of Television Producers and Directors' Director of the Year award.

Interestingly, his former collaborator, Roger Smith, later wrote the screenplay for a cinema version of *Up the Junction* when director Peter Collinson was keen to remake it as his début feature film. 'I couldn't reproduce the original, and didn't want to,' said Smith. 'So I centred it on one character who crosses the river, Polly, who was loosely based on Nell Dunn, but not specifically her. That character didn't exist in the book.'[31] The film, starring Suzy Kendall and Dennis Waterman, concentrated on the young Chelsea woman's relationship with a boyfriend, but it was an example of a cinema remake being outshone by its small-screen original. Loach had no wish to remake *Up the Junction* for the big screen, explaining, 'We felt we had done it as well as we could.'[32]

6

CATHY COME HOME

IF THERE WAS TRULY A Golden Age of British television, as opposed to a romanticised reflection on its formative years through rose-tinted glasses, *Up the Junction* and *Cathy Come Home* represent its zenith in contemporary drama. Anyone who thought the first play had made as big an impact as television ever could must have been unprepared for the shockwaves to come. Loach had shown that the new wave of small-screen drama could be relevant to the lives of people in Britain, with hotly debated, topical issues such as capital punishment and abortion. Now, with *Cathy Come Home*, he proved that television could speed up change. But it also served as a lesson: although highlighting a social scandal, it offered no political solutions, so its acceptance by those of all persuasions made Loach determined that politics would be at the core of his future work.

This new play originated in the same house as *Up the Junction*. Like his wife, Nell Dunn, Eton- and Oxford-educated Jeremy Sandford, the son of a book publisher, had observed at first hand the lives of those in Battersea after moving from fashionable Chelsea. When a neighbour and her children were evicted and placed in Newington Lodge, Southwark, an accommodation centre for homeless families provided by the then London County Council, he started to investigate the issue. ('Newington Lodge really did seem like a place that God had forgotten,' he said much later.)[1] As a result, he wrote articles about homelessness for Sunday newspapers and a radio documentary, *Homeless Families*, then the script that became *Cathy Come Home*. 'We hoped it would appear as a document in the 1964 General Election, as an indictment of Toryism, but we were unable to find anyone to back it,' said Sandford.[2] It was twice rejected by the BBC's 'Wednesday Play' bosses, Sydney Newman and Peter Luke, who took over from James MacTaggart. 'One commends his crusading spirit but this is documentary stuff . . . "The Wednesday Play" is not a political platform,' said Luke, quoted in a rejection letter from story editor David Benedictus.[3]

'Jeremy had submitted it with the awful title *The Abyss*,' recalled Tony Garnett. 'Then it was brought to my attention by Nell Dunn. I got the play off the ground and, with BBC management, I was a little economical with the truth over what it was about.'[4] The play was an uncompromising attack on council house waiting lists and the policy of separating husbands from their homeless wives and children, and generally a cry to help those whom the system allowed to slip through the net of the welfare state. It followed the story of Cathy, a young woman moving to London, meeting Reg and giving birth to two children. Then Reg loses his job as a lorry driver after an accident and they live with his unfriendly mother in Islington, move to a squalid council house from which they are evicted (a scene in which fear is etched into the toddlers' eyes as the door is hammered down), before an arson attack drives them from a caravan site, leaving social services emergency accommodation, a rat-ridden hostel, as the only refuge. Reg is separated from his family, and Cathy, by this time the mother of a baby daughter, eventually hands her elder son to a friend to look after, concerned about his welfare.

'It was a very dramatic story to make your toes curl,' said Loach, 'but the original script was very rambling. Tony and I talked about it with Jeremy, then I did some research with him, visiting hostels and homeless people he knew, and the two of us worked on the shape of the script, which was changed many times. [The play was billed "A story by Jeremy Sandford".] It became a horror story about the destruction of a whole set of family relationships and the string of events that brought it about.'[5]

All the stories in the resulting script were based on real events and Sandford had no doubt about who should take the title role: Carol White. So he was fortunate when she was turned down for the part of Bianca, alongside Richard Burton and Elizabeth Taylor, in director Franco Zeffirelli's Hollywood film version of *The Taming of the Shrew*. The actress heard the news while visiting Nell Dunn. 'You didn't get it?' said Dunn's husband, who was clearly pleased. 'I'm terribly sorry, Carol, of course,' he continued. 'It's just that I have been working on a play and I was rather hoping that you would do it.'[6]

Loach had his own reasons for casting White. 'Both Tony and I knew her, she had two small children and she was terrific in *Up the Junction*,' he explained. 'There was something quite touching about her performance – a warmth came through the screen and it made people want to watch. As well as being effervescent, there was a kind of sadness about her because you knew she was never going to get where she wanted to be; that was the impression she gave on screen. Really, she was just an ordinary girl with dreams, but too wayward ever to make them happen.'[7]

Loach saw something 'very solid'[8] in Ray Brooks, who was cast as Reg, although cameraman Tony Imi found him less convincing. 'To me, Ray was the odd one out,' he explained, 'because he was an established actor and the others were unknown people and played it real. He was the one who stuck out. I remember doing take after take with Ray because his performance was all too fine and studied.'[9] Brooks had already appeared in several feature films, including a starring role in *The Knack . . . and how to get it*, director Richard Lester's modish, fast-moving version of a stage play about a shy teacher (played by Michael Crawford on screen) who learns how to be successful with women from his lodger (Brooks). Lester had brought his surrealistic style to films after writing for the Goons on radio and, in making *The Knack*, pre-empted Loach's technique of shooting on the streets and catching the natural, unguarded reactions of real people.

Filming *Cathy Come Home* was a testing experience for Loach, with fourteen days scheduled on location and five short scenes to be shot in a studio in just a few hours. For the first time, all location work was filmed in sequence, according to the script, a practice that the director adopted in all his future work, wherever possible. 'It was an absolute scramble,' recalled Tony Garnett, 'because it was a hugely ambitious production, with filming in London, outside London and in Birmingham, and more than sixty speaking parts. I remember, when we were doing the scene out in Essex where the caravan was burned out, my assistant, Jane Harris, and I got in the car with *Spotlight*, the actors' directory, and went to that location to talk to Ken about casting for the next day. In terms of resources, it was like fitting a quart into a pint pot. It was a terribly difficult play to organise and John Mackenzie, the first assistant director, was one of the heroes of that film.'[10] (Mackenzie went on to become a successful director of films such as *The Long Good Friday* and *The Fourth Protocol*.)

A judge who issues an eviction order against Reg in one of the studio scenes was acted by Ruth Kettlewell, who had a reputation for playing battleaxes and found enough time to visit a magistrates' court to get a feel for the role of 'condemning those poor young souls'.[11] Barry Jackson, who was becoming typecast in television as menacing characters, played a rent collector banging at Carol White's door. Although the actor had a script, Loach prompted him to continue beyond the end of it and improvise. This was another technique that the director was evolving, seeing where the action led and using the unscripted material if it added to the drama. 'When I trained at LAMDA, we were encouraged to improvise,' said Jackson. 'It was unusual in television, but I had been forewarned, so I expected it.' However, the resulting realism was genuinely moving, even for one who was prepared for unpredictable reactions. 'It ended up rather distressingly, with Carol shutting the door on me,' recalled Jackson.[12] Further realism was added by using White's own sons, Sean and Stephen, as her children on screen.

Carol White with Ray Brooks and her real-life sons in *Cathy Come Home* [BBC]

Also unfamiliar to television drama viewers were locations that they normally saw only in documentaries. Gabrielle Hamilton, who played a social services department's welfare officer visiting an elderly man to explain why he should move to an old people's home, against his will, was left with a lasting impression of a Peabody estate where there was 'washing strung up across the courtyard of a very interesting tenement, with archways leading up to the various flats'.[13]

For Tony Imi, shooting *Cathy Come Home* was another exciting challenge, following the reactions to *Up the Junction*. 'Ken asked me what I thought we should do differently,' he recalled. 'I said: "I don't know, but let's just see how it pans out." Once again, we honed the work of not rehearsing. There would be a group of people, all chatting, and I was in the middle, trying to get sense out of what the scene was about; the energy there was incredible. At the same time, there were people on the film crew who had come up through the system and frowned upon it, saying: "This is very amateurish." I think, really, they felt out of it.'[14]

Cathy Come Home evolved the style of shooting on the streets that Loach had used in *Up the Junction*. 'The basic rule of standard film-making,' he explained, 'was that you empty the street, you put production assistants all round the corners, you stop anybody walking through and you shoot the scene. I started to encourage people to walk through so that you have a natural flow of people. Then it was another development to say we'll put the camera some way away and see how people around it respond. By having a documentary approach, we created a situation in which things were likely to happen, then filmed them. *Cathy Come Home* was the first example of that.'[15]

The play's final scene remains one of the most memorable in television history, hitting viewers like a punch in the stomach with its shock and raw emotion. As Cathy stands on Liverpool Street railway station, social workers suddenly move in to drag her two remaining children (one played by Carol White's son, Stephen) away so that they can be taken into care; their cries were real, as were White's own reactions. 'I really did get hysterical,' she said. 'I really felt that they were going to be taken away.'[16]

With the camera positioned well away from the action, which took place on the station concourse, Loach created a situation that was observed by rail travellers as real. He used hand signals to cue the actors playing social workers. 'We only had one shot at it, really, because you don't want to put the kids through that sort of thing more than once,' he said. 'It was upsetting to do it, although we were running around with a camera so fast and juggling so many elements that we didn't have time to dwell upon that while we were doing it. Those feelings hit you more in retrospect.'[17]

Tony Imi recalled feelings that *were* present at the time. 'Being with her own child made it more harrowing for Carol,' he said, 'and, while we were shooting, one woman dived out of the crowd, thinking the whole thing was real, and started freaking out, which made Carol start to do the same.'[18] Producer Garnett witnessed some of the filming on the station but admits he was not there for 'the crucial scene', adding, 'Frankly, I would have stopped it because I think life is more important than art. I don't think it's worth upsetting a child. That would have been one of the few disagreements that Ken and I had over fifteen years.'[19] But Loach insisted his pursuit of realism caused only temporary upset. 'The frame of the shot was only ten yards wide,' he explained. 'OK, they were taken, but they stopped twelve yards away and were then allowed back to their mother. It wasn't as if they were taken off.'[20]

The play finished with a caption that read, 'All the events in this film took place in Britain within the last eighteen months.' There followed other raw statistics that lay behind the human misery: 12,500 homeless in Britain and 4,000 children placed in care. Not only did this leave a lasting impression on viewers, but making *Cathy Come Home* had a profound effect on Carol White, who instantly became identified with the tragic role. 'In playing the part,' she said, 'I was frequently able to relate to some of the things I had seen in the hostels for the homeless when I did my research. The whole thing affected me enormously.'[21] People even approached the actress in the street, calling her 'Cathy'. 'I remember walking down King Street in Hammersmith,' she said twenty years later, 'and I was pushing my youngest son when someone came up to me and said: "Cathy, how are you doing?" I'm always remembered as Cathy. Even now, talking about it makes me feel emotional.'[22]

After its screening, *Cathy Come Home* had an immediate effect. Twelve days later, there was a public discussion in Birmingham, where Loach and Sandford talked about the issue of homelessness with city councillors, who were incensed at the portrayal of their city in the play but quickly abandoned their policy of separating men from their wives and children; this action was followed by some other local authorities. After a special screening was arranged for the Minister for Housing and Local Government, Anthony Greenwood, his Parliamentary Private Secretary, Wayland Young, and three permanent officials at the Ministry of Housing, Tony Garnett wrote to his BBC bosses, 'We were not challenged at any point either on our intentions in making the film or our facts.'[23] Although unhappy about the statistics shown at the end of the programme, the politicians did not dispute them.

Such was the public and political outrage after the screening of *Cathy Come Home* that it was repeated just six weeks later, followed immediately by discussions on both BBC1 and ITV. Laurence Evans, of the Local Government Information Office, who had asked local council officials to look out for mistakes in the play, protested in the BBC's *Twenty-four Hours* that it was unjust to welfare officers while, on the rival channel's *Frost Programme*, local government officers sought to defend themselves. Jeremy Sandford found himself in demand to speak at meetings of tenants' associations and the homeless, and wrote a novel based on the television production.

The play was repeated again in 1968, on the second anniversary of its original screening, after it won the prestigious Prix Italia award. It was followed with a postscript by Sandford updating the figures – an increase to 15,000 homeless people and 5,000 children in care, but acknowledgement that some action had been taken to alleviate the problem – and a discussion in *Late Night Line-up*, in which Anthony Greenwood declared that the film should become compulsory viewing once a month but maintained his view that the set of disasters befalling one family in it was not typical.

In the intervening two years, the Labour government had made some attempt to tackle the issue of homelessness by embarking on a national housebuilding programme and, through a White Paper, urging councils to abandon the policy of separating parents and children. Fifteen days after the first screening of *Cathy Come Home*, on the tide of public emotion that followed, Shelter was launched in the crypt of St Martin-in-the Fields Church, near

Trafalgar Square, by five Church housing association trusts. It mounted a publicity campaign to heighten awareness about the issue and appeal for donations, and frequently used clips and stills from the play for promotional purposes. The charity initially focused on four cities where the need was most acute, Birmingham, Glasgow, Liverpool and London, and worked with housing associations to improve what housing provision there already was and to create more. Des Wilson, Shelter's founding director, estimated that the first two screenings of *Cathy Come Home* were worth £500,000 to Shelter and referred to it as 'a scream of pain'.[24] Carol White also gave public talks to raise money for Shelter.

'There was quite a furore,' Loach commented three decades later, in his usual quiet, understated manner, but he came to realise in the wake of the television film's screenings that it had raised a social issue, put in the context of a personal tragedy, without outlining the political causes, so politicians of all persuasions adopted it as a *cause célèbre*. 'We were very suspicious of all those who tried to climb on the band wagon,' he said. 'We saw Anthony Greenwood and he tried to pat us on the head, and we were not of a mind to be patted on the head; we wanted to draw blood, really. But there was nothing in the film that suggested what ought to have been done, so I think that was the end of our reformist period.'[25] Loach and Garnett vowed to be more directly political in future, feeling that responsibility for the housing shortage should not be left to a charity. 'We said to ourselves,' recalled Loach, 'that, if we were to do a film like that again, we'd somehow have to tackle the ownership of the land, the building industry and the financing behind it. Otherwise, you're not really challenging anything.'[26]

Press reaction to *Cathy Come Home* largely followed this apolitical admonishment for a system that allowed homelessness to continue, with *The Times* headlining its review 'A searing indictment of housing conditions'.[27] But there were also the old criticisms about mixing fact and fiction, which conveniently sidelined the real issue, particularly in the *Sunday Telegraph*. Under the headline 'Play or propaganda?', its television critic, Philip Purser, slammed *Cathy Come Home* for 'sailing under false colours' by employing documentary techniques and, astonishingly, backed up his attack by asserting that Sandford 'fell back on statistics and snatches of tape-recorded testimony to shore up his case'.[28] Clearly,

Purser did not do likewise! In the same newspaper, a headline plea to 'Stop mixing TV fact and fiction' appeared over an article written by Grace Wyndham Goldie, who had recently retired as the BBC's head of talks and current affairs. A pioneer of those programmes over the previous twenty years, overseeing the development of series such as *Panorama* and *Tonight*, she described the 'semi-documentary' style as 'a new and dangerous trend in television drama'. She asserted that viewers expected images in news and current affairs reports to be 'an accurate reflection of the real world' and contended that the mix of 'the real with the fictional' might cast doubt on 'the validity of what has in fact been real'.[29]

Goldie was from the old BBC school of which the founding father was John Reith, the corporation's first director-general, whose idea of 'impartiality' was to write many of Conservative Prime Minister Stanley Baldwin's speeches during the 1926 General Strike and not allow labour leaders radio airtime during the dispute. The reaction of BBC establishment types such as Goldie was what led Loach and Garnett to keep the exact content of *Cathy Come Home* from their bosses in advance of transmission. A few weeks beforehand, Garnett, in a memo to head of plays and drama Gerald Savory, described it as a 'love story'[30] and let executives see it only after the programme billing had gone to press in *Radio Times*, ensuring that any ban would be as public as possible.

Exactly a year before broadcasting *Cathy Come Home*, the BBC had banned *The War Game*, director Peter Watkins's meticulously researched, shocking account of the predicted aftermath of a nuclear attack. In subsequent years, as Establishment figures gained control of both the BBC and the commercial television regulator, the Independent Television Authority (later the Independent Broadcasting Authority), censorship would become more commonplace – and Loach himself was the subject of it when he switched to making documentaries. Over many years following the screenings of *Cathy Come Home*, there were also attempts to discredit Jeremy Sandford's factual research and, in 1976, the writer publicly thanked BBC head of drama Sydney Newman, director of television Kenneth Adam and director-general Hugh Greene, who 'stood by the film' despite 'strong pressure [that] was put on the establishment of the BBC to recant, to "confess" that the picture was inaccurate, to apologise'.[31]

With *Cathy Come Home*, Loach and Garnett had crystallised their vision of telling truth outside the realm of an alloted slot, the television news, and shown that it could be acknowledged to be just as legitimate, if not more so. 'The idea,' explained Loach, 'was not to ask, "Is the play true?" but, "What truth is there in the play?" Those in authority were afraid that, if people did not know what was true and what was not, they would question the validity of the news. That was just what we wanted to do because the news is partial and a point of view; there's no such thing as an objective news report. The whole argument about objectivity is an impossible concept. The point is: what are they defending in the guise of objectivity?'[32]

In an attempt to repudiate the attacks on *Cathy Come Home*, Sandford wrote another television play, *Edna the Inebriate Woman*, about a down-and-out, which was directed by Ted Kotcheff in 1970. Unfortunately, by the time Sandford investigated the issue of homelessness once more, for the BBC documentary *Cathy Where Are You Now?* twenty years later,[33] he discovered that the problem had worsened as a result of cutbacks by both Labour and Conservative governments, and the eventual abandonment of a national housebuilding programme by Prime Minister Margaret Thatcher. The new statistics made grim reading: one million families officially accepted as homeless over the previous decade; homeless families in emergency accommodation rising from 4,400 to 38,000 over the twenty-five years since *Cathy Come Home*; single homeless sleeping rough rising from 1,000 to 6,000 in that time; and a dramatic reduction in the building of council homes, from 178,000 started in 1967 to just 12,000 in 1989.

The political arguments taking place among medical professionals in the mid-1960s were clearly illuminated in Loach's next 'Wednesday Play', *In Two Minds*, another drama centred on a social issue. It opens with a young woman, regarded as schizophrenic by psychiatrists of the old school, talking to her doctor. She tells him about the relationship she has with her mother, whose domineering, repressive nature is the real cause of her illness, in the view of a new wave of psychiatrists led by R.D. Laing. This was a firm repudiation of the traditional view that schizophrenia was something with which people were born and which could be treated and cured in the manner of a disease.

But this was not a typical Loach production. Indeed, he had little involvement in it until shortly before filming began. The driving forces behind *In Two Minds* were David Mercer, the fast-rising, Yorkshire-born playwright who had enjoyed success on television, and Tony Garnett, who studied psychology at university. Mercer had suffered a nervous breakdown before writing his 1962 play *A Suitable Case for Treatment*, an examination of psychiatric practice, which was turned into the film *Morgan*, about an artist's divorce pushing him towards insanity, and Garnett knew from the personal experience of someone close to him about the trauma of mental instability.

'The story of *In Two Minds* is the story of my life,' explained Garnett. 'David and I were very close friends and shared not only an interest in Marxism, but an interest in Freud. At that time, we were interested in the work of R.D. Laing, David Cooper and Aaron Esterson, and the double-bind theory and scapegoating within families – all those ideas that left-wing psychiatrists had made fashionable. David and I talked to Ronnie [Laing] and Esterson, and visited David Cooper's experimental ward. David had also been privy to my personal story and, out of all that, I commissioned him to write the television script. Initially, I was going to ask Roy Battersby to direct it, but he was working under Aubrey Singer, doing *Tomorrow's World*, and I couldn't get him out of that department in time because the BBC was so bureaucratic, so I asked Ken to do it.'[34]

For Loach, who 'used scripts to live off', Mercer was not the ideal writer. 'He cherished every word and we didn't really see eye to eye in terms of how filming should be done,' explained the director. 'I found sticking exactly to the working script a bit of a straitjacket and sometimes a bit artificial.'[35] By stamping his own mark on the script, Loach did not endear himself to Mercer. 'The relationship with David wasn't acrimonious, but he was not a writer I worked well with,' said Loach. 'A lot of the script was interviews and I felt that, if it were learned, I would never get that sense of people being put on the spot and searching for a reply. I thought it would be dead if I stuck to every dot and comma of the script. So, although I didn't get the cast to improvise the content, I asked them to rethink it through in their own words.'[36]

In Two Minds featured Anna Cropper as Kate Winter – 'I gave her a terrible hairpiece!' recalled Loach, lightening the discussion[37] – with experienced character actors George A. Cooper and Helen Booth taking the roles of her parents. The political nature of the subject-matter gave the play the hard edge that Loach sought. 'It was very contentious because it was saying that what is called schizophrenia can be an understandable response to an intolerable situation,' he said. 'This was about the politics of the family, which is always interesting and engrossing, and the way in which the parents might impose a personality on their child, which is usually a reflection of themselves. Most kids can brush that off but, if it becomes too oppressive, it gives the child real problems in differentiating their own personality.'[38]

Although Laing acted as a consultant to the play, *In Two Minds* simply took up his theories and projected them on to a fictional family. 'It was a completely invented piece,' explained Mercer. 'It wasn't a Laing case history – though it had all the characteristics of one. Laing was in any case ethically prevented from giving me access to his files. But, once you've grasped the Laingian idea of the schizogenic family, and if you can write, then you can invent a schizogenic family which has its counterpart in the real world . . . I didn't even know, when I was writing, that it was going to be given a documentary treatment by Ken Loach. I thought we'd be in the studio, with actors and constructed sets.'[39]

In reality, of course, Loach continued on his path of taking drama out of the studio. Alongside the debate about the causes of schizophrenia was the depiction of the almost brutal ways in which those diagnosed with mental illness were treated. 'We filmed all the real electric-shock treatment on real patients and they shook like mad,' recalled cameraman Tony Imi.[40]

Shooting this and the 'interviews', in the manner of current affairs programmes and documentaries, blurred the distinction between fact and fiction more than ever – and the debate about this continued in British newspapers – but Loach was successful in giving the issue of schizophrenia and its possible causes a wide airing. An hour after the screening of *In Two Minds* on BBC1, BBC2's *Late Night Line-up* provided psychiatrists with a forum for discussion. Inevitably, the agenda was set by the inclusion of professionals representing the old and new schools of thought, and the debate spread to the following day's newspapers. There were accusations that the play could frighten those who needed treatment and that others might believe their illnesses had been wrongly diagnosed or they were receiving the wrong treatment. 'One cannot calculate the effect of such a play on all the people who watched it,' wrote Henry Stanhope in the *Sun*.[41] It sounded like the bogus argument advanced by the BBC when it banned *The War Game* from being screened. At least, for the first time, the issue was in front of a mass audience, rather than just medical professionals; and it was one to which Loach would return.

A more obvious choice of subject for a mass audience was featured in his next 'Wednesday Play'. In younger years, the director had followed Nuneaton Borough Football Club's semi-professional side, until a love of theatre took over his life. But, since settling in London and buying a house in Barnes, he had found a renewed enthusiasm for the game and followed the fortunes of Fulham's Football League team. When Tony Garnett, a lifelong Aston Villa supporter, was approached with an idea for a play centred not just on a soccer club, but a real-life star, he had no hesitation in assigning it to Loach. Neville Smith, a Liverpool actor who had appeared in three of Loach's productions, *Wear a Very Big Hat*, *The End of Arthur's Marriage* and *In Two Minds*, was keen to write about the team *he* supported, Everton, who vied with Liverpool for success in a city split between two teams and two religious denominations, Catholic and Protestant. 'It was really about my family following Everton and a particular player called Alex Young,' explained Smith. 'He was beautiful and blond, and the play's title, *The Golden Vision*, described him.'[42]

The title also referred to the fans' expectations as they looked forward to the weekly game on a Saturday. The play, which reflected the passion held for football by millions of Britons, included a birth, a marriage and a death: the birth interfered with one of the fans getting to a match; the best man and groom at a wedding rushed off to a game after the wedding ceremony; and a lifelong Everton supporter's dying wish was that his ashes be scattered over the team's ground, Goodison Park.

Concerned that Smith had just one radio play behind him and had never previously scripted for television, Garnett suggested that he should team up with another writer. Loach recalled reading an article in *Private Eye* about Gordon Honeycombe, a newscaster with Independent Television News who had submitted a play to the BBC called *United!* and was perturbed that, after its rejection, the BBC launched a football serial under the same title. Honeycombe, who had acted alongside Loach once at Oxford University, was not a fan of football but recognised its potential on screen. 'I had never actually seen a game,' he admitted, 'but it was such a popular sport on television and I thought it would make an interesting series. I did my research via Chelsea and their manager, Tommy Docherty. After seeing the piece in *Private Eye* implying that the BBC had stolen the idea, Ken contacted me at ITN and brought me and Neville together. The two of us then had discussions with Tony Garnett, who fed us some ideas, and we went away and wrote the script. Because it was based on Neville's own family and experiences, he provided the bricks and I did the construction. I shaped it because I knew what worked in terms of a drama, but there was not much I could do with the dialogue because he was a Liverpudlian and he had all the jokes.'[43]

However, there was some friction between the two writers, leading to a falling out, with the result that Honeycombe's input was minimal. Fortunately, Smith's story was strong and those who acted in *The Golden Vision* contributed greatly to it. Liverpool-born Ken Jones, who had already appeared in two of Loach's 'Wednesday Plays', was cast alongside Smith, but the production was notable for being the one in which Loach began his practice of casting club comedians in acting roles. Having just made his first feature film, *Poor Cow* (see next chapter), and unhappy at the experience, he was keen to develop new ways of finding performers who would appear authentic on screen.

'What was significant about *The Golden Vision* for me was that we discovered a lot of Liverpool entertainers,' he explained. 'I found that most actors who came from Liverpool were straight actors who didn't have the humour and sharpness and spontaneity that I was looking for. So I went to a club run by Ernie Mack, who was an agent in Liverpool, and he introduced me to all the acts; they were terrific, with a raw energy and brightness. When they came to act in the play, they were absolutely true.'[44] One of the most significant pieces of casting was stand-up comic Bill Dean, who had a dry sense of humour and a pained expression, and went on to work with Loach five more times.

Another first for the director was taking one further step towards mixing fact and fiction by featuring, alongside the actors and comedians as fictional fans, the real-life Everton team and shooting interviews with manager Harry Catterick and some of the players (with their names appearing as captions on screen). 'Ken, Tony and I felt that, if we made a football film that was fictional, it would all fall apart once you get on the field,' recalled Smith.[45] So, in those days long before the Premiership became British soccer's top flight of teams, three of Everton's First Division games were filmed by the crew, which included cameraman Tony Imi, who had by then left the BBC but was hired by Garnett as a freelance. His biggest nightmare occurred at Highbury Stadium, where Everton took on Arsenal – and Alex Young scored. 'I had a zoom lens and knew there wasn't enough light to shoot something, so I didn't shoot it,' he recalled. 'The goal was scored and, because I missed it, we had to take it off a telecine recording.'[46]

Another nightmare at Highbury came when Neville Smith and the other 'fans' were intimidated by the threats of someone in the crowd. 'Ken told us to shout for Everton,' recalled Smith, 'but we couldn't because a drunken Scotsman produced a knife and said: "Shout for Rangers." Of course, we shouted for Rangers! Ken came up at half-time and said: "What are you doing?" I'm sure he believed we were having him on; by that time, the guy had wandered off.'[47]

Making *The Golden Vision* was a happy experience for all involved and Loach was pleased that it produced such a sense of camaraderie during filming. Alongside the birth, marriage and death in the story, he celebrated a landmark event in his own family during the shoot: the birth of daughter Hannah, in November 1967.

7

POOR COW

THE HARSH STREETS OF London, which in *Up the Junction* had vividly brought home to television viewers the realities of life for many people in Britain, were the setting for Ken Loach's first feature film. The opportunity to direct for the cinema was too good to miss and a natural progression for a drama-maker who had moved out of television studios with electronic cameras to real locations with a single-film camera. But Loach found himself making many compromises and his experience of working along-side unfamiliar people and with actors accustomed to being treated as stars convinced him that the big screen's conventions under-mined his intentions. 'I made a lot of mistakes with that,' he said. 'The actors had caravans. They'd be sitting in these luxury caravans for two or three hours and then get out to a tenement at the Elephant and Castle and say: "What shall we do now, duckie?" '[1]

Poor Cow began as a book by Nell Dunn, which she wrote after Loach made *Up the Junction*. The story was peopled with similarly authentic characters and, for the director, it was natural to cast Carol White in the leading role of Joy, who is married to a bullying criminal, Tom. When he is jailed for a robbery, she finds solace in the arms of the gentler, more sensitive Dave, but her happiness ends when he, too, is put behind bars for taking part in another violent crime. To support her baby son, Joy works as a barmaid and earns extra money by modelling at a seedy studio for 'amateur photo-graphers'. On Tom's release from prison, she gives him another chance but runs off when he beats her up. After walking aimlessly along the streets around Clapham Junction, she returns home to find her young son, Jonny, missing; after a frantic search, she discovers him in a derelict house. Realising that her priority in life is looking after the toddler, she resigns herself to living a treadmill existence with Tom, at least for the foreseeable future: her compromise between dreams and reality.

At the time, White's own account of the film brought home its realism and the touch of naivety that made her such a catch for Loach. 'Nell Dunn wrote it about a real girl she met in the slums,' said White. 'Gosh! I hope her husband in prison hasn't seen it, because she'll really get it. I guess he has, though. Do they show movies in prisons? We wanted to show what can happen to a girl in the slums. These people really exist. They don't ask for much in life, but their own lack of knowledge about life and their own ignorance about how to get a job and get out of their environment does them in. Even if you're pretty, your accent loses you the job, and you fall back on the easy way out – stealing, or nude modelling, or hitting the streets. I could've ended up like that.'[2]

Poor Cow focused on the drabness of life and thwarted hopes experienced by one woman, although she spoke for many. Loach adopted some of the techniques he had used in his television plays, such as Carol White telling her character's story through both voice-over and on-screen captions, and shooting in real locations across London, on the Isle of Sheppey, in Kent, and in the Brecon Beacons, South Wales, capturing the reactions of real people on the streets as he did so; the wistful pop music of Donovan was present throughout, its optimism and gentle strains in stark contrast to the despair and harshness depicted.

But there was no room in the production for Loach's professional partner, Tony Garnett. The driving force behind the film was Italian-born film producer Joseph Janni, a Jew who had fled with his family from Mussolini's Fascist repression and found success in Britain with 'kitchen sink' dramas such as *A Kind of Loving* and *Billy Liar!*. 'Nell Dunn was anxious that *Poor Cow* should be made as a cinema film,' recalled Loach, 'and her agent was in negotiation with Jo Janni. I was anxious that Tony stayed in the team because it had been very much a threesome with me, Tony and Jeremy [Sandford] or Nell. But Jo put quite a lot of pressure on Nell's agent and a certain amount on me to do the film with him as producer, so there wasn't a place for Tony in that set-up. I was very torn and think I made the wrong decision. I should not have done it with Jo; it would have been a much better film with Tony. But we would have had to hold out much longer and there was a question-mark over raising the money. I certainly felt uneasy at the time and I'm sure that Tony felt hurt – and he was right to feel that way. We were all quite naive about film.'[3]

Loach was also unable to use his favoured cameraman, Tony Imi, when Nat Cohen of Anglo Amalgamated, which financed *Poor Cow*, insisted on someone with more film experience. However, the picture adopted a documentary approach in keeping with the style that Loach had evolved, although with less handheld camerawork. As with *Up the Junction*, the director – who wrote the screenplay with Nell Dunn – made the film as a mosaic of 'snapshots' of Joy's life. Brian Probyn was hired as director of photography and, significantly, the camera operator was Chris Menges, who would influence the style of Loach's future work.

'The story demanded a lightness and simplicity,' said Loach. 'I had always shot on 16mm film, which gave a light look and the equipment was light, but we had to shoot this on 35mm. I felt weighed down not just by the equipment, but by the whole way the film was set up. The crew was huge, partly composed of people whom Jo Janni and his production manager knew from feature films and partly people I knew from television. The two groups didn't mix and I felt there was a kind of feeling of superiority from the film people, which was completely unjustified because the television people were quicker and brighter and sharper, while those I worked with felt the other lot were old-fashioned and stereotyped. It was the first film I had done and I was really way out of my depth in a number of ways. Knowing how to shoot it was one because it was midway between two styles, one of which was the handheld, very immediate style of *Up the Junction* and *Cathy Come Home*, and the other was the more reflective one that I was beginning to get interested in. Although I liked the pace and mobility of the handheld, I felt it had its limitations and could get tiresome, and that what was in front of the camera was more important than what the camera was doing. With an eight-week schedule for the film, instead of three for a television play, there was more time to construct the shots better, but I didn't know quite how to do it. I had this idea in my head that it would be interesting to cut from one scene to another only when there was a cut in time, so some of the scenes were far too long and it isn't fluent.'[4]

Obliged to shoot in colour for the first time, Loach was also keen not to 'end up with "nice" shots of slums and drab surroundings, which look attractive but make an entirely different pictorial comment to the one you intend'. His overriding aim was to portray the 'colossal waste' and Joy's 'great potential for enjoying life, for really living', but getting a 'raw deal' through her environment.[5]

Another compromise for Loach was accepting Terence Stamp, fresh from making Joseph Janni's production of *Far from the Madding Crowd*, as Dave, in preference to his own choice, Billy Murray. 'I had wanted an unknown actor for that role and felt Billy was a bit more authentic,' said Loach.[6] Murray, a graduate of the East 15 acting school, whose training had been partly funded by East End gangsters Ronnie and Reggie Kray, was cast instead as a criminal friend of Tom (three decades later, the actor became familiar to television viewers as corrupt copper Don Beech in *The Bill*). Loach had spotted Murray rehearsing the role of Demetrius in *A Midsummer Night's Dream* when he visited the drama school with *Poor Cow*'s casting director, Miriam Brickman. The director asked the budding actor to improvise a scenario in which he was being visited in prison by his wife or girlfriend. 'He told us we were supposed to be talking through the grille and the glass,' recalled Murray. 'I said to Ken: "How long is this guy doing?" He said: "A long time." So I said there would be no grille and glass. When he asked how I knew, I told him I visited people in prison and a friend of mine was doing fifteen years.'[7]

Later, a limousine was sent to collect Murray and take him to the World's End pub in Chelsea, where some potential cast members were congregating to take part in further auditions. 'Afterwards,' recalled Murray, 'Carol White said to me: "I hope you get it." I left and thought no more of it, until another limo came to take me to Jo Janni's office. Ken and Miriam were there and Jo was sitting behind a huge desk. He asked me: "Do you fancy playing any other part in this film? Pick a part." I was a drama student; I couldn't make a decision. He had clearly taken Ken's power away. Later, Miriam Brickman told me that Jo had given an ultimatum to Ken: he could have either Julie Christie and Billy Murray or Carol White and a name. But she told me not to worry because the people he wanted were Albert Finney, Tom Courtenay or Terence Stamp. She said: "I gave all three of them their first jobs, so I'll send scripts to them, as I have been asked to do, with a note saying, 'Don't bother to read it. I've got someone for it.'" Two weeks later, she told me: "I got Courtenay's and Finney's back, but Terence Stamp is dying to do it." Miriam was very apologetic and Ken said he had people for the other roles, but would I be part of the group, just to be in it.'[8]

However, Loach had no complaints about the star. 'Terence Stamp was fine,' he said. 'He was committed and worked very well. But, obviously, he brought with him memories of other parts. That was a concept that Jo Janni didn't understand. I had always been used to working collaboratively with Tony Garnett or whoever and we would talk things out, listen to what the other person thought, take that into account, then make a decision. If you're trying to work with someone who doesn't hear what you are saying, it's very difficult.'[9]

At least Loach had his own way in giving John Bindon his first acting role, as Tom. Bindon, who was known to Nell Dunn, had the authentic background sought by the director, having spent time in Borstal as a teenager and seven years in prison for assault. At the time of *Poor Cow*'s release, the film's publicist – mischievously or innocently – described Bindon as a former merchant navy deck-hand who subsequently worked in the antiques business, becoming 'something of an expert in detecting fake old paintings and furniture'.

During Loach's auditions, Bindon took part in an improvised scenario with Kate Williams, who landed the role of barmaid Beryl, Joy's friend with the contemporary beehive hairdo. 'Ken was obviously looking at the scene where he rows with Carol White,' recalled Williams. 'My brief from Ken was to goad Johnny into a row and make him see red. It worked remarkably well and I actually was very frightened. Johnny wasn't an actor and I couldn't tell whether he was acting or not, but Ken had to call a halt to the improvisation. He didn't actually hit me, but I was never sure that he wasn't going to. It was my first film and this was quite an initiation, not what I was expecting. But Johnny was very good, so he got the part.'[10] Bindon's criminal past proved invaluable when Loach needed to know how to stage the robberies featured in the film. *Poor Cow* also gave Malcolm McDowell his first feature film experience, as another of Carol White's string of on-screen lovers, although it was limited to a roll in the hay.

Shooting started in the spring of 1967 and the arrival of Terence Stamp on set immediately compromised Loach's working style. 'I told Carol White that there would be no caravans for actors,' he recalled. 'We would do it like we did television films: everybody just looked after themselves and stood in line for food. It had worked for us well in the past. Carol agreed to that and I told the production manager. Carol was shooting for a few days before Terence Stamp arrived, when we were filming in flats at an old Peabody's building in the Elephant and Castle with a narrow yard at the back. Suddenly, there was a huge kerfuffle of motor horns and people shouting. Into this narrow yard, they were trying to bring a trailer. "It's Mr Stamp's caravan," I was told. I was really cross. Obviously, Terence Stamp's agent and the producer had agreed he would have it, without telling me or Carol. She got very upset and thought she was being taken advantage of, so the next day another huge caravan appeared, even bigger. From then on, the whole character of the film changed and became like a big, old-fashioned feature film.'[11]

Loach's concerns paled into insignificance when he took them home, though. 'My father died during the filming of *Poor Cow*,' said his wife Lesley, 'and that was the worst thing in the world that had ever happened to me, so I got a bit cross when Ken came home once and said that Terence Stamp and Carol White were arguing about the size of their caravans. That was such a contrast to what I and my brothers and sisters were going through. I thought: "What a terrible business to be in." '[12]

Despite his frustrations, Loach displayed on set a talent for staying cool and never losing his temper, which became another of his trademarks. 'Ken got people to do things in such a gentle, mild-mannered way,' recalled Billy Murray. 'He never bullied and never played the director.'[13] After working so closely with Loach on *Up the Junction* and *Cathy Come Home*, Carol White knew exactly what he wanted of her. 'We had got to the stage where we communicated by telepathy,' she recalled. 'If something was wrong with a scene, we both knew what it was before we stopped to discuss it.'[14] The rapport they had built up over those previous productions meant that White simply handed herself over to Loach. 'I trusted him,' she explained. 'We just talked out each scene before we shot it, then we improvised it.'[15] The actress's own vulnerability was clear to others on the set, though. 'She was very nervous and unsure of herself,' recalled Billy Murray.[16]

The use of toddlers to play White's son in the film presented a different challenge, especially in scenes with Terence Stamp. 'It was a family affair,' she said. 'The little boy who played my child at the age of one-and-a-half was really my nephew, Simon. Simon hated Stamp and, every time Stamp had to come near us, Simon would cry. Then, when the child grew to the age of three, we used my own son, Stevie.'[17]

But one scene that filled White with dread was that in which Joy and Beryl model for the photographers, one of whom admits to having no film in his camera. 'So Ken took me down to this club where I watched this hard French piece pulling off her clothes and I was so embarrassed I walked out,' recalled White. 'Ken said I could wear a negligée, but when I got into the scene something remarkable happened. I was so involved that I started exposing myself all over and I just didn't care. I peeled everything off and actually enjoyed it and, every time I laughed out of embarrassment, Ken would just leave in all the laughs and blushes.'[18]

Laughs and blushes had already been experienced by two of the cast before the scene was filmed at a real photographers' studio in Pimlico. Kate Williams joined a fellow East 15 acting school graduate, John 'Ginger' Halstead, on a train from Ilford, in Essex, heading for Liverpool Street station. Although nervous about stripping on the first day of her first film, she felt more comfortable in knowing that a friend would be among those playing the photographers. Also with her was a case containing her 'pretties' – the underwear she had bought specially for her wedding the previous December;[19] a tight budget meant that cast members were asked to provide some of their own costumes. When the pair stepped off the train at Stratford, to change to the Underground, Williams realised she had left the case on the train. 'I didn't know what was in the case,' recalled Halstead. 'I jumped on the Tube train that had just come in and was going to Liverpool Street, and Kate said she would wait for the next mainline train. I arrived there first, found the lost property office, went in and said I'd left my case on the train. They discovered it had just been handed in and, when they asked what was in it, I told them it was clothes I was going to wear in a film. When they opened the case, there was all this ladies' underwear, so I came clean and said it wasn't really my case – it belonged to a friend and we were both appearing in a film for Ken Loach. Within minutes, Kate arrived, so we got out of that, they believed us and away we went for Pimlico.'[20]

When it came to shooting the scene, while White exposed more than she had intended, Williams clung on to her dignity. 'It's a tribute to Ken that friends remember me stripping off,' she said. 'In fact, I didn't strip at all – I was in underwear.'[21] But the seediness that was hinted at on screen crept into the filming. 'There was a real photographer there,' recalled Halstead, 'and, in the middle of filming, Carol got really pissed off and said: "Just a minute. I can hear film going round in someone's camera." Ken asked us all to stop, the backs of our cameras were opened and the real photographer was discovered with film in his. He was bounced off the set straight away.'[22]

Loach himself shot many feet of film while making *Poor Cow*, an early example of his practice of providing plenty of options at the editing stage, and created opportunities for authentic interaction and dialogue to occur. 'Before each scene,' Williams recalled, 'he briefed us on the bare bones of what was going to happen, let us pretty much improvise and shot a lot of footage. For the scene where Carol and I were eating burgers at an open-air café, which was in Richmond-upon-Thames, Ken told me to chat up real passers-by in the street and the assistants would have to run with clearance forms to get permission to use them in the film.'[23]

Although she played White's friend, Williams found that the star did not continue the relationship once the camera stopped rolling. 'There was no friction, but we didn't become close,' she recalled. 'Carol wasn't very chatty on the set, kept herself to herself and was quite private, but she was very pleasant and charming. She was comfortable with Ken and trusted him totally. He seemed to have the measure of her because it seemed to me he would cut the scene when he thought he had got the best of Carol. He was very caring and wouldn't exhaust her; maybe he sensed a frailty there.'[24]

A scene in which White visited the rent office was another example of improvisation. 'Ken told me she was coming to pay her rent,' recalled Ken Campbell, who played the rent collector. 'I asked him how much it was and he said: "What do you think?" So I replied: "About five pounds." So she came in and I told her it was five pounds. Ken then said: "Very good. This time, draw her attention to the girlie calendar on the wall." What we did was totally ad-libbed and we filled a whole roll of film up while Ken sat under the desk on Carol's side of the counter. There was one take where I accidentally brought my hand down on the edge of an ashtray and all the dog ends went up in the air and came down on Ken's head. I looked down and said sorry – and he kept that bit.'[25]

The pub scenes – astonishingly realistic for anything seen in a feature film before or since, as were the opening shots of White's character giving birth – included some of the repertory company that Loach had built up over the previous years and the gentle pop music was, briefly, in sympathy with its surroundings when White and Stamp were filmed enjoying an idyllic time on holiday in Wales. But Loach would later cringe at a scene of the couple kissing in front of a waterfall there. 'I'm not sure I could bear to see it again,' he said. 'I think we must have thought it was fun, really.'[26] A scene of White washing Stamp in a tin bath failed to get the desired reaction from the actor, so Loach quietly instructed the props department to fill the bucket with cold water.

Off screen, White had 'a brief but consuming affair' with co-star Stamp. 'We had slept together before, when I was seventeen and at the height of a wild period of promiscuity,' she revealed. 'In those days, I was more concerned with numbers than feelings. I wanted to sleep with as many men as possible and Terry happened to have been one of them.'[27] For the last two weeks of filming, which overran the eight-week schedule by four weeks, White darted between the *Poor Cow* locations and those for *I'll Never Forget What's-'is-Name*, for which director Michael Winner had signed her after she had made such an impact in *Cathy Come Home*.

Loach admitted that *Poor Cow*'s schedule overrun was 'a complete cock-up', explaining, 'It was partly my inexperience and partly the divisions in the crew and the production manager not knowing how to service what we wanted. I wasn't getting through the work in time and often there would be criticisms of the "rushes" [each day's footage] because they didn't understand the way I was going to shoot it. It was a constant battle to hang on to my method of doing it.'[28] Despite all this, *Poor Cow* was well received by critics on both sides of the Atlantic, with Dilys Powell of the *Sunday Times* contending that it was the working-class equivalent of the middle classes' *In Which We Serve* – 'often very funny, often bawdy, always miraculously fluent, as apparently spontaneous as if lived, not acted'.[29]

After contending with the overlapping schedules, White concentrated on her role alongside Oliver Reed and Orson Welles in the Winner picture, and her affair with Stamp fizzled out as her attentions turned to Reed and she enjoyed 'a sumptuous dressing room, a maid, caviare with my digestive biscuits and champagne everywhere but in the faucet'.[30]

While Stamp continued with a hugely successful career, White was embraced by Hollywood as 'the new Julie Christie' but never reached the heights enjoyed by that British actress. She went to live in the United States and enjoyed all the trappings of stardom, leaving behind 'the draughty dressing rooms at the BBC and film budgets that counted every penny'.[31] But the 'Battersea Bardot', as she was christened in the press, failed to make it big and fell into a cycle of sex, drink and drugs. After a brief, disastrous return to Britain, when she was sacked from a starring role in Nell Dunn's West End stage play *Steaming*, she headed back for the States, where she died of liver damage, at the age of forty-eight, in 1991.

Meanwhile, John Bindon won acting roles in films and on television off the back of his appearance in *Poor Cow* but eventually returned to his criminal ways – even being acquitted of murder, on the grounds of self-defence – and died of cancer in 1993.

As for Loach, he realised that he did not want to learn the conventions of feature films if *Poor Cow* was the template: he would carve out his own style. 'There was a value in doing it as a first feature film because it taught me all the things that I should never do again,' he said. 'Being browbeaten by a producer is one that hasn't happened since. I did a two- or three-picture deal with Joseph Janni. The first was to be *Poor Cow* and the second an adaptation of a David Storey book, *Flight into Camden*, set in the West Riding of Yorkshire and about the relationship between a man and woman who move to London to escape their families, but Jo reneged on making it, saying: "The North is finished in films." I said: "It's still there, Jo." But he simply felt it was a trend that had gone out of fashion. After *Poor Cow*, I wanted to get out of the remainder of the contract, and a lawyer friend, Irving Teitelbaum,

managed to do that.'[32] Loach also had another gripe – shooting his
début feature film in colour. 'You can't stop colour being pretty,' he
said. 'I think people would have taken *Poor Cow* a lot more
seriously if it had been done in black-and-white. As it was, they
lumped it in with the Swinging Cinema – which I loathe anyway.'[33]

However, thirty-two years later, homage was paid to Loach and
Poor Cow when director Steven Soderbergh incorporated scenes of
Terence Stamp – with Carol White and John Bindon, combining the
tender and criminal sides of his personality – into the American film
drama *The Limey* as 'flashbacks' in the story of a vengeful convict,
newly released from prison, travelling to Los Angeles in an attempt
to discover who murdered his daughter. In the intervening years,
Loach chalked up a body of work, made in his own uncompromising style, that would earn such respect.

Loach directed Carol White and Terence Stamp in *Poor Cow*
[Fenchchurch Films-Vic Films]

PART III

KES AND THE PROBLEMS OF INDEPENDENCE

8

A WET SUMMER IN BARNSLEY

THE SOUTH YORKSHIRE countryside was where Ken Loach discovered a hive of political awareness that would feature in many of his films and television documentaries. He also developed a new style of detached, observational film-making, in sharp contrast to the in-your-face, handheld-camera-on-the-run mode that had become a trademark of his 'Wednesday Plays'. In the summer of 1968, making what became one of British cinema's finest masterpieces, Loach shot the gentle but essentially tragic *Kes* in and around Barnsley, where the idyllic Yorkshire landscape was tempered by scenes of coal mines and industrial activity.

Barry's Hines's novel *A Kestrel for a Knave*, about a fifteen-year-old boy, Billy Casper, who finds satisfaction in training a rare bird while facing a certain future down the local pit, provided Loach with the compelling story and visual possibilities to carry the social message that the British school system was failing many pupils by not recognising their full potential. 'For all the liberal aspirations of trying to draw things out and not push them in, the objective role of a secondary modern is to produce a certain amount of unskilled labour,' said Loach. 'The school, and the youth employment officer, can't recognise that this boy has qualities, or they've got to find someone else to fill his manual job from the pool of eleven-plus failures.'[1]

In 1968, as the regime of Hugh Greene at the BBC was in its death throes, signalling the end of the Corporation's liberal era, in which radical ideas had found a voice, Loach and Tony Garnett left to set up their own production company, along with talent agent Clive Goodwin and Garnett's friend and solicitor, Irving Teitelbaum. With the decision to adapt Barry Hines's book as their first project,

Kestrel Films was chosen as the company's name and Loach was guaranteed to have Garnett as his producer, ensuring that he would never again have to accede to the demands of an outsider, as in *Poor Cow*. A small amount of money from the National Film Finance Corporation enabled Kestrel to set up and run an office.

Garnett had been alerted to the talents of Hines by Alfred Bradley, a legendary radio producer at BBC North in Leeds, and read the writer's first novel, *The Blinder*, about a young footballer, as well as a few radio scripts. 'I asked to see Barry,' recalled Garnett, 'and he came down to London. I said to him: "Would you like to do a 'Wednesday Play'?" He said he would very much like to, but he had a book going round in his head and felt that was what he should write next. That immediately showed his integrity because the advance on a literary novel was very small compared with the money for a "Wednesday Play". I told him I respected that but, if he ever felt like writing one, just to let me know and, in the meantime, would he let me have a look at the book when it was finished. A year later, the typed manuscript of *A Kestrel for a Knave* landed on my desk. I thought it was one for the cinema and Ken would be the best director for it.'[2] Loach, similarly impressed by the story, was in agreement and both of them joined Hines in adapting the book for the screen, although the original narrative was written in such a simple, visual way that, according to Garnett, this amounted to little more than 'a cut-and-paste job'.[3]

A Kestrel for a Knave emanated from the views that the writer, from Hoyland Common, near Barnsley, had formed after seeing both sides of the educational divide in his own life, as a child and an adult; he also shared with Loach a mining family background and experience as a teacher. The son of a miner, Hines had attended Ecclesfield Grammar School and hated it, but lived for sport. After working as an apprentice surveyor at a local mine for several months and loathing it, he returned to school to take A-levels – also playing football for England Grammar Schools – then trained as a PE teacher at Loughborough Training College. 'When I moved to London and taught sport in a comprehensive, I started reading for the first time, mainly Graham Greene and other books of the 1930s and 1940s,' Hines recalled. 'Then, I started going to the theatre and arthouse cinemas, and developed an interest in the arts. So I began writing short stories for myself.'[4] Films such as *The*

Loneliness of the Long Distance Runner and *Saturday Night and Sunday Morning* were also influences. 'It was the first time the North was represented honestly,' said Hines, 'and I thought: "My God! You can write about the area and people you know."' Writers like Stan Barstow, Keith Waterhouse and Willis Hall were a big encouragement; I was reading the novels and seeing the films.'[5]

After marrying, he returned to Hoyland Common and taught at St Helen's County Secondary School, in Athersley. Hines's new interest in writing led him to pen *Billy's Last Stand*, about the village coalman, and send it to Alfred Bradley; it was eventually produced as a radio play on the BBC's Third Programme (and later performed at London's Royal Court Theatre). After giving up full-time teaching, Hines wrote his first novel, *The Blinder*, the story of a schoolboy who was a footballing genius as well as being academically brilliant; in other words, it was a combination of autobiography and wish-fulfilment.

With *A Kestrel for a Knave*, he opted for a more realistic account of life for the many who were regarded as cast-offs when they failed the eleven-plus. 'There were always people who thought the grammar schools shouldn't go,' explained Hines. 'But, having been a teacher and become more and more political the older I got, I was always for the comprehensives because of the sheer waste. There was a feeling among those that didn't make it to grammar schools that they'd had it; they went to work down the pit or on a building site and that was it. It was almost impossible to realise any latent talent.'[6] (Proposals for comprehensive schools had been launched by the Labour government in 1965 and, four years later, 124 education authorities would have their plans approved, leaving thirty-nine under the selection system.)

Hines found like minds in fellow former grammar school boys Garnett and Loach. 'Tony and Ken came up to Hoyland Common,' he recalled, 'and we went on a walk round the woods at the Old Hall Farm, which was actually used in the film as Monastery Farm, where the boy finds the hawk, and just chatted to make sure we were on the same wavelength – it wasn't a story about falconry! The book was political, saying that the Billy Caspers of this world were regarded as washouts and failures and no good at anything. I was trying to show that, in different circumstances, Billy was a clever boy. He wasn't an academic, but he wasn't thick; it was more to do with motivation.

Once he got this kestrel, he realised he didn't know what to do with it. It's not like having a young magpie or crow, which you just keep, then let go. A kestrel is not a pet, like a dog or a cat; in order to keep this hawk and look after it properly, he needed a book, so he went to the library and bookshop. What is in these manuals is ever so complicated but, because the motivation was there, he read the book and then he was able to train the hawk.'[7]

The idea of featuring a bird as the boy's motivation was influenced by Hines's younger brother, Richard, who kept a kestrel in the shed at the bottom of the writer's garden; both brothers learned how to rear and fly the bird. 'I became obsessed with hawks after reading a book called *The Goshawk*, by T.H. White,' recalled Richard Hines. 'In the book and film, Billy gets on the wall at Monastery Farm and gets the kestrel from the nest. I did that at the Old Hall in real life years earlier, climbing up the wall during the night, when it was dark.'[8]

With his adaptation of *A Kestrel for a Knave*, Loach began a pre-production process that he would follow in all his subsequent work. 'Barry showed us the places we had imagined in the book, including the school he had taught at,' recalled Loach.[9] After seeing the Old Hall Farm and St Helen's County Secondary School, the director found a retired miner's house on a Hoyland Common estate to use as the Casper family's home, the Rockingham and Skiers Spring collieries at nearby Birdwell for scenes of Billy's miner brother at work, a field near Hines's Hoyland Common home, where Billy flies the bird, the Cudworth Hotel pub, where his mother and brother enjoy a night out, Barnsley Civic Library, which he tries to join, Clayton's Betting Shop in Lundwood, where he fails to place a bet for his brother, Savage's fish-and-chip shop in Hoyland Common, where he spends the money, and Barnsley Market, where he walks with the kestrel on his wrist; the James Miles Bookshop, in Leeds, was also used, for the scene in which he steals a book about falconry.

Although school scenes were shot at St Helen's, Loach scoured three schools in the Barnsley area to find his Billy Casper and cast other child roles. 'One of the ideas of the film,' he explained, 'is that every boy and girl has huge potential without space to develop and there are pre-arranged slots ready for them as manual labourers. We thought that, if our thesis was correct, within this group of boys, there would be one who could bring Billy Casper to life.'[10]

After seeing almost 200 children, Loach invited about thirty of them to the Queen's Hotel, Barnsley, and put them through two scenarios: Billy's school playground fight with MacDowall and his visit to the library to find a book on falconry. 'For the first one, we were given a script, but there were no lines for the library sequence,' recalled David Bradley, who landed the leading role. 'Whereas the previous three kids had gone straight up to the librarian and asked for a book, I elected to do something different. I walked around the walls of the room, as if looking at different shelves. Eventually, the librarian said: "Excuse me, can I help you?" I replied: "It's all right. I'm just looking for a book." We then started to get very gently into a conversation.'[11]

Bradley, the waif-like fourteen-year-old son of a Barnsley miner and a seamstress, had acting experience in just three school panto-mimes. Like Billy, he lived on a working-class estate, had failed his eleven-plus and had an interest in nature, although he did not come from a broken home, like the hero of the book. 'There were others who were good, but David was extraordinary and very, very talented,' Loach recalled.[12] There were other considerations, how-ever. 'We knew immediately that David was just perfect for the part,' said producer Garnett. 'But we agonised over our choice for weeks because we knew that we were going to make a big difference to this young lad's life. He told us that he had the choice of going down the pit or getting a job at the Co-Op when he left school – so acting was the only way out for him.'[13] When he received the letter from Loach inviting him to take the role, Bradley recalled in wonderment, 'It was written in purple ink. I'd never seen purple ink before!'[14]

The casting of Bradley and others in the picture set another benchmark for the way in which Loach would work in future. The realism for which he was known in television plays such as *Up the Junction* and *Cathy Come Home* was translated to the big screen via his method of finding people who could relate to the characters they were playing, which often meant using non-professional actors. Boys were chosen from the many he met at the real-life schools, but he found grown-ups to play teachers by visiting a Leeds variety agency, continuing the practice of casting performers from the Northern club circuit, as he had just done in his television play *The Golden Vision*. He was impressed by their ability to think on their feet and their lack of self-consciousness and, in speaking with local accents and adapting the script to their own words, they sounded natural. 'They learned their lines, then Ken allowed them to dirty them up – to say them in their own way,' recalled Barry Hines.[15] Several of the cast went on to turn professional as actors and become household names.

Rotherham-born Lynne Perrie (real name Jean Dudley), who played Billy's neglectful mother, whose husband had walked out, was a cabaret singer with club experience in Britain, Germany and South Africa, and had appeared on the same bill as the Beatles, the Rolling Stones and Sacha Distel. She subsequently acted in television plays and, most memorably, took the role of Ivy Tilsley in *Coronation Street*. Her brother, Duggie Brown, a stand-up comic who later found fame on television in *The Comedians* and acted with Loach three more times, played the milkman from whom Billy steals. Freddie Fletcher, who was cast as Billy's bullying brother, Jud, was also a local club comedian who worked by day as an interior decorator but went on to act professionally. Joe Miller, a South Wales-born comedian who had appeared in the television show *Blackpool Night Out*, played Billy's mother's date in the pub scene. Such entertainers were members of the Variety Artists Federation, which was affiliated to Equity, thus enabling Loach to avoid breaching union agreements.

Casting the role of the tyrannical sports master, Mr Sugden, proved more difficult, until Brian Glover went to meet Loach after asking Barry Hines whether there might be a role for him in the film. Glover, a Sheffield-born English teacher who had worked with the writer at Longcar Central School, in Barnsley, and performed as a professional wrestler by night, under the name Leon Arras, gave a memorable performance on the games field, showing the character to be a frustrated Bobby Charlton who takes over a school football match; it is one of the funniest scenes ever shot by Loach. 'Because he was a teacher, Brian could control the kids and I was able to set up incidents for him to respond to,' explained the director. 'The humour in it was the teacher dealing with the boys and taking the mickey out of them, but not realising they are taking the mickey out of him as well. Brian cottoned on to that exactly. He was like an overgrown schoolboy, but never went too far because he was a teacher.'[16]

Zoë Sunderland, a librarian at Barnsley Civic Library, played herself. In similar vein, the role of headmaster Mr Gryce was taken by Bob Bowes, the real-life head of Ashton School, and one of St Helen's own teachers, Trevor Hesketh, who had amateur acting experience at the town's Wishing Well Theatre, was cast as a pompous teacher. Billy's maths teacher was played by Geoffrey Banks, a newsreader at BBC radio in Manchester, who also acted in amateur theatre and taught French. Bernard Atha, a club entertainer and dancer who lectured in humanities at Huddersfield Technical College and was responsible for student counselling and vocational guidance, was clearly suited to the role of the youth employment officer who interviews Billy. (Atha became a regular representative of officialdom in Loach's work over the next decade. He was also a Leeds city councillor who served as Mayor more than thirty years later and was appointed an OBE.)

Two Liverpool comedians who had appeared in *The Golden Vision* also took part in *Kes*. Bill Dean played a fish-and-chip shop owner and Joey Kaye was an entertainer in the pub. The only professional actor to appear in the film was Lancashire-born Colin Welland, as compassionate teacher Mr Farthing, who encourages Billy's enthusiasm for training the kestrel and asks him to tell the rest of his class about it. However, Welland was cast partly because of his experience as an art teacher before turning professional as an actor and becoming known as PC Graham in *Z Cars*. Loach directed him in three episodes of the programme and the pair, who both lived in the south-west London 'village' of Barnes, remained friends, although by the time of *Kes* the director had moved to a Georgian terrace on the Kentish Town–Highgate border, in North London. 'Ken isn't the sort of bloke to cast you because you're a friend,' said Welland. 'He cast me because I was what the character was: I had been a teacher in a secondary modern in Leigh, in Lancashire, exactly the same sort of school as the one in *Kes*. He would probably have cast me if I had not been an actor. I was so delighted to work with him again.'[17]

Welland reverted to teacher mode by spending five days in charge of his screen class before filming was due to begin and many pupils insisted on finishing the assignments he set them. Just three days before the cameras were set to roll, Richard Hines found a baby kestrel in a nest at the Old Hall Farm and named him

Freeman. During filming, he was to look after the bird, whose real gender was never determined but was female in the story, as well as two other hawks supplied by a gamekeeper on an estate at Wentworth, near Doncaster, to act as understudies in case of loss, accident, illness or poor performance. To capture and 'man' these hawks – named Freeman, Hardy and Willis, after the shoe store chain – the Hines brothers had to apply to the Home Office for a licence, to comply with the Protection of Birds Act 1954.

Over the next month, much of the birds' training was to take place in front of the cameras. Freeman was the main bird used on screen, but both the others were seen and Richard Hines gave the child star special responsibility for Hardy. 'Although I didn't know anything about kestrels, I did marvel at them,' said Bradley. 'They're such stunningly beautiful birds. Freeman would fly straight at me, very low, perhaps eight to nine feet off the ground, whereas Hardy used to fly high and then swoop down.'[18] The teenager was given just fifteen pages of script and had to promise not to read the book to find out how the story ended. (These were the beginnings of Loach's practice of handing out pages of script as filming progressed – with some lines blanked out.)

David Bradley in
Kes
[Kestrel Films-
Woodfall Films]

But, with cast and crew assembled in South Yorkshire, disaster struck: the film's backer pulled out. National General, a Hollywood production and cinema-owning company keen to break into the British market, had agreed a £165,000 budget in a deal with Tony Garnett through its London subsidiary, Carthay Centre Productions. 'The money just fell away,' explained Garnett, 'so Ken and I went up and down Wardour Street [capital of Britain's film industry], trying to raise cash. People just sniggered and said the film was about the wrong kind of bird. It was getting desperate because the chicks were about to fly the nest and we couldn't do the movie without the kestrels. Also, we had a conscience about the crew because they would have been out of work, so I called a meeting at my house and told all the heads of department that the money had fallen away, we weren't sure whether we could put the film together and they were free to take other work. Every one of them said: "We want to do this and we'll stick with it." '[19]

A fairy godfather arrived in the person of Tony Richardson, a British film legend who had directed classics such as *The Entertainer*, *A Taste of Honey*, *The Loneliness of the Long Distance Runner* and *Tom Jones*. He heard about Loach and Garnett's plight and, through his association with United Artists across the Atlantic, used his reputation to pick up the phone and get an instant deal. 'Tony heard we were in trouble and asked to see us,' recalled Garnett. 'We went to the West End offices of his company, Woodfall Films, in Curzon Street, and he asked how much we wanted. I told him £165,000 and he said: "All right. Come back this afternoon." We returned at five-thirty and he was in the middle of trying to set up his own movie, *Laughter in the Dark*, starring Nicol Williamson, and was having problems with that. He had come off *Tom Jones*, which made a fortune for United Artists, whose London office had already turned down *Kes*. As soon as Los Angeles had woken up, he rang United Artists. In one phone call, we got the money. He said: "Go off and make your film." Of course, $400,000 was nothing to them and they didn't want to say no to Tony. Thanks to him, we were able to go ahead.'[20] In fact, United Artists made Richardson agree a cross-collateralisation deal for *Kes* and *Laughter in the Dark* under which, if either film went over budget, that would have to be paid for from the profits of the other. Richardson left Loach and

Garnett to film without any interference, although he helpfully thought of the title, *Kes*, towards the end of the shoot. (Kes was the name that Billy gave to the hawk; *A Pocket of Silence* was a title previously mooted.)

That summer in South Yorkshire was remembered by all those who took part with incredible affection, despite the fact that it was one of the wettest in living memory. Just as Loach had effectively created his own Everton supporters' club in *The Golden Vision*, he established a 'family' feel during the shooting of *Kes* that would become one of his trademarks, alongside his reputation for maintaining a calm set and never shouting 'Action!' or 'Cut!', preferring to let events establish themselves naturally before the camera. 'All the people involved came from within a few miles of each other, so there was a really strong sense of community,' he recalled. 'That most of the cast were untrained as actors proved to be a great advantage because they were drawing on their own experiences. This meant they had a remarkable ability to make a fictional situation believable in front of the camera.'[21]

Colin Welland, thrown back into his real-life days of teaching, recalled, 'It helped considerably that I was surrounded by real kids and real people. It was a terrific experience. I look at the film now and remember it as if it was a part of actual events in my life.'[22] In one of the classroom scenes, Welland's character asks Billy to regale his friends with an account of how he trained the kestrel. 'The whole class was enthralled by Billy's story and their reactions were completely real,' said Welland. 'It was completely unrehearsed. We were genuinely moved and that's what comes across. That's what makes the scene so vivid.'[23]

For David Bradley, it *was* a part of his life – indeed, a life-changing experience. He recalled the filming, during his school holidays, as 'like being at Blackpool Pleasure Beach every day', explaining, 'It was one rollercoaster ride to the next.'[24] A car picked him up at seven-thirty to take him to each day's location, filming would finish at four in the afternoon, then he learned the rudiments of kestrel training, before returning home for a meal and to learn his lines for the following day. Richard Hines took the youngster through the training process: attaching a swivel to the jesses (leather straps fitted to the falcons' legs to hold them) and a leash to the swivel; the 'manning', to get the falcons used to humans by carrying them on the glove; flying the falcons to the glove, first on a creance (a long, tight line), then freely; and, finally, 'stooping' the falcons to the lure (a string with a leather pad with a pair of bird's wings and meat fastened to it). Critical to the filming was the fact that these falcons fly only when they are hungry, so the weight of the three kestrels had to be monitored carefully and they could appear before the camera only for a short time each day.

Like Billy, Bradley had a morning paper round, which meant his day started at six-thirty. 'It wasn't affecting my acting,' recalled Bradley, 'but Ken and Tony noticed I was looking tired and asked me what I did in the morning. When I told them I delivered newspapers, they offered to pay my wages not to do it. We were often shooting six days a week and, a few weeks into filming, in September, I told Tony that I wouldn't be available on Saturday afternoons any more because I sold football programmes for my local team, which allowed me free admission to Barnsley's matches. So I also got a couple of quid for not selling programmes.'[25]

As filming progressed, Barry Hines saw the vision of his book unfolding before his eyes. 'It was cold and overcast the whole time, but everyone had a marvellous time,' he said. 'With all the laughter going on during filming, I knew for certain that we'd be laughing at the finished thing. But the most exciting thing for me was seeing that Ken Loach was succeeding in capturing the spirit of my book.'[26]

Loach's new, observational style of filming, which became his standard, was influenced by the Czech New Wave directors, such as Jiri Menzel, Ivan Passer and Milos Forman, as well as Chris Menges, who had been the camera operator on his first film, *Poor Cow*, and subsequently worked in that capacity alongside Czech director of photography Miroslav Ondrícek on *If . . .*, director Lindsay Anderson's public-school satire. 'I had seen the Czech films and liked their photography and the lenses they used,' said Loach. 'I tend not to use the wider lenses, just a narrow range that corresponds to your eye's range. You get frames that are more pleasing.'[27]

Menges felt that the results of his collaboration with Loach were the consequence of a shared vision that found an outlet with Barry Hines's story. Like Ondrícek, Menges had a background in documentaries and he admired the Czech's fictional pictures with director Milos Forman, especially *Lásky jedné plavovlásky*

(*A Blonde in Love*). 'His early films were superb,' said Menges, 'but the one I worked on, *If . . .*, was much less satisfactory. It's down to a meeting of minds and a sympathy for the story. Ken and I were trying to find a very sympathetic, almost gentle, way to capture the performances. He said I was the person who showed him the way, but really we were learning together by the experience. On *Poor Cow*, we lit the actors and then they did the performance, but with *Kes* Ken wanted something more simple and observational, to illuminate a room and let the performance develop within that room so that we weren't putting marks down and telling actors where to go. They could live in the reality as they found the situation and we could capture the performance.'[28]

One method that Loach instituted to heighten the reality for those appearing in front of the camera was to move the film crew as far away from the action as possible. 'The priority is to get a performance that people will believe, that has originality and spontaneity,' he explained. 'If you put the technical apparatus too close to the actors, they will find that a distraction. So, if you can remove the lights and the boom from being in their eye-line and set the camera back, it gives them the freedom to relate to the other people in the scene.'[29]

It might have seemed impossible to do this when one scene with David Bradley, Colin Welland and the kestrel had to be filmed in the garden shed where Billy keeps the bird, but Loach simply found a small hole through which to shoot, leaving the performers alone in their own space. 'We were in total silence,' said Welland, 'and you couldn't help but respond to it and feel the awe that Barry Hines tried to describe in his script. A lesser director would have had the camera there, sat behind it and taken one wall out, but Ken allowed the reality to unfold, totally undisturbed by the camera.'[30]

Using natural light as far as possible became another Loach filming method and, as with *Poor Cow*, he would have preferred to cement the realism by shooting in black-and-white, but United Artists stipulated that *Kes* must be made in colour. So, to avoid ending up with picturesque scenes of the Yorkshire countryside, the film stock was preflashed to desaturate and take some of the colours out.

The filming style adopted by Loach arose partly out of the logistics. 'Although the budget for *Kes* was quite small for a feature film,' explained Tony Garnett, 'there were no expensive stars and we were able to shoot for seven weeks, in locations that were close together, and shoot a quarter of a million feet of 35mm film; that was a huge luxury.'[31]

Throughout filming, Barry Hines's house at Hoyland Common was used as the production office. 'I didn't even have a telephone then,' he recalled. 'The company put a phone in, on a little landing going up the stairs; they were on the phone all the time. What was good about it was that United Artists never checked up on this and I kept the phone for a year or two afterwards!'[32] To get documentary-style pictures of the streets of Barnsley – such as small boys seen wearing pyjamas on their doorstep – Loach would send the film crew off for a coffee and roam around in a van, with just the cameraman and sound recordist in the back.

Realism was everything for Loach, who used the element of surprise to elicit natural performances from his young cast. When Billy is among five boys sent to the headmaster's office for a caning, a younger sixth one is told to take a message to the head. None of them expected a real caning to be administered, which it was, least of all the twelve-year-old, Martin Harley; his tears were as real as his protestations. Barry Hines, who was present for most of the filming, recalled, 'Ken said to Bob Bowes, who played the head: "Every time that little lad opens his mouth, tell him to shut up. Don't let him get the words out." You see the panic on his little face, but afterwards Ken explained to all of them why it was necesary and they understood, so they didn't bear any grudges.'[33] Director of photography Chris Menges was also prepared for the scene. He recalled, 'Ken whispered in my ear: "They are going to be walloped." I thought: "Christ! We're going to beat children up and what happens if I miss it!" It's a scene that millions of people have lived for real in schools, though.'[34]

As with the moment in *Cathy Come Home* when the children are taken away from Carol White, Loach justified such realism, affecting children, with the need to portray reality. 'They were going in for a caning but weren't sure what was going to happen and it stung for a minute or two,' he said. 'Kids were getting the cane routinely every day and it's a very important scene because the headmaster is going on about the collapse of standards and how people don't respect authority in the way they used to, but he is so blind to the fact that he canes the wrong boy. The young boy got a couple of strokes, but we gave him extra pocket money afterwards and, within seconds, he was smiling through his tears.'[35]

In fact, the group of boys were far from happy after the caning had been administered on the first take. 'I had never had the cane and Ken or Tony had assured us that we wouldn't really get caned,' said David Bradley. 'So we didn't put our hands out how we knew they should be put, lowering your thumb as much as possible and gently flexing your fingers so that the cane hits flesh, as opposed to bone, when it really hurts. When we were actually caned, we were really upset, not in terms of tears, but angry we had been lied to. So we decided that we wouldn't do it again and went on strike. Ken and Tony got together, then came back and said a couple of the caning takes could be done from behind and we could wear gloves, but they would have to do the actual shot from the front one more time and would pay us an extra ten shillings [50p] for each hand caned, which would include those with gloves on. The younger boy wasn't caned again, though. In total, the rest of us made £3 10s [£3.50]. We realised that it had to be real, but it was the shock of having trusted these people over several weeks and, suddenly, we were told that we didn't have to worry about this scene because we wouldn't really get the cane, but we did.'[36]

Loach, who did not recall making any firm statement about what would happen to the boys when they entered the head's office, was looking for a similarly realistic reaction to the killing of Billy's kestrel by Jud, the result of Billy's failure to place a bet for his brother. In reality, a dead bird was found by the British Falconers' Society, with the help of veteran anthropologist John Murray of the Royal Edinburgh Museum, but as much as possible was done to convince Bradley that this was one of the kestrels he had helped to train. 'David had realised that, somewhere along the line, there would have to be a dead bird,' explained Barry Hines. 'He had seen the lads getting the cane and the realism that had gone through the film, and he was very troubled.'[37] Hines's brother, Richard, recalled, 'Before the scene was shot, I was in the dinner queue with David and Freddie Fletcher when Ken came up and said to me: "Go with Freddie now, Richard." He was letting David think that we were going away to kill the hawk. Just before filming, I put jesses on the dead hawk and placed it in the dustbin.'[38]

But Bradley insisted he never believed the bird was one of those with which he had formed a bond. 'Barry and Richard tried to prepare me for the fact that, come the end of the film, they would have to put my kestrel, Hardy, down unless they could find a dead one,' he explained. 'Then, suddenly, about a week before we were to shoot that sequence, Hardy went missing, so training during the last week was purely with Freeman; Willis had already flown back to the wild. I interpreted it that they were trying to make me believe my kestrel had been killed, but I didn't believe they would do such a cruel thing. When I saw the dead kestrel, I couldn't tell that it wasn't Hardy, but I was convinced that they couldn't do something so nasty.

'What actually gave me the feeling of great grief or anger was not the kestrel, but what had happened before shooting the scene. After filming something else in the morning, I arrived at the canteen caravan late for lunch, they had my favourite meal on the menu, shepherd's pie and apple crumble with custard, and hadn't wiped it off the blackboard. When I asked for it, I was told they had run out and they hadn't put any by for me. I was really pissed off by that, so I elected not to have any lunch and went to pig out on fresh fruit. As I ate it, I thought about what had happened and concluded that they were trying to upset me, and realised I had to go along with their wishes. I was obviously affected by the fact that there was a dead kestrel, but I didn't believe it was Hardy. I went away in denial, not believing they would do that.'[39]

David Bradley with (left to right) Richard Hines, Tony Garnett and writer Barry Hines
[Kestrel Films-Woodfall Films]

Although the film followed the novel, the ending was changed. 'In the book,' explained Barry Hines, 'Billy gets into a closed-down cinema through a window, sits there and projects on to the screen his life and what is on his mind. He wants his dad to come back; when he was a little boy, he used to go to the cinema with his dad, then his dad left home. It wouldn't have worked at all cinematically, so in the film he buries the dead hawk under a hedge bottom.'[40]

Making *Kes* was one hurdle overcome – and Loach trimmed £10,000 off the budget supplied by United Artists – but getting it screened in cinemas was another. Tony Garnett's own initial reaction to the broad Yorkshire accents in the film and some incidents of swearing provided a warning of what was to come. 'We went to see the rushes in the cinema in Barnsley,' said Richard Hines. 'As we walked back to the hotel afterwards, Tony Garnett had a face like thunder, so my brother, Barry, asked him what was wrong. "We are going to end up with an X-certificate film that's not understood five miles outside Barnsley," he said.'[41]

Garnett himself faced the wrath of the film's backer. 'United Artists weren't interested at all,' he recalled. 'I showed it to one of their executives, Eric Pleskow, who was in London as part of a visit to Europe, just him in the viewing theatre and me biting my finger nails at the back. When it finished and the lights came up, he got up, walked down the aisle and, as he passed me, he didn't even break his stride. "I would have preferred it in Hungarian," he said.'[42]

Britain's leading cinema circuit, Rank, through which United Artists distributed in Britain, then left *Kes* on the shelf, seemingly bemused at how to market the film, which did not fall into any conventional category. With the threat of it being dumped, Kestrel director Clive Goodwin whipped up press interest in the picture. In September 1969, Loach and Garnett hosted a special screening in the private cinema at Bowater House, Knightsbridge, which had been used for the preview of the animated Beatles film *Yellow Submarine* more than a year earlier. Screenings followed at the London Film Festival two months later and some hope of a cinema release came when Britain's second-largest cinema circuit, ABC, agreed to take *Kes*. Even then, the film was shown only in ten towns in the North of England, with a premiere in March 1970 in the city of Doncaster – in South Yorkshire, but more than ten miles from Barnsley.

United Artists refused to let *Kes* be selected as an official entry at the Cannes Film Festival, although it was featured there in the

Critics' Week line-up. Then, as if the annual South of France bash categorised it as 'arty', *Kes* received a London release at The Academy, an arthouse cinema in Oxford Street, indicating that United Artists still had no idea how to market the film. Such was the critical praise heaped on it as a result of all these screenings that *Kes* finally went on general release almost two years after filming ended in South Yorkshire. Defying some criticism that it should be subtitled because of the broad Yorkshire accents, the film was recognised as a classic and the publicity surrounding it had helped to promote sales of Barry Hines's book, which became a set text in school examinations. The Society of Film and Television Arts honoured David Bradley with a Most Promising Newcomer Award and Colin Welland as Best Supporting Actor in its film awards.

In 1999, by which time it had established a reputation worldwide, *Kes* was reissued to mark the thirtieth anniversary of Loach and Garnett's first feature film together; it was also number seven in the British Film Institute's list of best films of the twentieth century, behind *The Third Man*, *Brief Encounter*, *Lawrence of Arabia*, *The 39 Steps*, *Great Expectations* and *Kind Hearts and Coronets*.

Lynne Perrie, Brian Glover, Freddie Fletcher and Duggie Brown, all virtual unknowns until they appeared in *Kes*, went on to act professionally. Meanwhile, David Bradley, whose performance validated Loach and Garnett's reasons for turning Barry Hines's story into a film, proved that there was life for a Barnsley schoolboy beyond the local pit, but his fate made him a popular candidate for 'Where are they now?' features over the following decades. With the opportunities given him by the film, Bradley went on to act on television, in series such as *The Flaxton Boys* and *A Family at War*, as well as *Kisses at Fifty*, a 'Play for Today' written by Colin Welland. On reaching the age of sixteen, he changed his professional name to Dai Bradley because an older namesake was already a member of Equity, then performed alongside Anthony Hopkins, Derek Jacobi and Joan Plowright in Peter Hall's National Theatre company, winning international recognition once more by playing the troubled teenager, Alan Strang, in a two-and-a-half-year world tour of Peter Shaffer's play *Equus*, which included a run on Broadway. He was not offered the chance to repeat the role in a film version (fellow Yorkshireman Peter Firth won the part) but was subsequently seen on screen in *Zulu Dawn*. Then, in the 1980s,

9

THE RANK AND FILE

BY 1968, THE SWINGING SIXTIES had revealed its flipside: while some still valued 'the pound in their pocket', others looked around and saw a world of chaos. During that cataclysmic year, people took to the streets of Western capitals to protest against the United States' war in Vietnam, with sit-ins of students at universities and workers in factories; Americans questioned that distant war for the first time when news film showed their troops under siege during the Tet Offensive; another conflict raged and famine proliferated in Biafra; American black civil rights leader Martin Luther King and presidential candidate Robert Kennedy were both assassinated; Soviet tanks rolled into Czechoslovakia; civil rights marches highlighted injustices in Northern Ireland; and Conservative MP Enoch Powell fanned the flames of racial hatred with his 'rivers of blood' warning against further immigration.

In the same year, Ken Loach's disillusionment with the Wilson government led him to start attending meetings of the Socialist Labour League, which later became the Workers' Revolutionary Party. Its declared aim at the time was 'to prepare and mobilise the working class for the overthrow of capitalism, the establishment of working-class power and the building of a socialist society',[1] with its policies based on the theory of Marxism as developed by Lenin and Trotsky. Another visitor to the party's regular Friday meetings was his former collaborator and university contemporary Roger Smith, who had been in Paris during the May protests. Loach never became a member of the SLL, membership of which was banned by the Labour leadership. 'It was part of the process of hearing other people make sense of what we were witnessing and trying to find an analysis that explained why the Labour government acted in the way it did,' he said. 'By and large, it supported the employers, when it had been elected to be on the other side. The answer clearly was historical and I started to read the history of that struggle. The Socialist Labour League had a diaspora of people who were being drawn into politics and would evaluate the ideas, read the books and go and discuss.'[2]

Having established with Tony Garnett the need to be more overtly political in their work together, Loach found a major influence on his developing political consciousness in Jim Allen; their director–writer partnership was to last, on and off, for almost thirty years. However, their first work together, *The Big Flame*, marked the end of the BBC's radical era that was epitomised by such 'Wednesday Plays'. After his long battles to shoot on location and with a new regime at the BBC insisting that in future all plays should have no more than ten minutes of outdoor filming, Garnett announced he was leaving the Corporation. 'For three years I was in the middle of the BBC row about plays – and the argument about whether they should be documentaries or theatrical,' he explained. 'I simply got sick of it.'[3]

Writer Jim Allen made Ken Loach's films more overtly political
[Paul Chedlow/ Parallax Pictures]

The Big Flame, a story of dockers striking for a living wage and job security, returning to work after six weeks to take over the running of the docks themselves and facing a bloody battle when the government sends in the Army, was clearly relevant to the troubled times – but, for BBC management, dynamite. Filmed entirely on location in Liverpool over twenty days in early 1968, before Loach and Garnett made *Kes*, it was twice scheduled and cancelled before finally being screened in February 1969; the play became a hot potato when the real-life worker sit-ins followed the filming. 'It looks for and deals with real social issues, and that is what some people at the BBC will not allow,' said Garnett at the time. 'When you get a writer who is prepared to put his guts on the screen, then it is a privilege to produce his work. But the time has come when that isn't possible for the foreseeable future at the BBC.'[4]

Allen, a straight-talking Mancunian who spoke in thick tones and with a broad accent, had started writing for 'The Wednesday Play' in 1967, when Garnett commissioned *The Lump* from him. This followed his departure from the scriptwriting team on *Coronation Street*, after his idea to kill all the residents in a coach crash during a mystery tour of the Lake District was rejected. Born in the working-class Manchester suburb of Collyhurst, the son of Irish Catholics, Allen began to read voraciously after being imprisoned for riotous behaviour outside a pub in occupied Germany while serving with the Army during the Second World War. Through jobs as a labourer in the building trade, a docker and a miner, and reading the works of Marx and Engels, his political education took root and he preached against social democrats in the Labour Party and Stalinists in the Communist Party. He joined the Revolutionary Communist Party, which became the Socialist Labour League in 1958, causing him to be expelled from the Labour Party. Articles he wrote in *The Miner*, a rank-and-file newspaper that he also edited, led him to be blacklisted from Lancashire coal mines after coming into conflict with National Union of Miners leaders who belonged to the Communist Party. Returning to the building industry, he similarly found himself isolated because Communist Party members monopolised the shop stewards movement. Inspired by his work on *The Miner*, he tried his hand at writing for television with a play about a hod-carrier; it was rejected by Granada Television, but the Manchester-based ITV company recognised his talent and, in 1965, offered him a job on *Coronation Street*.

After watching *Cathy Come Home*, Allen contacted Tony Garnett and was commissioned to write *The Lump*, the story of how casual labour was exploited in the building trade – an issue that was to provoke a national builders' strike the following decade. Drawing on his own experiences, this was the first example of Allen's writing proving to be prophetic, as *The Big Flame* would be. *The Lump*, screened in 1967, was directed by Jack Gold, one of many creative talents fostered by Garnett; others included writers David Mercer, Leon Griffiths, Charles Wood and Peter Nichols, and directors John Mackenzie and Christopher Morahan. Among those who worked for different producers on 'The Wednesday Play' were writers John Hopkins, Robert Muller, John Mortimer, Alan Plater and the 'non-naturalist' Dennis Potter, and directors Charles Jarrott, James Ferman (who gave up directing to become the country's chief censor, at the then British Board of Film Censorship) and Peter Duguid. But Garnett's fierce determination to produce political and relevant plays made them the most biting and carved him out as one of the most important people to shape British television drama. In partnership with Loach, the results were electrifying.

It was only time before Garnett introduced Loach to Allen, who had by then left the Socialist Labour League but continued to support its policies. 'Jim was political to his fingertips,' said Loach. 'He came on the scene at the time Tony and I felt we needed to make a firmer commitment to a position to the left of the Labour Party, rather than just being dissatisfied and criticising. He had connections with left-wing organisations and we started talking more specifically about another political agenda.'[5] Garnett had no doubt that *The Big Flame* was a play for Loach to direct. 'Ken and I were so close, socially and politically, and our working relationship was two sides of the same coin,' said the producer. 'I knew Ken would make a brilliant job of it.'[6]

Loach was enthused when he saw the script but discovered a creative friction that he would endure throughout his subsequent years of collaboration with Allen. 'I was immediately impressed with Jim's writing,' he said. '*The Big Flame* moved us on to another level: it became about that word so beloved of political people, "struggle", not just a social phenomenon where a victim is cast, as in *Cathy Come Home*. It was about the working class struggling to assert its power. I wanted to make the events live, but I don't think Jim really understood that actors couldn't just say what he wrote and it would work. He was always very protective of his lines but, to get a script to spark, you have to create room. He could be a real bugger, sitting there on location, with the script right in the actors' eye-line; I was always having to move him out. But he always liked the results.'[7]

The director had twice previously filmed in Liverpool, for *Wear a Very Big Hat* and *The Golden Vision*. With *The Big Flame*, he recognised the city's importance as a centre of industry and political awareness. Trotskyism had taken hold among workers on Merseyside more than in any other area of Britain; the seeds of what became Militant took root there, particularly in the Walton Labour Party. Now, Loach saw in Allen's script the commitment and integrity to put in front of television viewers an uncompromising and persuasive argument for workers determining their own future. 'The Big Flame was important to me because it posed the question of workers' control, which means a great deal to me,' said Allen.[8]

The play charted what was to become one of Allen's constant themes: the selling out of rank-and-file trade unionists by their leaders. It recalled a real-life dockers' strike after the introduction of mechanisation to accommodate container transportation and the Devlin Report's recommendation of decasualising the workforce. But, instead of caving in as a result of divisions in the Transport and General Workers' Union's leadership, as actually happened, the workers are seen to take over the docks and run it for five days, until the Army moves in to crush them.

Allen received some help with research from a former Liverpool docker, Peter Kerrigan, who had led the real-life strike and was a folk hero in the city; Loach cast him in a lead role. (Liverpool agent Ernie Mack, who again provided many variety acts to take straight roles, ensured that Kerrigan had the required Variety Artists Federation membership by securing him bookings as a raconteur.)

But Loach's own research almost caused The Big Flame to turn to ashes. 'We needed the co-operation of the Mersey Docks and Harbour Board in order to be able to shoot on the dock,' explained Garnett. 'This was hardly a film of which they would approve, considering it depicted a big strike with them as the villains and ended up with the workers declaring a Soviet [Communist-style] occupation on the docks. I was in delicate discussions with them, and the BBC management had no idea what we were doing, but had a very indulgent hands-off policy, which is what they were like then.

'There's an innocent side to Ken that can't believe anybody would want to stop him doing what he wanted to do. While I was in London, battling the BBC for resources, he was in Liverpool showing the Mersey Docks and Harbour Board the script. I went mad when I heard and had to race up to Liverpool and take the management out to a very alcoholic lunch, paid for by the BBC, where I had to swear blind that the script that they had been given was not the film we were intending to make and salvage it by getting permission back to film on the docks. I was economical with the truth; I didn't exactly lie to them, but I reassured them because I felt they wanted to feel better about it. They were very wary, but we succeeded in receiving enough co-operation to get it done.

'Remember that we didn't quite have the reputation then that we individually have now, so they would not have seen us coming. Also, in those days, there had been hardly anything on the BBC that was political in a left-wing sense, certainly not in drama. It's difficult now to appreciate the prestige of the BBC in the eyes of the ordinary citizen then; organisations like the Mersey Docks and Harbour Board weren't sophisticated about the media and they implicitly trusted the BBC. For quite a number of years, I was able to reap the benefit for our films of that implicit trust because, as soon as we said we were from the BBC, doors opened and no questions were asked.'[9]

The ambitious production was a difficult one to mount, another example of 'putting a quart into a pint pot', as Garnett recalled.[10] Although the story of 10,000 dockers demanded a large cast that would have been possible with a feature film, Loach had to do his best to work within BBC budgets, creating almost sixty credited roles, with many more 'walk-on' parts taken by real-life dockers. Having seen the benefit of casting non-professional actors in *The Golden Vision*, he also tried to push back the boundaries to create more 'real' people on screen. 'We would have dockers as extras, then give them a few lines to say,' explained Loach. 'That way, they were like promoted extras, rather than fully blown actors, but we made sure they were paid the going Equity rate for what they did. We were doing a film about trade unions, but we were in a battle with the actors' union. With *The Golden Vision*, we had wanted variety acts to be able to join Equity, which had a closed shop. We were supportive of that, but our position was that they should be allowed in because they were already entertainers. It was a tense relationship for some years because the Equity officials were responsible to their members. My position was that my first loyalty was to the film.'[11]

The two leading characters on the unofficial strike committee running the dispute in Allen's script were played by Peter Kerrigan and professional Liverpool actor Norman Rossington, and Ken Jones – a native of the city and veteran of three previous Loach 'Wednesday Plays' – acted another leading light among the dockers. Godfrey Quigley took the role of the blacklisted labour organiser, Jack Regan (before the creation of the tough television policeman of the same name), a Communist-turned-Trotskyist who masterminds the docks occupation, run by a port workers' council, and envisages a 'big flame' of political feeling igniting across the country. Indeed, as the fictional element of the play flickers to a conclusion, news of such actions is heard on the radio – 'our socialist-romantic last scene', as Garnett described it.[12] It is preceded by the sight of the four strike leaders being sentenced to three years' imprisonment.

The Big Flame was filmed in the documentary style of Loach's previous 'Wednesday Plays' and his ruses for eliciting natural reactions were as cunning as ever. 'Those playing the dockers had to assemble at the Adelphi Hotel bar at eight one morning, ready to film a fiery meeting,' recalled Ken Campbell, who played a reporter. 'Then they were told that nothing would happen before eleven, then twelve. So they all got as pissed as rats, before finally setting off for a derelict warehouse. On the way, they met a genuine docker who thought he had to go to the meeting as well, and did so to the end. The genius of it was the state they got into for the scene after all the drink they had consumed.'[13] Loach was less impressed with one 'reporter' who was told to give his name and the newspaper he represented before asking a question and said, 'Joe Bloggs, *Daily Globe*,' as broadly instructed. 'Ken went quietly potty,' recalled Neville Smith, who played a member of the strike committee. 'That's the danger of improvisation. When it works, it works well, though.'[14]

Almost a year after filming had finished, as he held his breath and finally hoped that *The Big Flame* would be screened, Tony Garnett mischievously wrote in *Radio Times*, 'If anyone should still doubt that it is fiction, we have set it in the future – as no documentary could ever be.'[15] But that assurance did nothing to stop many newspaper critics from weighing in once more with their 'drama or documentary?' cries. The casting of Peter Kerrigan in a lead role confused one critic to the point of 'accepting' that he was an actor but asserting that his 'thick, stumbling and uninflected voice' indicated otherwise.[16] In fact, Kerrigan subsequently carved out a distinguished acting career, topped by a towering performance in Alan Bleasdale's anti-Thatcher rallying cry *Boys from the Blackstuff* as a former docker dying of a long-term illness and enjoying a final trip, in his wheelchair, round the deserted, decaying Albert Dock.

Kerrigan also acted in Loach's next two television plays, both continuing the theme of working-class struggle and the divisions between trade unionists and their leaders. Jim Allen found another strike to dramatise when employees at Pilkington's Glass Works, in the Lancashire town of St Helens, took industrial action in 1969 and asked him to tell their story. Almost 9,000 went on strike for seven weeks and won a £3-a-week wage rise, but 600 were sacked because they withdrew their labour in support of a fellow worker, 250 were shut out and blacklisted by firms in Merseyside and South Lancashire, and 350 were re-employed, but not reinstated, thereby losing rights built up over as long as thirty years.

Allen and Loach took the script to the writer's old employers at Granada Television, but it was turned down. 'They backed off because Pilkington's Glass Works was a big, important firm in their region and they didn't want to offend it,' said Loach.[17] Returning to the BBC, the pair made *The Rank and File* for the new 'Play for Today' slot, which had replaced the golden era of 'The Wednesday Play'. Over the next decade, this strand would feature early works by writers Alan Bennett, Colin Welland, Trevor Griffiths, Alan Bleasdale and Mike Leigh, as well as more established ones such as John McGrath, Dennis Potter and Jack Rosenthal, although it rarely boasted the cutting edge of drama that its forerunner had pioneered.

Garnett was busy on another project, so Graeme McDonald produced *The Rank and File*. With the more tolerant BBC regime consigned to history, Loach was compelled to shoot the play well away from St Helens so that the connection with the real-life strike was not immediately identifiable. Instead, he filmed in Stoke-on-Trent and, although the director was happier with his own work on the play compared with *The Big Flame*, it carried a sense of *déjà vu* after its predecessor. As well as Peter Kerrigan, others who were transplanted from that to *The Rank and File* were Bill Dean, Tommy Summers, Johnny Gee, Bert King, Neville Smith, Ernie Mack and Joan Flood.

At the same time, shooting was taking place in Liverpool on *Gumshoe*, director Stephen Frears's first feature film, a crime comedy written by Neville Smith and starring Albert Finney (Frears had also signed up Chris Menges as director of photography before Loach could secure his services, so Charles Stewart worked on *The Rank and File*). This meant that some of the Liverpool contingent taking part in both productions – Smith, Dean, King and Mack – were constantly moving between the two locations.

The television play showed how families were affected by the strike, with brother fighting brother, but the violence became a bit too real in one scene. Johnny Gee, more used to playing the guitar in clubs, took the role of a striker who is the victim of underhand manoeuvres by the management while walking home from a demonstration. 'A van pulled up with a group of hired heavies who offered me a lift,' he recalled. 'They were dressed in workmen's clothes and I, as my character, thought they'd been involved in the demonstration, so I got in. When they reached an area of wasteland, they stopped the van, burst open the back doors and lifted me bodily out. I knew what was going to happen and I had been told to go down and cover myself when these extras went for me with the insteps of their boots. I also thought one of them was going to simulate a headbutt, but he grazed my cheekbone. Whether my evasive action stopped it being worse or whether he aimed badly, I don't know.'[18]

The following day, Gee's friend from the clubs, Bill Dean, tried out a prank that backfired. 'It was a freezing-cold morning and we had a scene where we had to put up posters with a bucket of paste,' explained Gee. 'Bill told Ken about my hammering the previous day: "I think we had better do it again because Johnny was laughing when they were kicking him." Ken said: "Were you laughing? If I see it in the rushes, there will be trouble." I told him I wasn't and he said I could get my revenge. "I'll tell you what," he told Bill. "Johnny can stand on your shoulders." I'm about fourteen stone and I worked my heels into Deanie's shoulders and then dropped an enormous blob of paste down the back of his neck. He went crackers – and Ken used it in the film. "You pig bastard!" Deanie screamed. He always used that phrase.'[19]

Allen certainly found an effective mouthpiece for his political views in *The Rank and File*. The play closed with Peter Kerrigan's words, 'I think that we're about two steps off a police state or a fascist state. That's the only description that you could ever give to any system that wants legislation to curb workers fighting for their rights . . . I go along with Trotsky, that life is beautiful, that the future generations cleanse us of all the oppression, violence and evil, and enjoy it to the full.'

Loach completed a trilogy of consecutive television plays about grassroots trade unionists with *After a Lifetime*, Neville Smith's moving story inspired by the death of his own father, told through the fictional events of the days leading up to his funeral. Made in

1969, before *The Rank and File*, but screened shortly afterwards, this was Loach and Garnett's first programme to be shown on ITV, the result of a two-year contract to make single dramas for London Weekend Television, one of the channel's two contractors based in London. A separate company, Kestrel Productions, consisting of Loach, Garnett, their accountant, Michael Henshaw, Irving Teitelbaum and former 'Wednesday Play' producer Kenith Trodd, was formed specifically for this purpose; it was a partnership, as opposed to a limited company, because, with all projects underwritten by the newly launched commercial company, there was no apparent risk. London Weekend Television was headed by former BBC1 controller Michael Peacock as managing director, the Corporation's ex-head of music and arts, Humphrey Burton, and respected political interviewer David Frost.

Shot beautifully by Chris Menges and directed with great sensitivity by Loach, *After a Lifetime* was set in Liverpool and again featured some of the city's regulars, including Smith, Peter Kerrigan, Bill Dean, Johnny Gee, Joan Flood, Mike Hayden, Bert King and Ernie Mack. One valuable new find was Jimmy Coleman, who played Smith's brother in the Catholic family. A building labourer by day and singer-guitarist in the city's clubs by night, he had previously been a docker who took part in the real-life Liverpool strike and appeared in *The Rank and File*. 'There's a strain of militancy in all of us because of our working-class situation,' he said. 'I was one of the militants.'[20]

The brothers' father was remembered as a militant trade unionist who took part in the bitter 1926 General Strike, but the political points were more implicit and less on the surface than in Jim Allen's screen tracts on industrial relations, and there was frequent humour to alleviate the serious content. In one memorable scene in *After a Lifetime*, Smith, Coleman and Dean carry a carpet down a street to spruce up a room for the wake because the family's own carpet is in shreds. As the loud-mouthed, bigoted Uncle Sid, Dean was establishing the character that would win him legions of fans many years later: grumpy pensioner Harry Cross in the Channel Four soap opera *Brookside*.

'I wrote *After a Lifetime* three years after my father's death and large parts of it were autobiographical,' recalled Smith. 'My father was very quietly political, not a loud voice. He worked for Dunlop, as a pipefitter's mate in Speke, and was a rank-and-file trade unionist in the engineers' union. When I cried in the film, sitting with the coffin, they were real tears. On the last day of filming, we had a wrap party and then I had a phone call to say the house where my mum and brother lived had burned down and they were made homeless. It was gutted and everything my father had owned went in that fire. It was very ironic.'[21] The play's title was agreed on after other ideas were rejected. 'Originally, it was called *A Kind of Hush*,' explained Smith. 'I liked that, but Ken and Tony hated it. Then they called it *The Pope and Alan Ball*, before I said no and we came up with *After a Lifetime*. [Loach recalled reading Walter Allen's *All in a Lifetime*.] They used to have competitions for titles, with a bottle of whisky as the prize.'[22]

More than eighteen months after it was made, *After a Lifetime* was finally shown, spurred on, as with *Kes*, by Tony Garnett's decision to arrange a private screening for the press. Although, at the time of the preview, LWT claimed that there had been problems with the 'quality of print', with Equity over the use of non-professional actors and with the seventy-five-minute length of the play, Garnett insisted that the running time had been agreed with the ITV network and discussions with the actors' union had been completed.[23] The Independent Television Authority also insisted on two sexual references in the dialogue being cut,[24] before it was broadcast four months later in the 'Sunday Night Theatre' slot.

Throughout the 1970s, Garnett, as a freelance, flitted between two-year contracts at the BBC and other work. By the time *After a Lifetime* was broadcast, Kestrel's deal with LWT had finished. The original management team's up-market new programmes failed to attract enough viewers for the commercial network and, with a financial crisis looming, Michael Peacock was sacked and half of the executives left. A 'saviour' appeared in the form of Rupert Murdoch, the Australian media mogul who would later take on the British newspaper print unions (although he was soon eased out of ITV because of his press interests).

On his return to the BBC in 1970, Garnett faced questions about his political affiliations. Fifteen years later, it was revealed that MI5 'security' vetted BBC staff through the personnel department, particularly targeting those who were active in left-wing politics. As later happened with attempts to blacklist directors Roland Joffé and Roy Battersby, Garnett was employed because some executives were prepared to stand up to 'the man in the mac' at Broadcasting House and the MI5 vetoes, arguing that his talent overrode any political objections. Loach was never aware of himself being vetted. 'I was probably seen as a softer option,' he said.[25]

A Kestrel Films production of the time was Loach's first documentary; *In Black and White* was also the first major example of his work being censored. It was commissioned by the Save the Children Fund, which wanted to promote its activities in Britain and Africa, and LWT provided two-thirds of the budget in return for the right to screen the film. Jeremy Seabrook, who was writing a book about the rising resentment and bitterness in Blackburn over immigration,[26] researched the documentary, which was shot in that English Northern town, in Kenya, which had won its independence from Britain in 1963, and in Uganda, where colonialism ended a year before that.

'Initially, I thought it was going to be about the fund doing good work and saving children,' recalled Loach. 'But, when we were making it, we discovered that they were operating in conjunction with Kenyan businessmen to develop and educate a strata of black kids who would become the new middle class and Civil Service for the new Kenya. We shot in one particular school financed by the Save the Children Fund, where the whole practice was like a British public school: they wore uniforms, saluted the flag and were taught about manners and behaviour in the same way, and the library was full of books such as *Biggles*. Also, the headmaster was alleged to have shot more people during the Mau Mau uprising than anyone else; he bagged a lot of scalps. A black American teacher there was absolutely outraged by what was going on and said it was an exercise in neo-colonialism. All the teachers had to dress like Westerners, but he bought some shirts from the market in Nairobi and was told he wasn't allowed to wear them. We included all that in the film and the Save the Children Fund were outraged. They threatened to sue us for not making the film we said we would. In the end, we did a deal and the upshot was that they took away the cutting copy of the film and they wanted to destroy it, but we negotiated that it should stay in the British Film Institute vaults, never to be shown.'[27]

Kestrel Films director Irving Teitelbaum recalled, 'The Save the

Children Fund was a charity with royal patrons and existed through donations. They felt the film was hostile and, not surprisingly, were extremely upset, with the result that there was a legal dispute. I think Ken and Tony had managed to get a lot of material, like *The Big Flame*, that created a fuss through the BBC, which was a kind of indulgent parent, but it was much tougher in the outside world.'[28]

Loach aso fell foul of the Central Office of Information when, keen to dispel the image of the insensitive careers officer seen in *Kes*, it commissioned him to make a sixteen-minute 'vocational guidance' film. For *Talk About Work*, Loach filmed young people in different jobs, discussing their progress. Unfortunately for the COI, one worker on the assembly line at Ford's Halewood car plant did not stick to their desired script. Loach recalled, 'He said: "If I do this for another ten years, I'll be dead; it's a terrible job and completely destroys your brain." We included it in the film and, lo and behold, the Central Office of Information said: "You've broken the contract; we don't want to hear this." So that was squashed as well!'[29]

Kestrel's decision not to make commercials but to accept commissions for documentaries such as *In Black and White* and *Talk About Work* seemed to have highlighted the impossibility of producing films to the satisfaction of other organisations, which had their own vested and political interests. Two years of operating as a freelance outside the security of the BBC had provided Loach with his first experience of dealing with the uncertainties that were to dog him over the next two decades. He would have to fight harder than ever to get films made and contend with controversy and censorship. Five years inside the BBC had cushioned him from a cold, harsh world, but the Corporation itself was changing and taking the carpet away from under those who had been given such artistic freedom. Perhaps only by leaving, and weathering the storms that would result from sticking to his political principles, could Loach further his career and be true to himself. Over the coming years, many plans came to nothing, including further scripts by Neville Smith (one about a group of lads on a package tour and another set in a bra factory). In the meantime, he worked with another writer for a second time – on a remake of their first play together.

10

FAMILY LIFE

THE SUCCESS OF *Kes*, after its troubled road into cinemas, made it easier for Tony Garnett to get another Ken Loach film off the ground. Ironically, it was one for which the director had no great enthusiasm. Garnett's own traumas, reflected in David Mercer's *In Two Minds*, made him determined to remake that 'Wednesday Play' as a feature film. 'Ken was quite reluctant, as was David,' recalled the producer. 'It's the only subject where I've insisted we had two bites at the cherry, for my own personal reasons. It was so important to me, to do with a woman in my life and a painful time. Although it wasn't necessarily a sensible thing to do, it was almost an obsession in me to try to understand what had gone on. David had also known this woman, but he didn't want to do it and Ken wasn't keen to do it again. I was absolutely determined we *would* do it again and had to persuade them.'[1]

Having made *In Two Minds* in a documentary style centred on interviews with the troubled young woman and her parents, Loach sought a different approach for the film and found a suitable title in *Family Life*. 'Unlike with *Kes*, I didn't have a strong cinematic view of it,' he explained. 'It was very much about the internal family relationships. In the television version, you didn't see the therapist on camera, but in the film I wanted to have him in the scene. When the therapist is effectively the camera, you have nothing to cut to because it's a dialogue with the people he's talking to and the therapist himself. That was the biggest change from the TV version.'[2] A real psychiatrist, Michael Riddall, took the Laingian role of the pioneer in a National Health mental hospital who encourages patients to live as a community and discourages the use of electro-convulsive therapy and chemotherapy, before he moves to another hospital, his experimental ward is closed and the old regime is reinstated.

As with the original 'Wednesday Play', the teaming of Loach and Mercer was not an ideal one. 'I wanted to explore the therapy sessions so that people saw the mother, father and daughter searching their minds, being taken unaware and revealing things the actors didn't know they were revealing,' said Loach. 'But David Mercer was a writer who wrote very precisely and wanted the full stops and punctuation observed. That was a real tension that never resolved itself and Tony was stuck in the middle. It wasn't a particularly easy relationship and I found David difficult to talk to.'[3]

The director was greatly aided in making the film come alive by those he cast in the lead roles. A new family was created, with another great Loach find, Sandy Ratcliff, as the troubled nineteen-year-old, Janice. A photographic model who later found fame as Sue Osman in the original cast of *EastEnders*, she had little acting experience beyond BBC schools programmes, but a background that helped her to live the character. 'When I was about ten, my school sent me to the Tavistock Clinic,' she explained. 'I was a grade-A student who was also trouble – a bit rebellious – but that was all.'[4] This rebellious streak led Ratcliff to be expelled from her Islington girls' grammar school. Later, she took up modelling, bought a flat in Carnaby Street and worked as a waitress and disc-jockey. Photographed by Lord Snowdon, she was tipped to be one of the faces of the 1970s. 'I had been a stylist, before a couple of photographers kicked me in front of the cameras,' said Ratcliff, 'but I was never truly comfortable in that position. Then I did some work for *Honey* magazine and a couple of schools programmes, very much in drama-documentary style, made by Julian Aston. He suggested I contact Kestrel Films. If he had told me it was for a lead role, I would never have gone for it.'[5]

Janice's father was played by Loach faithful Bill Dean, by then also a regular in television sitcoms, and the search for someone to act her mother led to another classic find. The director discovered Grace Cave on the Walthamstow Conservative Association's ladies' committee. With only limited experience in amateur dramatics, she was the living version of David Mercer's character, the domineering mother who represents traditional 'family values' and is in conflict with a free-spirited daughter: in Cave and Ratcliff, Loach once more blurred the distinctions between real life and fiction. 'Grace was extraordinary,' he recalled. 'She absolutely stood by everything the character said. When actresses play a woman like that, they may tend to make a judgement about the character, even subconsciously, and you see it in their performance. I wanted someone whose belief in what they were saying absolutely shone through their eyes and the only way to do that was to get someone who really did hold those beliefs. So I thought: "Where will I find someone who will uphold traditional 'family values'?" That had to be among the ranks of the Conservative women. I tried out various scenes with half-a-dozen and there were several who were quite terrifying.'[6]

Sandy Ratcliff (centre) in *Family Life* with Bill Dean and Grace Cave [Kestrel Films/BFI Collections]

Another change from the television original was the addition of the teenager's boyfriend, Tim. The role was taken by Malcolm Tierney, a Mancunian who was able to draw on his own, unsettled family background to empathise with the story in *Family Life*. 'As a child, I went through a period when my parents would break up, but my father always came back,' he explained. 'It was pretty awful and I was torn between the two of them, so I would go silent. One day, when I returned home from a birthday party, my father asked how it was and I told them about it. Both my parents were weeping with laughter and I brought them together again. But, academically, it was hopeless because I couldn't do homework there. There was one period when my dad went into hospital for a whole term and my performance improved enormously.'[7] Tierney found his salvation in attending art school, where he took part in plays, then worked for six years as a commercial artist and textile designer, before training as an actor and turning professional. At the time of *Family Life*, he had gained most of his experience in theatre. His girlfriend, actress Kika

Markham, had starred in Loach's first television play, *Catherine*. 'I knew David Mercer, who had been Kika's boyfriend until about a year before we met,' he recalled. 'When I met Ken, he said the role I was going for wasn't quite written. I think he wanted a boyfriend for Janice, someone who understood her quirkiness and provided a voice that wouldn't be proselytising but have a rebellious attitude towards society. He turned out to be an artist, but maybe that came out of what I had done.'[8]

For personal reasons, Chris Menges was unable to shoot *Family Life* – made by Kestrel Films, with a budget of less than £190,000 from Anglo-EMI – so Charles Stewart once again stepped in as director of photography. Interiors were done in a specially constructed prefab in the Hertfordshire town of Hemel Hempstead, north of London, and filming also took place in hospitals where former schizophrenic patients and members of R.D. Laing's community participated in group therapy scenes.

Sandy Ratcliff attended such sessions and talked to psychiatrists when Loach took her to various mental hospitals in preparation for her role. 'It was very powerful stuff for me,' she recalled. 'Then, when we were filming, I didn't have a day off because my character was needed all the time, so it just took over my life for that period of time, but it was enough to turn my life around and make me look at all this that I had never looked at before – mental health generally and how we dealt with it. That's when I remembered going to the Tavistock Clinic.'[9] Throughout the shoot, Loach forbade Ratcliff from washing her hair and, when she cheated, it became a battle. 'Ken stopped me wearing make-up,' she explained. 'I couldn't wash my hair for seven weeks; he used to examine my head to see I hadn't cheated. He made me let the roots show their natural colour.'[10]

Tierney's role as her boyfriend, Tim, required him to ride a scooter, so he had to enrol for a three-week course of lessons and take a test. 'That was a huge sword of Damocles hanging over me,' recalled the actor. 'I was told that, if I didn't do it, I wouldn't be able to shoot the scooter sequences. The test was on the day we were doing the scene where Sandy and I painted the garden gnomes blue. At one point, Ken said to me: "Put her on your shoulders." Suddenly, I realised she was squirting the oil-based paint on my hair. I had to take it in good part, but it then started to rain and I needed to go to Woolwich for the scooter test. So I put my helmet on, set off and managed to pass. Afterwards, I looked in the mirror and saw I had a blue-streaked face!'[11]

When the cast and crew took a collection for striking postmen, it drew from Grace Cave the reaction that might have been expected of her. 'She was very pissed off with all the people constantly coming round and collecting money for the strikers' families!' recalled assistant cameraman Ivan Strasburg.[12] Cave became a source of mischief for Loach throughout the shoot. 'Ken had me and Billy Dean winding up Grace off set,' said Malcolm Tierney, 'and, on set, he would throw things in provocatively and half-wink at us.'[13]

The director also achieved an authentic shot of children caught in the crossfire of a blazing row by sending Tony Garnett in to create an argument with Dean. In another scene, two orderlies had to be seen restraining Tierney, and Loach ensured that they would have to make a real effort. 'When we rehearsed it with Malcolm,' said Chris Webb, an actor who was starting to do stunt work, 'I told him: "When we come to film it, do it as rehearsed, otherwise you'll get hurt if you're not careful." We then went out of the room and Ken apparently said to Malcolm: "I want you to resist them as much as you can." We came back in and he just went bananas and I had to grab him and hold him against the wall while Sandy was there screaming.'[14]

One person unwilling to be part of Loach's manipulation, though, was Ann Penfold, who played a nurse at the mental hospital in a scene where Janice is forced to take medication. 'Ken took me aside and asked me to wrench Sandy's arm up behind her in the tussle, in order to elicit a real scream of pain,' she recalled. 'I refused on the grounds that an actress worth her salt could cry out convincingly without a work colleague having to inflict actual pain.'[15] Loach later denied there was any intention to cause real pain.

Doremy Vernon, who played a nursing sister, simply found surrealist humour in the surroundings. 'We were in a television room at the hospital and there was a man who had gone mad because he had become involved with computers early on,' she said. 'The film camera was set up and he kept on going up to it and saying: "I'm Telly Welly Wells." It was pure Spike Milligan.'[16]

As with its television forerunner, *Family Life* sparked controversy and discussion about the conflicting ideologies and approaches to schizophrenia. The picture was a commercial failure in Britain, leading to problems in finding backing for future projects, which meant that Loach did not make another feature film for seven years. In France, it was initially banned from cinemas by the film censors, on the grounds that it might incite people to commit suicide. After newspapers pointed that the film had been screened at the Cannes and Berlin Film Festivals with no fatal results, the ban was lifted and *Family Life* attracted huge audiences, helped by being in the right place at the right time. 'It happened to open in Paris just months after the literate French had discovered R.D. Laing, so he was of the moment there,' said Tony Garnett. 'That film definitively created Ken's reputation in France.'[17] In the United States, it was retitled *Wednesday's Child* ('Wednesday's child is full of woe,' according to the rhyme).

Appearing in *Family Life* had an effect on the careers of both Sandy Ratcliff and Malcolm Tierney. The actor went on to play villains on television while Ratcliff eventually landed a steady stream of work as a jobbing actress before her role in *EastEnders*, although her life proved as erratic as that of Janice in the film and she had conflicting feelings about making it. 'I wasn't trained, so I got quite cross during the filming,' she said. 'I took Jan home with me a little bit and found it really hard. I wanted her to be stronger, because she wasn't schizophrenic, just a scapegoat, the victim of the family. It upset me. So did watching women of my mother's age having electric-shock treatments. When the filming was over, that was it; I felt abandoned and got quite depressed for a while. Then, for a couple of months when the film came out, I was being invited to every party going and even went to Budapest to represent Britain with *Family Life* at a film festival. But I wasn't working most of that time and there were times when I didn't have the bus fare to get to places I was supposed to be going.'[18]

In the vein of Carol White and John Bindon, fact and fiction collided – but Ratcliff proved to be a survivor. Shortly before joining *EastEnders* the following decade, she became addicted to heroin and, after treatment, served eight months in Holloway prison for conspiracy to supply cannabis. Then, in 1991, she gave an alibi in court to a lover of ten days who was found guilty of killing two women. 'Anybody who knows me knows I wouldn't protect a man who killed a woman,' said Ratcliff. 'I gave him an alibi and I stand by it. He must have done it because he was found guilty, but he certainly didn't do it when they said he had. The police got their timings wrong. I then just dropped out of the limelight and had more than one breakdown; it was awful. Then, I did some counsellor training and started driving London ambulances.'[19]

Just like many characters featured in Loach's films, Ratcliff's own problems seemed unresolved. 'I always felt I had nowhere to go but down after *Family Life* because it gave me so much personal publicity, and I got enormous respect for playing that role,' she said. 'I sometimes regret doing it, but I wouldn't not have done it. That's how my life has gone: things just turn up. I think my family was slightly dysfunctional, too. My parents were always quite rigid and had to live through me right up until their deaths; they were rather possessive of me. I don't think I realised that at the time of *Family Life*, though. I've had periods of depression in my life, which I've learned to deal with.'[20]

Loach's own family life was turned upside down shortly after he finished shooting the film. Although work often took him away from home for months on end, he enjoyed time with his wife and children. 'Ken has been a fantastic father,' said Lesley Loach three decades later. 'He loved it, especially when they got a bit older. He taught them to write, helped them with their projects, and took them to libraries and the boys to football matches. He would also take them on trips on the Tube, usually to museums!'[21] Film sets were not a place for families, though. 'I went up to Yorkshire when he was making *Kes*,' said Lesley. 'We had three children then, but Ken couldn't cope with a family *and* making a film. When he makes a film, he is a film director; he isn't a father or a husband. The best time is when he is editing. He loves it and he is home at a reasonable time.'[22]

It was during the editing stages of *Family Life* that tragedy struck. On 2 May 1971, Loach was driving his Triumph Herald estate, with sons Stephen and Nicholas, wife Lesley and her eighty-five-year-old grandmother, Jane Greenwood, as passengers, on a notorious two-lane stretch of the M1 near Watford where there was no crash barrier along the central reservation. Suddenly, a wheel came off a Triumph Herald coupé travelling in the same direction in the left-hand lane, resulting in Loach's car spinning across the

carriageways into a bridge parapet crash barrier. His five-year-old
son, Nicholas, and Lesley's grandmother died in the accident,
Loach's jaw was broken, his wife had multiple injuries and seven-
year-old Stephen was to suffer greatly from the loss of his brother.

Lesley Loach with children (left to right) Stephen, Emma, Hannah
and James [Sophie Baker]

The shock was felt by all those around the director. 'It is still so
vivid,' said Tony Garnett more than thirty years later, 'because I
was often at Ken's house and close to the kids and, for me, it was
like my own family.'[23] But Loach felt an obligation to complete his
work on *Family Life*. 'He eventually came back into the editing
room and carried on,' recalled Ivan Strasburg. 'He was walking
around for weeks with his jaw wired up.'[24]

Lesley Loach, who spent six weeks in hospital, was initially kept in
the dark about the deaths. 'I was very badly injured,' she recalled, 'so
they didn't tell me what had happened for about three weeks because I
was on a breathing machine; they thought I might cry, and you can't
cry on a breathing machine. Actually, I didn't cry for months. I was
quite ill when I came out of hospital and couldn't do much or walk far
or care for three children, so Ken had to stay and look after me for a
bit. My mother and Ken's mother each came for a while, too.'[25]

Although Loach spent more than a year at home, close to his wife and their three surviving children – Stephen, three-year-old Hannah and James, who was almost two – he found it difficult to confront his grief. 'When I was having a bad time, it didn't coincide with when Ken was having a bad time, so we would never talk about it,' said Lesley. 'I really don't know how we got through it. I think we were both in shock. We didn't deal with it very well as a family. I used to talk to the children because they would always ask questions, but I could never talk to Ken; the whole thing was just too painful. It was an area neither of us would dare go into. We very rarely go to the cemetery together, either, because it is still pretty awful. Over the years, though, things have got easier and we can talk about it more now.'[26]

Practical repercussions of the crash continued for several years. When it was discovered that the other car's wheel, which disintegrated, had a six-inch rusted crack in it, the Loach family decided to sue the driver. But he pleaded that the car had been serviced and had passed an MOT test only a month earlier and the vehicle examiner in the case agreed that this would not have been discovered in such a test. The Loaches then decided to sue the driver's insurers and garage jointly, but the garage went bankrupt and the insurance company contested the case on the grounds that its client had not been negligent. Psychiatric reports on Loach's son Stephen reported that he had hallucinations of his dead brother at night and, with the case constantly adjourned and the consequent stress, the family decided to withdraw the compensation claim in October 1975, leaving them with a legal bill of £909.30. 'Since the emotional strain was proving too great for my family,' said Lesley Loach, 'I wrote to our solicitor telling him we could stand no more and to abandon the whole thing.'[27]

Almost eighteen months after the accident, the Loaches had celebrated the birth of their second daughter, Emma. 'We decided we would have another child,' recalled Lesley, 'because our elder daughter, Hannah, said: "We're supposed to be four children, but there are only three of us." It was very nice to have another baby.'[28] By then, her husband was easing himself back into work, but, if he found it difficult to discuss his son's death with his wife, he would certainly not broach it with others. 'It's something you neither recover from nor want to recover from,' he reflected. 'If I were to talk about it publicly, I think I would feel too exposed.'[29]

11

DAYS OF HOPE

AFTER A YEAR'S BREAK, Ken Loach eased himself back into work
with a first for him on screen – an adaptation of a classical work.
He filmed *A Misfortune*, based on a Chekhov story about a
woman's adultery, for BBC2's Saturday-evening arts compendium,
Full House. 'It was an easy way of getting back into work and quite
an unpressured situation,' he explained. 'It was just a half-hour film
and the short story already existed, so all I had to do was adapt it.'[1]

Producer Melvyn Bragg, a fellow student at Oxford University,
commissioned Loach to make *A Misfortune* as part of a series of
Chekhov and Joyce film adaptations. Loach and Tony Garnett had
previously discussed with him the possibility of turning his first
novel, *The Hired Man*, into a film after they founded Kestrel, but
their conversations failed to bear fruit. 'I think I was too stuck in the
mud at the time,' admitted Bragg. 'Ken and Tony wanted to take
the book as the basis for a film, but I rather wanted the film to
follow the book. I didn't quite get the hang of what they were up to
and regret it now. I should have let them get on with it. When I
returned to the BBC on *Second House*, as it originally was, I said
I would produce ten films based on short stories of Joyce and
Chekhov and, rather airily, said I had great people like David
Storey to write the scripts and others like Ken Loach and Karel
Reisz to direct them, on tiny budgets. Bill Morton, the editor,
accepted the idea.'[2]

Of course, Loach had classical experience in repertory theatre
and at Oxford University – where Bragg, one year his junior, saw
him in a Restoration comedy and considered him to be 'very funny
indeed'[3] – and his outlook reflected that of the Russian playwright.
Both recognised the need to paint the grim reality of hopelessness

and despair experienced by some people so that alternatives could be considered.

A Misfortune, Loach's first production with designer Martin Johnson, filmed in Norfolk during the summer of 1972, featured three well-seasoned classical actors who were inducted into the director's way of performing. 'He said he wanted to make it like real life,' said Lucy Fleming, 'and not to think about acting it, just to *be* it. I found it quite difficult. We had a script, but very loosely based on the story, and Ken was very keen for us to interact with each other. When I arrived at the hotel before filming, I found a note under my door. It was written to me as my character, as if a note from my lover, who was played by Ben Kingsley, about how we must meet. At first, I thought: "This is odd." When it came to filming, we weren't allowed any make-up at all, which, of course, was right for a girl in those days, and it was a much looser way of working, which I loved. In a party scene, I had to play the piano and Ken was very keen that I learn it and play it as much as possible. I'm about the most unmusical person you could think of, but there was a lady there who taught me.'[4]

While Fleming prepared for her role with piano lessons, Loach gave Peter Eyre, who played her cheated-on husband, a book on pre-revolutionary Russia to digest. 'After reading it,' recalled the actor, 'he asked me, with a group of extras around us, to tell them the content from a conservative imperialist point of view, then he said to do the same from a revolutionary slant and, finally, he said: "Now, do a mix of both. If you mix imperialism and a bit of revolutionary together, you will end up by speaking Chekhov." That, of course, was correct.'[5]

While shooting in a large, cold house in Norfolk during the early winter of 1972, the cast and crew had one eerie moment. 'For a scene with someone in bed, we put some lights up and the room got really hot after being very cold,' recalled Loach. 'The sound man was saying: "There's an electrical fault." So we looked around and the noise got louder and louder. We discovered that a lot of flies had hibernated behind the wallpaper and they all woke up, and we were engulfed with them in the room.'[6]

Loach followed *A Misfortune* with a major television epic, three years in the making, that also harked back to the early twentieth century. *Days of Hope* was writer Jim Allen's *tour de force*, a history of the labour movement over the ten years from wartime 1916 to the General Strike, centred on the experiences of one farming family in the north-east of England. 'We're not paddling around on folksy nostalgia,' explained Allen,[7] at a time when television was brimming with historical series and period dramas such as *Upstairs Downstairs*, *The Onedin Line*, *Lord Peter Wimsey*, *Sam*, *South Riding*, *Edward the Seventh* and *The Stars Look Down*. Loach was keen to kill a few myths about British history. 'The traditional view is that England has always been a peaceful and stable society where violence is a teenage aberration,' he said. 'We wanted to show that England is founded on a violent past which involves the forceful suppression of dissent.'[8]

Days of Hope started, in 1972, as another Allen drama about an industrial dispute, the 1921 Durham miners' lockout, which Loach and Garnett hoped to make as a Kestrel feature film. After it was rejected by various companies, including Paramount Pictures and the London office of American International Productions, they took the idea to the BBC and developed it as a four-part television film. Like all his dramas with Garnett and Loach, Allen worked closely with the producer and director. 'Ken is very much a hands-on director,' said the writer. 'He's involved in every stage of the scripts. I might write half-a-dozen scenes, then we sit down, tear it apart and put it back together. It's the only way to make it work. Because we have the same politics, basically, that's no problem. When you write in isolation, you can't see the wood for the trees. Ken is like a laser beam. I curse him at times, but he's always right. He will come and look at the material and say: "That's great, Jim, but I think this." And he is right, because I've been so deep in it that I can't see it. That's how we develop the script together.'[9]

This was a method that also worked well during Loach's collaborations with his other regular writers, Barry Hines and, later, Paul Laverty. For many years, the director gained the best of both worlds by interspersing the uncompromising political bullets of Allen's work with more gentle, observational scripts by Hines. Laverty fell somewhere between the two camps but was closer to Hines in that most of the political messages were implicit in his scripts, rather than explicit.

Allen's *Days of Hope* script, researched from history books, memoirs, diaries and local newspaper reports, featured three pivotal characters in their formative years: Ben Matthews, his elder sister, Sarah, and her husband, Philip Hargreaves. Ben starts as a sixteen-year-old who longs to fight in the First World War, while Philip is a conscientious objector and Christian Socialist in hiding from the police who is conscripted to France, court-martialled as a deserter and saved from execution only by a last-minute decree. Episode 2, set in 1921, sees the beginnings of Ben's conversion to Communism. Having previously joined the British Army serving in Ireland, he is among troops sent to the mines when pit owners lock out the workforce in an attempt to make them accept wage cuts, but he deserts on the way to Durham and is jailed for three years. By Episode 3, three years later, Philip has risen from union official to become an MP in the first Labour government, under Ramsay MacDonald, and is living in London, where Ben joins him but causes a rift by joining the Communist Party; Philip urges unions not to create division in the labour movement while his party adopts previous Tory strike-breaking plans in case of an emergency. Stanley Baldwin's subsequent Conservative government puts those into effect when confronted with the General Strike in the final episode, when Sarah is working with Ben as a Communist organiser. This new analysis of a critical time in the British labour movement's history proved to be Allen's definitive work on his theme of betrayal; the political and industrial struggles from that time also clearly bore comparison with those in the early 1970s, when the country endured inflation and a policy of wage restraint, under both Conservative and Labour rule.

'*Days of Hope* grew out of Jim's, Ken's and my political interest and commitment,' explained Garnett. 'The idea was to show ten years of betrayal in the Labour Party and the trade union leadership. It ended up in defeat and the idea was that, if we showed how that came about, we could warn everybody to ensure it did not happen again. We could see that Labour is never "in power"; it is only ever "in office". You just watch trade union officials who can't wait to get to the House of Lords and see them becoming servants of the permanent government and junior members of the Establishment, and being more and more removed from the genuine concerns of people. It was just as true in the Seventies as it was in the Twenties.'[10]

Days of Hope was a television epic, three years
in the making [BBC]

Faced with the daunting task of casting almost ninety roles, Loach started by making a list of 'Some Tyneside Actors', which included Alun Armstrong, and 'Actors – Mostly Yorkshire Born, but might cope with the Geordie accent',[11] such as Brian Glover (although he did not finally appear). Before scouring North Yorkshire and County Durham, the main locations for filming of the first two episodes during the second half of 1973, he saw some London-based Northern actors in February of that year. Armstrong was among five who he noted were 'reasonable Geordies seen in London, but hardly worth getting up for very small part that can be glorified extra'.[12]

The leading role of Ben was filled when an out-of-work young actor, Paul Copley, was sent in Loach's direction. He had been working as an actor-teacher with a Theatre in Education company attached to Leeds Playhouse and, in the city's BBC studio, recorded his first role for radio – teacher Mr Farthing in *Kes*, as played in the film by Colin Welland. After watching *Family Life*, Copley yearned to work with Loach, a burning ambition fuelled by his admiration of the director's 'commitment to socialist principles and his political and artistic integrity'.[13] He then moved to London to live with his new bride, actress Natasha Pyne, eventually found an agent, Chris Long, and filled in a long 'resting' period with supply teaching and casual driving work. 'Having made an SW7 delivery in a van I was driving,' recalled Copley, 'I decided to make a detour and call in to see Chris Long at his office in Kynance Mews. He wasn't there. The only person in the office was a temp and she had nothing to do with the theatrical business. We talked; she recognised my Yorkshire accent. She said that she had recently been on a camping trip in the Lake District and two people in the next tent had mentioned that Ken Loach was about to make a film for the BBC which required genuine Northern accents. Did I want her to ring the BBC? Why not? She did and, what's more, she arranged an appointment for me: BBC TV Centre, East Tower. I was astonished.'[14]

When Copley travelled to White City to meet Loach, he made the error committed by many others before and since, of mistaking the director for an 'assistant' and chatting away, unaware of the 'audition' taking place. Realising that time was passing and he needed to deliver the Steenbeck film-editing machine in his van in the car park below, the actor stopped talking about his family, teaching, and living in London, and said, 'Look, I'm sorry about this. The chances of getting this job are probably slim and, if I don't get the Steenbeck delivered, I won't have the van driving job either. Could you ask Ken Loach how long he's going to be because I'm going to have to leave very soon.' To which the 'young production assistant' responded, 'Oh, sorry. I'm, erm, I'm Ken Loach!' Copley recalled, 'I was pretty mortified but tried not to show it, apologised a lot and left – absolutely sure that the job was out of the window. Ken, however, had got exactly what he wanted – a chat/interview untrammelled by stiffness or embarrassment on my part and an insight into what made me tick as a person. Given that Ben Matthews in *Days of Hope* is pretty unworldly-wise and naive at the start of the story, I hadn't yet ruled myself out of the job!'[15]

After a further meeting, with Loach, Allen and Tony Garnett, Copley was offered the role. He immediately identified with the character through having been brought up in the Yorkshire farming village of Denby Dale, training as a lance corporal in the Combined Cadet Force while at school and gaining experience as a student union official during teacher training. But Loach realised that such a role in a historical saga required the actor to be fully conversant with the politics of the time. 'Because the character was political, Paul had to know what the ideas were,' he explained. 'He was absolutely right for the role and made it his own; he had a vigour and energy and brightness in his eye that was very good.'[16]

In preparing to play Ben, Copley appreciated the help given him by Loach. 'He guided my research and reading so that I felt able to join in the argument and debate without hesitation by the time Films 3 and 4 came along,' explained the actor. 'He gave me suggestions for a reading list, which included the writings of Marx, Engels and Lenin, as well as those of outstanding radical and socialist politicians, writers and commentators. I was reading Robert Tressel, Beatrice Webb, Keir Hardie, the *Morning Star* – anything that would broaden my understanding of socialism and social injustice/justice. He encouraged me to keep an open mind when I visited political meetings and gatherings. During the months before filming, Natasha and I researched all shades of Left opinion and strategy, and attended meetings of all kinds – from Communist Party of Great Britain meetings and cultural events to Actors' Equity meetings!'[17]

The two other major roles, of Philip and Sarah Hargreaves, went to Nikolas Simmonds and Pamela Brighton, Peter Kerrigan stayed in type as leader of a local branch of the Communist Party in London, and Liverpool agent Ernie Mack and comedian Joey Kaye were cast once more.

Filming took place in North Yorkshire, around Ripon and Masham, and in County Durham, South Wales, Rochdale, Bristol and London. In a scene showing conscientious objectors in France, shot in Pembrokeshire, Nikolas Simmonds was teamed with Peter Armitage (noted by Loach, in the auditions, to be 'squarely built, good Yorks lad'[18]) and delivered one of Jim Allen's classic lines: 'The only war worth fighting is the class war.' Armitage himself ventured: 'The only way to end war is to establish socialism.' Scenes of troops in Ireland in that first episode were shot in Tenby, on the south-west tip of Wales, where the actors were not welcomed by the locals. 'We had to get all our hair cut off,' recalled Jimmy Coleman, who previously appeared in *The Rank and File* and *After a Lifetime*. 'In the evenings, when we finished filming, we went out and were getting treated with a lot of disrespect because people genuinely thought we were soldiers, and there was a little argy-bargy in certain clubs. In one, all the locals set against us and I thought there was going to be murder.'[19]

Some of the soldiers were played by Northern comedians, including Duggie Brown in his third role for Loach, and this helped to bring lightness to the filming of some harrowing scenes. After one in which a squaddie was blown up by a landmine, the director prepared his army for what was to come. Paul Copley recalled, 'His direction went something like this: "He was your friend and comrade, and you know that just over that hill he's been blown apart. As it sinks in that you're not going to see him alive again and that this could have been any one of you, you get to your feet and make your way up the hill – slowly at first. The lightheartedness is gone. You're all shattered and alert for danger now. So just think about the importance of what's just happened and we'll turn over. All right, Hal?" Hal Nolan replied: "Certainly, Ken. But first a song!" Then, parodying bad club singing, he launched into: "If a picture paints a thousand words . . ." Everybody roared with laughter – the bubble of concentration was burst, but the moment was very funny. Everybody saw the funny side, including Ken, and the situation was soon back in serious, workmanlike mode.'[20]

As usual in a Loach film, reality spilled over on screen, making Copley feel he owed it to all those taking part not to let them down, particularly in a scene of a miners' meeting in a village hall. 'Many of the men playing pit deputies and union activists had actually worked down the pit or were union officials, and their experience and commitment gave the scenes tension, truth and immediacy,' he recalled. 'Actors like myself and Alun Armstrong knew that to be other than truthful would be to let these hard-working local men and women and their ideals down – we couldn't have done that.'[21]

Stephen Rea, who was recommended to Loach because of his experience in alternative theatre, was cast in the small role of a reporter interviewing Philip Hargreaves after he addresses the Transport and General Workers' Union meeting in the third episode. 'That scene was improvised,' explained Rea. 'Nikolas Simmonds was playing a working-class guy moving towards the Establishment. As a left-wing journalist, I was challenging that and asking him hard questions about where his commitment was going to lie now he was inside the system. When the director of photography said he wanted to shoot the scene again because there was a flare in the camera, Ken said: "I like flares." He liked the fact that viewers knew it was a film. In another scene, where I was watching Nikolas speak at a political meeting, they couldn't afford to fill the auditorium with extras, so they literally had cardboard cutouts of people, lit joss-sticks and a pall of smoke went up.'[22] Interestingly, although Rea recalled the first scene to be improvised, it was scripted, a reflection of Loach's willingness to allow actors to work around the writer's words.

Despite the budgetary constraints, Tony Garnett regarded it as a major triumph to have secured BBC backing for the series, with each episode ranging from eighty to 135 minutes. 'On location, Ken was always complaining he didn't have enough time, money or resources, but I bust a gut getting all that I did out of the BBC,' he explained. 'It was a huge production, by any standards, and they wouldn't do it today. But directors are *supposed* to be like Oliver Twist and ask for more. I remember having to drive it through in order to get it made, having to say no to Ken, telling him that whatever he didn't get in on that day on that location wouldn't be in the film because we had to move from Rochdale to Bristol the next day. Of course, he didn't like it, but he had to take it because, in the end, I told him that the unit was moving. Ken will push and push and push for what he wants and squeeze out what he can, but ultimately he is a realist and a grown-up, and he's not one for childish tantrums. He lives in the real world and has a reputation for staying within budget. You use as many resources as you possibly can, then cut your cloth accordingly. Once again, it was putting a quart into a pint pot, but we never fell out. Considering the pressure we were under, there was remarkably little tension.'[23]

Emotions exploded only once *Days of Hope* – billed as 'a series of four films from the Great War to the General Strike' – reached BBC1 screens in the autumn of 1975. Immediately after the final episode was broadcast, the *Tonight* programme, on the same channel, featured a debate that included Jim Allen and William Deedes, editor of the right-wing *Daily Telegraph*, which predictably had attacked the drama as 'sheer propaganda'.[24] Interviewer Sue Lawley said to Shaun Sutton, the head of BBC drama group, 'You haven't answered Bill Deedes's point when he says that there are things

about plays like this, with this sort of "propaganda" in them, which
. . . people in the BBC would not notice were left-wing.' Sutton
responded, 'I am quite capable of noticing that they are left-wing. I
think any large artistic group will always contain a certain number of
people of left-wing persuasion. This is absolutely inevitable and I
think it perfectly right. In the last two years, we have presented less
than ten plays of this nature before *Days of Hope* – less than ten out
of 850 original drama transmissions. That seems a very fair proportion to me.'[25] Equally predictably, the *Daily Mail* headlined a
feature, 'The most powerful TV plays of the year . . . or just a
political broadcast for the Far Left?' Novelist John Braine told the
paper the films were slanted against the Establishment and said of
the conscientious objector scenes, 'I was so angry I couldn't take any
more and almost kicked the set in.'[26]

Such reactions only served to show that those responsible for
Days of Hope had hit a raw nerve. 'I enjoyed it immensely!' recalled
Tony Garnett. 'We thought that, if the right-wing press was saying
this, it had all been worth it.'[27] As with *Cathy Come Home*, there
were attempts to discredit the drama, highlighting inaccuracies
such as the wrong cap badge on a uniform. 'If people are upset with
the political stance,' continued Garnett, 'they will find some tiny
thing that you've got historically wrong and say: "If they can't get
these little things right, obviously the whole thing's rubbish." '[28]
Loach simply responded, 'Those critics never confronted the arguments and counter-arguments in the script, which are very subtle
and brilliant writing. That muscular fighting for ideas is like Shaw
but, to me, it's much stronger than Shaw. Jim's writing is the red
meat of revolutionary socialism; he never took the easy shortcut,
never made an assertion that wasn't earned through the arguments.'[29]

Days of Hope, whose style of filming confirmed that Loach had
firmly left behind the handheld-camera approach that had marked
his early years in television, also had an impact beyond raising the
hackles of right-wing critics. Just as Alan Parker, Britain's most
successful modern-day film director in Hollywood, cited *Cathy
Come Home* as 'the single most important reason why I wanted to
become a film-maker', Stephen Frears said, 'There isn't one cinema
film which compares in importance with *Days of Hope*. Not one.'[30]
The four-part drama, over almost seven hours of television, had

ripple effects abroad, too. A producer with Boston television station WGBH subsequently asked Loach to direct some episodes of a planned series on that country's labour history. He replied that he was 'committed to a couple of projects which should occupy the next two years' and added, 'Also, I'd find it difficult to work in an environment and idiom where I didn't feel at home.'[31]

Loach himself had been acclimatising to a new domestic environment since moving with his family from London to the Somerset spa town of Bath in 1974, as his elder son Stephen approached secondary-school age – 'I just wanted to bring the kids up in a better way, in a less oppressive city,' he explained[32] – and one of his professional commitments was another Barry Hines script, set in the South Yorkshire countryside that he had embraced in *Kes*. *The Price of Coal* started as a single play, *Meet the People*, about the preparations for a royal visit at the fictional Milton colliery, but Loach and Tony Garnett felt that something else was needed to counterbalance the hilarities of bosses rushing around to make long-needed repairs, paint the pithead white and tear down girlie calendars while workers watch with humorous scepticism. 'It was a very funny screenplay, a lovely comedy,' Garnett recalled, 'but it would have been too easy to give the impression that it's a lot of fun being a miner.'[33] So Hines agreed with Loach and Garnett to write a linked second play, *Back to Reality*, in which there is a pit explosion that kills two miners.

In casting *The Price of Coal*, Loach returned to the Leeds theatrical agency that had supplied him with some of the comics who appeared in *Kes* and auditioned many at the City Varieties Theatre in that city and others at the Ardsley House Hotel, Barnsley. One of those, Duggie Brown, took the role of the assistant colliery manager, with Jackie Shinn – also a real-life pit deputy at Brodsworth Colliery outside his native Doncaster, with experience in a mine rescue team – as his superior; Bobby Knutt, from Sheffield, and Stan Richards, a Barnsley performer who shortly afterwards found long-running fame as Seth Armstrong in the soap opera *Emmerdale*, played workmates at the coal face. 'Those comics were part of the culture,' said Hines, who accompanied Loach for the casting interviews. 'Even though most didn't work at the pit, they were brought up in pit villages.'[34] Some real mining apprentices were used as extras, found on a day-release course at Barnsley Technical College.

The Price of Coal was shot at the disused Thorpe Hesley pit, near Barnsley, during the glorious summer of 1976, a sharp contrast to the weather when *Kes* was filmed. Because it would be impossible to film inside the mine itself, an underground tunnel was dug through a slag heap and a 'coal face' created, covered by a tarpaulin; a paddy train was installed and the old cage that took colliers below ground was sent part of the way on its trip to show the screen 'miners' on their way down. When a brick was discovered propping open a window because the sash had gone, this was incorporated into the first play, with an apprentice being despatched to paint it.

Stan Richards recalled the Loach style of coaxing performers to give their best that was familiar to those who worked with him. 'Every time we did a take,' he explained, 'Ken told us: "That was brilliant. One more time." Then, he said: "We will do it again and, this time, don't stop at the end of the script. Carry on and do some more." And, because we were club comics, we found it easy to ad-lib. At one point, I said to Barry Hines: "What do you think about what we're doing to your play?" He said: "Actually, I think you're quite enhancing it." '[35]

Richards also observed another Loach trait. 'He would take a couple of pebbles from the pit top in his hand and toss them in the air, then eventually throw them away,' he said. 'I once said to him: "What are you trying to do? Practise to get on the cabaret circuit?" He said: "No, I have a problem, so I stand and do this. Once the answer has come into my head, I chuck them away because I don't need them any more. It saves me buying worry beads!" '[36]

In the final scene of the first play, Loach added his own humour to the story and achieved a lifetime ambition. 'A helicopter was hired and the management were lined up outside the office,' recalled Hines. 'There were two real brothers, one of them with a bald head that was very shiny. It did look a bit odd, the sort of thing that would make people laugh if he walked on stage like that as a comedian [which he was]. So Ken said to him: "It might be better for the filming if you wear a hairpiece." When they lined up for this last scene, Ken told the helicopter pilot: "I want you to come down in the middle of the yard, well away from the line of dignitaries." The helicopter came down, a long way from them, and there was a gentle breeze. Then, for the next take, Ken said to the pilot: "This time, I want you to come down as near as possible to them." It came down only about ten yards away from them, the hairpiece started coming off and the man's brother reached over to try to hold it on as it was blowing away; there was dust flying up and the whole thing was chaos. Tony Garnett turned to me and said: "He's been waiting to do that all his life." And Ken had told [cameraman] Brian Tufano to go in close because there would be no second go at that.'[37] As a result, the unscripted action subsequently appeared on screen.

Referring to 'Ken's obsession', Garnett explained, 'It started when he was quite young and he's always been intrigued with people who have wigs and hairpieces, particularly men. I can remember, way back in the Sixties, we would be sitting in a café in Soho, because he loved tea and a bun, and he would go: "There's one! There's one!" "What?" I said. "I've got a sighting," he would say. There would be someone with a wig, but I could never tell. It just amused him. So Ken was absolutely delighted to put that gag in at the end of *The Price of Coal*. That probably made the whole film for him. Someone should write a PhD on Ken's obsession with wigs and hairpieces!'[38] Loach's explanation was simple. 'If you've got a trained eye, you can spot one a mile off,' he said.[39]

The Price of Coal, screened just three years after a national miners' strike had brought down Edward Heath's Conservative government, depicted the humour and camaraderie of this group of workers, as well as the everyday dangers they faced underground. As the 1970s progressed, Loach saw the Wilson and Callaghan Labour governments continue to offer no radical alternative to Toryism and, in 1977, stood firmly by his principles when informed that the Prime Minister wished to recommend him to be appointed an OBE in the Queen's Silver Jubilee and Birthday Honours List. He responded, 'Thank you for your letter of 18th May concerning the possible inclusion of my name in the forthcoming Honours List. However, it would be incompatible with the views I and my colleagues have consistently expressed in our films for me to accept such an award, and I must therefore decline the Prime Minister's suggestion.'[40] The days of hope betrayed in the 1960s, as earlier, were now no more than a flickering light at the end of a long tunnel.

12

END OF AN ERA

JUST AS THE DOOR appeared to have firmly shut on socialism, Ken Loach was approaching the end of another chapter: his professional partnership with Tony Garnett. Throughout the 1970s, the producer had found it increasingly difficult to get Loach films accepted for television or the cinema. A Jim Allen script about 1920s Ireland, Nell Dunn's *The Girls*, set in a South Wales factory and following a young woman's self-discovery, and a documentary telling the story of Chinese table tennis players visiting Birmingham and seeing local people's homes, social clubs and canteens all came to nothing. At the same time, there was no lack of offers from producers and writers who wanted Loach to work on their projects. 'Play for Today' scripts by Trevor Griffiths and John McGrath were mooted, as were an HTV adaptation of a Janina David book, *A Square of Sky*, and a United Artists cinema film of the John Galsworthy novel *The Apple Tree*. But Loach simply felt that these were 'outside' projects that did not emanate from his own commitment and enthusiasm.

When Garnett was promised money from a French company, provided that the resulting film starred an actor from that country and was a children's story, Loach opted for a book he had found on his own children's shelves. *Black Jack*, a 1968 novel by Leon Garfield – the author of *Jack Holborn* and *Mister Corbett's Ghost* – was the tale of an eighteenth-century highwayman who escapes the gallows and the body-snatchers who believe him to be dead, and abducts a young draper's apprentice, Tolly. When they rescue Belle, a girl on the way to the lunatic asylum after being mistakenly diagnosed as mad, the children become embroiled in Black Jack's adventures.

Loach adapted the book himself, transplanting the action from London and Surrey to North Yorkshire, where, during the filming of *Days of Hope*, he had discovered countryside that had changed little over the intervening two centuries. *Black Jack* became a curiosity among Loach films. Although its low budget – just £500,000 – resulted in a slightly unfinished production, the director showed a fresh approach in his way of putting period drama on screen, without being weighed down by heavy costumes and stilted dialogue. 'You can't make a historical film in Surrey today,' explained Loach. 'We wanted the landscape of North Yorkshire and the dialect of South Yorkshire. In the book the speech is unaccented, but if you do a period film in contemporary middle-class English it always turns the speakers into figures at a fancy-dress parade. I took a liking to Yorkshire because of the use of old forms of speech – thees and thous and arts. They are echoes of the past and yet it is a very contemporary dialect. It is Arthur Scargill's dialect and you can't get more contemporary than that.'[1]

Ever socially and historically conscious, Loach also saw the film as a means of portraying the pre-Industrial Revolution English landscape and the harshness endured by those who lived in it. After his forays into the world of schizophrenia and psychiatry, there was an added attraction in the story of Belle, which was drawn from Garfield's experience of working in a mental hospital, where he researched bio-chemistry shortly after the Second World War. 'My inspiration for Belle was the real case history of a girl who had contracted scarlet fever and, as a result, could only remember things for fifteen seconds at a time – or a minute at the most,' said the author. 'This was twelve months after her illness. She suffered a form of reversion in which she went back to childhood and threw tantrums like a four-year-old. This was what got me thinking about Belle's predicament and child-like innocence when I started writing *Black Jack*.'[2]

Despite these reasons for wanting to make *Black Jack*, Loach later admitted, 'It was a little bywater, really, rather than the main thrust of what we wanted to do.'[3] The promise of French money, alongside that from the National Film Finance Corporation, also meant changing the leading character to a Frenchman. As a result, Black Jack was played by Jean Franval, a former singer in bars, cabarets and clubs in the South of France who progressed to straight acting roles after appearing at Paris's Olympia Music Hall. Dozens of televison and film roles followed in various European countries, although he had never previously appeared in a British production.

To find the child leads, Loach returned to Barnsley, where he had discovered David Bradley ten years earlier while casting *Kes*. After seeing several hundred children, he chose fifteen-year-old long-distance lorry driver's son Stephen Hirst, from Worsburgh High School, Whitecross, to play Tolly, and twelve-year-old Louise Cooper, a miner's daughter who attended Bradley's former school, St Helen's, to play Belle. 'It's very difficult for a child to portray insanity,' said Loach. 'We looked at all the pale, thin girls we could find, but when we saw Louise we knew at once that our search was ended. She has an extraordinary sensitive face that really haunts you.'[4]

Six weeks' filming in the late summer of 1978, mostly around Masham and Ripon, was hampered by incessant rain and interruptions from an RAF flight path overhead. 'It was a difficult shoot, under quite difficult conditions,' recalled director of photography Chris Menges, 'and it didn't quite gel, particularly because of the budget.'[5] Menges shot all exteriors on Super 16 film to give grainy images but needed to switch to 35mm to avoid the colours becoming garish for interiors, where natural light was used as much as possible to reflect the fact that rooms at the time of the story were illuminated by a few candles or an oil-lamp; candles with thick wicks were used to boost the 'natural' light in rooms where the camera found dark, sinister corners.

A particularly colourful scene in the film is that featuring a travelling fair – brought to life by Loach's production designer, Martin Johnson – and its array of lively characters, such as a quack physician and a troupe of dwarfs. ('Tom Thumb's Army', consisting of Malcolm Dixon, Mike Edmonds, David Rappaport and Tiny Ross, subsequently appeared in the fantasy adventure *Time Bandits*.) Rather than adding a music soundtrack afterwards, Loach intended to use some of these people to play instruments on screen, as they would have done in the eighteenth century.

'I have a fairly puritanical attitude to music,' he explained. 'I have some sympathy for the position that the film should be able to exist without music telling you what to feel and that something horrible is going to happen around the corner. But sometimes music can sustain a feeling generated within the film or make another comment by putting the scene in a different light or adding its own reflection. It was different with the early "Wednesday Plays", where the music was part of the world of the film and belonged to the characters, rather than film music put on afterwards. In *Kes*, John Cameron's music was used to endorse the idea of the bird as having qualities that you also wanted to attribute to Billy. John said he would use an oboe rather than a flute, which maybe would have been the obvious instrument, to give a more reedy sound, making it more earthy and less ethereal.'[6]

In his preparation for *Black Jack*, a phone call to top folk music producer Bill Leader led Loach to Bob Pegg, who had enjoyed cult status during the 1970s with the folk-rock band Mr Fox. Having studied traditional music at Leeds University and written two books on the subject, he was initially employed as a 'fixer', to hire other musicians. Pegg brought in veteran Irish singer, musician, actor and storyteller Packie Byrne as the flute-playing quack physician, Dr Carmody, and Dave Chatterley to play the hurdy-gurdy, which was mimed to by one of the dwarfs. The extra requirements of a period drama also brought money to the local economy. Kneale Pearce, owner of Ripon Dental Laboratory, recalled, 'The make-up girl asked if I could make some grotty-looking dentures for two of the actors. I did one set for the male villain, who visited the laboratory to discuss the level of "grottiness" requred, and another for an actress, duplicated from an old set provided by her. Each set was made with broken and blackened teeth.'[7] A garage in the nearby village of North Stainley provided transport to move carts and carriages between locations, with one long trip to Whitby for the harbour scene at the end of the film.

While shooting the opening, hanging scene in a dell at Studley Royal's deer park, outside Ripon, on an unusually sunny day, dozens of villagers from miles around were bussed in as extras. They had no qualms about getting into character. 'We were peasants and I had blacked-out teeth,' recalled Margaret Crosfield. 'My children, who also took part, didn't recognise me after I had been made up. It was a hot day and someone stepped on a wasps' nest. One of my children, Sarah, was in a bodice and a wasp went down the front, which caused a brief commotion!'[8] While the locals took all that was thrown at them in good humour, some of the cast were less enthusiastic about one unscripted incident. 'The Frenchman had a pee against a tree,' recalled Bob Pegg, 'and some of the actors were shocked because there were children present. They were outraged about what in France would be normal behaviour!'[9]

In line with his usual policy, Loach dished the script out to his cast on a daily basis and told the child leads not to read the book, so they knew nothing of the story they were 'living'. As filming went on, Pegg was one of the first to notice the effects of the tight finances. 'Halfway through the shoot, the catering budget must have collapsed,' he recalled, 'because the food changed character, from being quite opulent to very spartan. Then I was informed that I couldn't have my hire car any longer, which made it impossible for me to get to the set because I was living in Hebden Bridge, which would have meant getting a couple of trains and a bus, but Tony Garnett sorted it out with the accountant, Bob Blues.'[10]

In the editing stages of the film, Loach decided that some extra music needed to be added to the soundtrack after all, so Pegg was called back to compose some and he subsequently went to Twickenham Studios to record it. He played wind instruments himself and was joined by Dave Chatterley on hurdy-gurdy and classically trained Leeds viola player Mark Uttley. 'There was a stagecoach chase, for example,' recalled Pegg, 'but the two coaches didn't look as if they were going very fast and it was hard to differentiate between the two, so I was asked to write music that changed when the shot switched from one to the other. The sound man responsible for the studio recording gave me timings for several scenes and I went away and wrote the music. Then, I went into the studio at Twickenham where the *Star Wars* soundtrack was recorded and the pictures came up on the huge screen, but the timings I had been given for the coach chase weren't exact. However, I had already written my music and the film was already edited, so the music didn't change exactly with the cuts. That involved extra expense because they had to go back and re-cut the film to fit the music.'[11] Loach recalled, 'We had run out of money by the time it came to dubbing and mixing the sound; it was dubbed in a day-and-a-half, instead of a couple of weeks.'[12]

Black Jack received appreciative reviews but failed to gain a widespread cinema release in Britain, although it was more successful in Jean Franval's native France and won the Cannes Film Festival's FIPRESCI Award, voted for by international critics. The picture kept Loach working but did little to further the screen ambitions of any of those involved. Indeed, Stephen Hirst – unlike David Bradley – showed no desire to make a career out of acting after his experience in a Loach film. Instead, he followed dozens of his fellow school-leavers by taking a job down a local pit. 'I am sure he could have been an actor if he wanted,' said Loach, 'but he wanted to be part of his own community and that's what they do. It sounds like a proper sense of proportion to me.'[13]

For Loach and Garnett, the years of fighting to get films made had taken their toll, and Garnett was frustrated, ready to look for pastures new. '*Black Jack* is something I should never really have done,' he said. 'That arose when we couldn't get anything else made, because of the subject-matter and the fact there was no such thing as the British film industry. It was a question of both wanting to make something and earning a living. One of Ken's children was reading *Black Jack*, Ken said he had found the book and, frankly, I wasn't keen; I just wasn't interested. Out of loyalty to Ken, which is never a good reason, I did get involved and then we had to have a completely miscast French actor to get the French money. It was a nightmare getting the finance together. Consequently, I didn't give it much attention and I did a bad job on it. We didn't fall out, but we became a little bit estranged.'[14]

Garnett's memories of *Black Jack* demonstrated not just his lack of enthusiasm for the project, but perhaps an acknowledgement that he knew then that his partnership with Loach had run its course and the two of them had different ambitions for the future. 'I searched and searched, read lots of books and chose this one very carefully,' recalled Loach of his research. 'It certainly wasn't as casual as Tony makes it sound! Also, Jean Franval was very committed and brought a strong presence to the film.'[15]

Although Loach and Garnett would remain friends, the partnership was over. With fifteen years of being able to rely on a like-minded and supremely talented producer behind him, Loach had to face an increasingly chilly world on his own. At the same time, he saw the need to return to political film-making to respond to the radical right-wing policies of Britain's new Prime Minister, Margaret Thatcher. Meanwhile, Garnett made his own directing début with the feature film *Prostitute*, then left for the United States. 'I was moving in other directions and needed to get away, to get some distance from this country,' he said. 'I was personally going down a cul-de-sac, both creatively and politically. I felt my generation of the Left had blown it and I was exhausted.'[16]

In Bath, Loach found other diversions. He was briefly involved with local writers as an executive committee member of the Playwrights' Company, which was founded in 1978 to promote the production of new plays and stimulate theatre writing. He also found a new football team to support in the semi-professionals of Bath City, seeing them win the Southern League championship in the 1977–8 season, before joining the newly formed Alliance Premier League, which later changed its name to the Football Conference. 'I just enjoyed standing on the terraces,' said Loach.[17]

High-speed trains ensured that the director could reach London in little more than an hour and he saw the opportunity to make a children's television series, *Garfield's Apprentices*, based on the *Black Jack* author's novellas about eighteenth-century apprentices. The idea was received enthusiastically by Lewis Rudd, Southern Television's head of children's programmes, and plans were made to shoot six one-hour films but, with no foreign producer coming forward to contribute finance, the series was abandoned. 'It was quite a bold project and a costume drama of any ambition needed co-production money,' said Rudd. 'We tried for finance from Germany, but we couldn't get the budget together.'[18]

Loach, who acknowledged that his talent was not for pitching ideas and finding finance for productions, needed an anchor. 'I had a spell not knowing quite what to do, when I was really struggling,' he said.[19] A helpful word from Chris Menges to Charles Denton, who had built up the documentaries department at ATV, Independent Television's franchise holder in the Midlands, was to set Loach on a different course . . .

PART IV

THE LEAN YEARS AND CENSORSHIP

13

PASTURES NEW AND OLD

KEN LOACH'S FIRST documentary for ATV amounted to a low-key return to his own theatrical roots. In *Auditions*, he followed three eighteen-year-old dancers as they came to the end of a summer season in a Marti Caine show on the Wellington Pier in Great Yarmouth, on Norfolk's east coast, and set out to find more work in a precarious business, just as he was struggling to do. 'I was always stage-struck,' Loach explained of his motivation for making the film. 'I loved hanging around theatres and thought there was something really quite appealing and interesting and funny about that idea.'[1]

The one-hour documentary saw Loach reunited with Chris Menges – who filmed it in the director's favoured black-and-white – as they followed these young women all over the country during the late summer of 1979, witnessing their constant setbacks and interviewing them about their hopes and ambitions. It was also notable for giving Loach his first credit as a producer, although more significant for the fact that film editor Jonathan Morris worked with him for the first time. Finding the documentary difficult to classify, ITV eventually screened it in a late-afternoon children's slot over Christmas 1980.

Appealing as it was, *Auditions* did not provide ATV with a weighty film like those that had become a hallmark of its factual output on the ITV network since Charles Denton – who had been with Loach on the same BBC directors' course – left Granada Television's *World in Action* in 1974 and helped to set up the company's documentaries department. Three years later, when he rose to the rank of ATV's programme controller, Richard Creasey became executive producer of documentaries, nurturing a team that could boast journalists and film-makers such as John Pilger, Antony Thomas, Adrian Cowell, Michael Grigsby and Brian Moser. Creasey drew the battle lines with the Independent Broadcasting Authority, which demanded 'impartiality' and 'balance' under the Broadcasting Act, and gradually established a right for his enviable line-up to make 'personal view' documentaries. Pilger's hard-hitting films, presented by a journalist who arrived at the truth by using a subjective approach and discarding the myth of 'balance', had been a frequent target of the IBA. Tackling the Authority head-on, Creasey used those documentaries as the cornerstone of his successful campaign, although Pilger found much less interference when he tackled foreign subjects. Loach would later apply the same approach to making documentaries in Britain, with disastrous results.

Phil Askham starred in the television drama *The Gamekeeper*
[ATV Network/BFI Collections]

In the meantime, he developed another idea with ATV that was in much more familiar vein – a television adaptation of Barry Hines's 1975 book, *The Gamekeeper* – thanks to the way in which the ITV company blurred the demarcation lines between programme areas. 'I was very keen to take advantage of the fact that we had drama-documentaries as a slot,' explained Creasey. 'I wanted to see if we could explore not the drama-documentaries in the way Antony Thomas was doing for me, but the pure drama, and do it as a documentary. I was extremely attracted to the idea of saying to Ken: "Do something on real life, but make it as a drama and I will pay for it as a drama-documentary." That meant discussing it as that with the unions and using magnificent documentary editors such as Roger James. Also, Ken realised that he could work again with Chris Menges, one of the great cameramen, and I created a publishing environment, where I was the head of the department and my job was to enable people like Ken to work on such projects. That combination was extremely attractive from Ken's point of view.'[2]

Making *The Gamekeeper* as a drama fitted in with Loach's own views on restrictions imposed by documentaries. 'It's the difference between a pamphlet and a novel,' he explained. 'Sometimes, it's quite useful to write a pamphlet but it can never dig as deeply as a novel.'[3] The story was set in the South Yorkshire landscape familiar to Barry Hines, where the feudal system lived on. It followed a year in the life of a fictional steelworker-turned-gamekeeper, George Purse, as he lovingly rears chick pheasants through the seasons, then watches as their lives are ended by his master, the often absent duke, whom he despises. At the same time, he chases away poachers and children who trespass on the rich man's estate, and his wife complains about the low wages. However, he reflects that this job gives him more satisfaction than his years in a nearby steel mill.

It was another Hines social commentary highlighting the differences in Britain's class-ridden society. The title role was taken by Phil Askham, a former miner who lived in Hoyland Common and previously had a small part in *The Price of Coal* and played the hangman in *Black Jack*. A friend of Barry Hines's brother, Richard, he ran a business in nearby Hoyland selling and repairing cash registers, and enjoyed outdoor pursuits such as shooting, hare coursing and fishing.

Hines's book was based on a real-life gamekeeper called Trevor Jones, on the Fitzwilliam estate at Wentworth, near Rotherham. The writer walked around the estate with him and attended a grouse shoot. 'We went up on the moor with the real posh set,' recalled Hines, who still wrote in longhand, using a Biro on foolscap paper, before sending his scripts to a typist. 'As we were waiting for the grouse to come over, Lord Somebody-or-other said to me: "I saw that film *Kes* at Balmoral with the Queen." Those people were always grumbling they never have any money or any land. You're standing on this moor and as far as you can see is their land, but they've got no money and no land! Then I wrote the book, which is about class, not gamekeepers. You don't have to say anything; you just show it.'[4]

On the other side of the class divide, Loach saw a growing political awareness among those in a county affected over the previous decade by disputes in its two major industries. 'The people of South Yorkshire must be among the most politically sophisticated in the country with the experiences of the miners' strikes and the steelworkers' strike under their belts,' he reflected. 'Yet estates like the one shown in the film still exist side by side with the pits and steelworks. In this area the social implications of the gamekeeper's job are sharply revealed.'[5]

Making *The Gamekeeper* was Loach's happiest experience while working freelance, on a contract basis, at ATV, which became Central Independent Television in the 1982 ITV franchise reshuffle. 'It was something that could only really be done for a big company because I had to go back to film several times over the course of a year,' he said.[6] The need to mount four separate shoots, around Wentworth, meant that Chris Menges and Charles Stewart shared the photography between them.

Much enjoyment was gained from transporting some of Britain's genuine aristocrats to the woods where filming took place. The 'toffs' included Jonathan Bulmer, of the cider family, and Dai Llewellyn, playboy brother of Princess Margaret's one-time lover, Roddy. 'They were all first-rate Hoorays who were up there for a laugh,' recalled Loach. 'Also present were their attendant wives and girlfriends, who were a sight to behold. The pivotal character was Rupert Dean, a Bertie Wooster–P. G. Wodehouse sort of figure who put the group together. They were very funny and took it in good part. There was more shooting to do with the setting up of the actual pheasant shoot than they had expected. They got a bit impatient and were clearly more keen on getting the fowl out of the air than they were in making the film.'[7]

The Gamekeeper received its first screenings at the Cannes, New

York and London Film Festivals, before its ITV broadcast, publicised as a 'dramatised documentary', in December 1980 – a week before *Auditions* was screened. Thanks to the international activities of ATV's distribution arm, ITC, it was shown in cinemas abroad and, with the advent of satellite and cable television in the 1990s, it found an extended life on channels such as FilmFour.

Loach grabbed the opportunity to get feature-film status for his next project after ATV, worried about the possibility of losing its ITV franchise, set up a film subsidiary, Black Lion. (In fact, ATV was forced to reform itself as Central Independent Television.) A French company, Mk 2 Productions, agreed to contribute to the £506,000 budget, in return for European rights outside Britain. Loach was contracted to ATV for a year's work on the production and Kestrel Films secured an agreement with the various unions allowing for general theatrical distribution in Britain through Artificial Eye, following a television screening.

Looks and Smiles started out as a Barry Hines story about courting, with its title taken from a line in Tolstoy's *Anna Karenina* in which the grandmother explains that it was conducted in the same way by all generations – through looks and smiles. This developed into a story of disaffected youth and the increasing prospect of finding no jobs, a theme that became more relevant in the wake of Margaret Thatcher's 1979 General Election victory in Britain, as unemployment soared to one-and-a-half million and inflation to almost 20 per cent in the year following the Conservatives' win. Unfortunately, this topicality was never projected enough to make *Looks and Smiles* a strong political voice against Thatcherism, even though the Iron Lady had been in power for almost eighteen months when filming began in the autumn of 1980. Whereas, more than ten years earlier, *Kes* had depicted children being reared for manual labour, *Looks and Smiles* showed their prospects to be even bleaker. In Sheffield, a city with a worldwide reputation for its steel industry, recession had hit hard: one unemployment office where filming took place displayed a card advertising 'The Job of the Week', where once there had been dozens.

The central characters were unemployed school-leavers Mick Walsh, played by seventeen-year-old Graham Green, whom Loach discovered as an apprentice mining fitter on day release at Barnsley

Technical College, his friend Alan Wright, acted by Tony Pitts, who was a trainee truck mechanic in Sheffield, on day release at a college there, and turned eighteen during filming, and Mick's girlfriend, shoe shop assistant Karen Lodge, a role taken by sixteen-year-old Newcastle policeman's daughter Carolyn Nicholson, who was studying for A-levels. 'Equity had always been very hostile to Ken working with non-professionals,' recalled Irving Teitelbaum, the Kestrel Films board member who stepped in as producer following Tony Garnett's departure. 'We had lengthy negotiations with them about the leads, but they gave permission in the end.'[8] Phil Askham followed his central role in *The Gamekeeper* by playing Green's steelworker father.

Loach introduced Green, who came from nearby Thurnscoe, to jobless youngsters so that he could get a feel for his role. 'Until I met them I hadn't really understood how down you can be or how embarrassing it is if you can't buy the sort of things you're used to,' he admitted.[9] Nicholon was pessimistic about her own chances in the north-east of England. 'Unemployment here is really bad,' she said. 'I don't think I'm going to be able to stay in Newcastle, because there's no chance of getting a job. Most of my friends have stayed on at school because there are no jobs for them if they leave. The ones who have left are unemployed. It's a way of life in Newcastle.'[10]

As soon as he heard he had landed a role, Pitts resigned from his mechanic's job at a Sheffield garage. 'Despite the fact that I had only two months left of an apprenticeship and they had invested thousands of pounds in me, they said I could go that minute,' he recalled. 'They just got shut of me.'[11] In the story, which Hines turned into a novel, Pitts's character joins the Army after finding no other work. The necessary look was a bit drastic for a teenager used to enjoying nights out and female company. 'I was spiky-haired and had to have all my hair cut,' he explained. 'At the time, it would have hampered my chances with the ladies on the streets of Sheffield.'[12]

Looks and Smiles was filmed in black-and-white by Chris Menges over six weeks, mostly in and around Sheffield, but with two days in Barnsley and several in Bristol, where Karen's father in the story lives with his girlfriend and baby. Premiered at the 1981 Cannes Festival, where it shared a new award as Best

Contemporary Screenplay and beat the official British entry, *Chariots of Fire*, it was shown at the London Film Festival before its first British television broadcast the following year, and subsequent theatrical release. Neither Graham Green nor Carolyn Nicholson decided to pursue an acting career – Green returned to a local pit and Nicholson to her studies – but Tony Pitts went on to play Archie Brooks in the television soap opera *Emmerdale* for ten years, before turning to writing.

For Loach, the film was a lost opportunity. 'I think we missed creating the outrage in the audience that should have been there,' he said. 'In *Looks and Smiles*, as in *Poor Cow*, the way I was working seemed tired and lethargic. My memory is that the sequences had lost their energy. I needed to quicken the pace next time.'[13]

14

QUESTIONS OF CENSORSHIP

THE GHOST OF Robert Maxwell looms large over the most sinister case of censorship in British commercial television. It was unfortunate for Ken Loach that he should have switched to making documentaries at a time when the crooked media tycoon and former Labour MP was abusing his power as a director and major shareholder of Central Independent Television to further his own business interests. This came in the wake of Maxwell's rescue of the British Printing Corporation, with a survival plan that relied on union co-operation, and at exactly the time he was buying the *Daily Mirror* and needed to negotiate new deals with the printers' and electricians' unions. To ensure cordial relations with the unions, especially the electricians, he put subtle pressure on the television company's board to suppress *Questions of Leadership*, in which Loach gave union members the opportunity to call their leaders to account.

One of those criticised, Frank Chapple, the right-wing general secretary of the Electrical, Electronic, Telecommunications and Plumbing Union – who later became Lord Chapple of Hoxton – also tried to get the programmes, or at least his contribution to them, banned. Maxwell was able to ensure they were by turning to his advantage the conservative views of many on the Central board, some of whom voiced a concern that showing support for left-wing programme-makers would threaten the company's reputation.

Loach quickly found who called the shots when he waded into documentary-making with the same passion that marked his politically charged dramas for the BBC. Throughout the 1970s, the roll-call of programmes subject to censorship by both the BBC and ITV regulators was notorious. The most frequent victims of all were those about Northern Ireland, where a new war had raged since 1969, under the euphemism of 'The Troubles'. Within two years, the board of governors at the BBC and the board of members at the Independent Television Authority (later the Independent Broadcasting Authority) were vetting all programmes on the subject.

One of the great *causes célèbres* was *South of the Border*, a film in the *World in Action* series, which already had a history of run-ins with the ITA over the notions of 'impartiality' and 'balance'. The Authority said that the documentary, about how the violence was causing political pressures in the Irish Republic, was unacceptable for transmission because the London, Belfast and Dublin governments were not represented. Ten years later, *World in Action* withdrew another film, *The Propaganda War*, rather than adhere to the IBA's demands that it remove footage of both IRA hunger striker Bobby Sands's strike and the open coffin of the fourth hunger striker to die, Patsy O'Hara, lying in state, guarded by hooded gunmen.

This was the climate in which Loach sought to make television documentaries. *Questions of Leadership* had its roots in another programme, which gave him a warning of what was to come. In between shooting *The Gamekeeper* and *Looks and Smiles*, he returned to South Yorkshire to film interviews with steelworkers who had just staged their first national strike in more than fifty years. Less than a year after Margaret Thatcher's election victory, British Steel plants across the country closed when they took industrial action for thirteen weeks during the first quarter of 1980 in pursuit of a 20 per cent pay claim after being offered just 2 per cent when inflation was running at 18 per cent; plants in the private sector followed. Just like those in *The Big Flame* and *The Rank and File*, the steelworkers were striking for a living wage. They ended up with 11 per cent, plus another $4\frac{1}{2}$ in return for new working practices and productivity deals, but the result was tantamount to signing their own death warrant. In the following months, the Consett works, in County Durham, was closed with the loss of more than 3,000 jobs and short-time working came to 17,000 of South Wales' 24,000 labour force; the 'streamlining' continued.

Some trade unionists felt let down by their own leaders, echoing the theme of betrayal featured by Loach in his plays with Jim Allen, and the director was keen to give them a voice. So Barry Hines helped him to assemble rank-and-file members to discuss the strike with their leaders, as well as others whose jobs depended on the steel industry, in a filmed debate over one-and-a-half days at Sheffield Hallam University. 'It was a different way of discussing politics,' recalled Loach. 'I tried to get away from the way interviewers sit there with their own agenda and fit the discussion into it. That broadcasting person was taken out and we had the direct confrontation between the two sides of the argument, putting the steelworkers face to face with the people who had led the strike. It wasn't like anything they had ever faced before, where there's usually a moderator who won't let the dog get to the rabbit. Here, they were being seized by the throat by these guys whom they go out of their way to avoid.'[1]

The footage was edited down into a one-hour documentary, titled *A Question of Leadership*, and scheduled to be shown nationally by ITV on 5 August 1980. Shortly beforehand, ATV formally withdrew its offer of the film to the network, claiming that it did not comply with the IBA's guidelines because the union leadership was inadequately represented; this was, in reality, a response to the authority's objections about the programme's political 'imbalance'. Certainly, the leaders did not emerge favourably from the debate, with one South Yorkshire steelworker saying, 'We had no leadership in this strike, from the top, none. They gave us no direction, they gave us no bloody help, and what help they did give us was very, very limited.'

ATV's decision to withdraw the film, after offering it for screening, came just four months after its drama-documentary *Death of a Princess*, made by Antony Thomas, had caused a rift between the British government and the Saudi Arabian royal family, and within sight of a new round of ITV franchise bids. (A decade later, the removal of Thames Television's London weekday contract was widely seen as the Conservative government's reprisal for that company's *This Week* film *Death on the Rock*, about British SAS troops shooting dead, in cold blood, four unarmed IRA suspects in Gibraltar.)

'It also has to be put in the context of the many conversations we previously had with the IBA about "personal view" films,' said Charles Denton, ATV's programme controller. 'There had been a lot of kerfuffle about "personal view" documentaries because the Authority had gone on and on about the need to preserve objectivity and not to have one viewpoint stressed to the detriment of a balancing viewpoint that would be put within the same schedule, ideally in the same week. Out of that, we had to start showing a lot of "personal view" films to the Authority – you might say for vetting, but they would say for their advice on those that they thought were getting close to infringing the Broadcasting Act. Later on, we got into what we were allowed to say in *Spitting Image*, a programme that was completely over-the-top and calculated to offend in a number of ways, which was, of course, unlawful.

'To the Authority, I would say that Ken was seen as a left-wing firebrand – that's one of the reasons we wanted him to make films for us. He had proposed *A Question of Leadership*, Richard Creasey had backed it and I backed Richard. David Glencross [the IBA's deputy director of programmes] saw it and we had a lot of conversations with him. He believed it was unbalanced and putting a partial view of contemporary events that wasn't acceptable under the Broadcasting Act. But Ken wasn't seeking balance; he was seeking to reflect a point of view of the silent working population. It was taken out of the schedule and we failed to come to an agreement with the IBA about its political balance.'[2]

However, a suggestion was made that the film should be cut by twelve minutes to allow a studio discussion to be added, giving stronger representation to the British Steel Corporation or trade union leaders. It took ATV six months to find space at its Birmingham studios for this and, in April 1981, James Bellini chaired a talk with steelworkers' union general secretary Bill Sirs and Welsh TUC general secretary George Wright, as well as two of those who took part in the original film, British Leyland car worker Alan Thornett and South Yorkshire steelworker Bernard Connolly. Finally, *A Question of Leadership* was screened on 13 August 1981, one year after its planned transmission date – but only in the ATV region. 'The steam had gone out of the argument by then,' explained Charles Denton. 'We never offered it back to the network but were able to show it in our region because Clare Mulholland, the IBA's regional officer, saw it and agreed it could be scheduled. She is a very rational human being, more inclined to be libertarian in her views than proscriptive.'[3]

Loach reflected on the way censorship worked. 'Where there is a film that is likely to present points of view – calmly and articulately – which are outside the views which are commonly held to be acceptable, then it will probably be shown to the IBA,' he said. 'The IBA will make overt or covert remarks and then the programme-makers are encouraged to change the programme themselves. They haven't been censored. The programme has not technically been offered for view. This is a common practice. In this case it was over a body of opinion which had not been expressed in the news coverage during the steel strike and which criticised the conduct of the union leadership from the union members. Because the news hadn't covered it, when we showed that opinion, the IBA said it was not representative.'[4]

The arrival of Channel Four in Britain appeared to signal the opportunity for a more diverse range of views to be broadcast. Many ITV companies, including Central – ATV's successor in the new franchise allocation – made programmes for the new channel, which had a remit to transmit radical, 'alternative' material. Loach might have been encouraged when its commissioning editor for single documentaries, Paul Madden, agreed that the *Question of Leadership* idea could be broadened to tackle the same issues of democracy in all unions. As a result, Loach shot *Questions of Leadership* during the summer of 1982 and edited the footage the following winter and spring into four one-hour documentaries.

The first film examined the 1980 closure of the Laurence Scott engineering works in Openshaw, Manchester, the steel strike of the same year, labour relations at British Leyland and disputes involving the train drivers' union ASLEF and National Health Service workers; the second was a critical look at the 'undemocratic' practices of the electricians' union, EETPU, and included an interview with its right-wing leader, Frank Chapple, who remained a member of the Labour Party despite having signed the Limehouse Declaration, which showed his support for the new Social Democratic Party; the third focused in detail on industrial relations at British Leyland, in particular the sacking of its much maligned convenor Derek Robinson and the management's subsequent attack on the shop stewards' movement; the fourth was a day's discussion at Warwick University, where rank-and-file critics – including Alan Thornett and Bernard Connolly, who had taken part in the debate in *A Question of Leadership* – put their grievances to some of those broadly sympathetic to the approach of union leaders, such as Ken Cure of the engineering workers' union, Labour MP John Golding and Kate Losinska of the Civil Service union, the CPSA.

Questions of Leadership gave rank-and-file trade unionists a voice

During the interview with Frank Chapple, by the *Guardian*'s labour correspondent, Keith Harper, the electricians' leader made clear his support for free-market forces. 'I would oppose a pay cut,' he said. 'I would expect the management to put instead of pay cuts a way of reducing labour unit costs, maybe with some more redundancies or a bit more unemployment.' To the question of whether he agreed with those on the Left that full employment in Britain was a possibility, he responded, 'Well, the illusions of the Left I find surprising because there has been so much happened since the Russian Revolution to prove that those illusions are illusions.' Chapple further declared that he did not regard himself as a socialist, but a social democrat, and could foresee circumstances under which he would leave the Labour Party. When Harper persisted with questions about branch reorganisation within the electricians' union, Chapple walked out, saying he would not talk about internal union matters. 'It's just a set-up,' he said. 'It's another one of these deliberate things aimed at making a monkey of me and the union.' The only problem Chapple faced was that he was being interviewed in his own office! The film crew was eventually asked to leave.

Chapple immediately wrote to Roger James, who produced the

series, asking that his interview should not be used, but James replied that it would. Through his solicitors, the union leader then complained to Central that the interview breached the agreement made about the subject-matter to be discussed.[5]

In the meantime, the programmes were edited, with the on-screen title, *Questions of Leadership*, followed by the subtitle, 'Problems of democracy in trade unions . . . Some views from the front line'. Although originally commissioned as a single documentary, Channel Four accepted that the material warranted more time, although the channel's executives have subsequently differed in their accounts of whether three or four programmes were to be broadcast.

In May 1983, the series was submitted to Channel Four, whose solicitor, Don Christopher, checked it for any possible legal ramifications. He reported to Roger James the following month, 'I will be telling Colin Campbell [Central's company secretary and legal officer] that in my view the legal risks associated with the programmes – and I have now seen the VHS of programme 4 – are acceptable so far as Channel Four is concerned in view of the information you kindly provided.'[6] Christopher later confirmed, 'I was absolutely happy with the programmes legally. I felt that, if there were elements that were potentially defamatory, Central had produced to me evidence to defend any proceedings.'[7] But, behind the scenes, trouble was brewing.

Over the previous eight months, another battle had been raging between Central and the IBA – one that set a precedent and established a new ruse for diluting dissident voices, without appearing to constitute outright censorship. John Pilger's documentary *The Truth Game*, which challenged the Establishment view that more and more nuclear weapons were needed to make the world a safer place, was pulled from the ITV schedule of 23 November 1982 only nineteen days in advance. The IBA insisted that it be postponed after the Authority's full board viewed the film at the recommendation of David Glencross. The deputy director of television demanded that a 'complementary' documentary be made to offer other views, despite the fact that *The Truth Game* adhered to the IBA's guidelines for 'personal view' programmes. Pilger's previous films had conformed to those rules, too, and some had been 'balanced' by others in general terms. For instance, his 1970 *World in Action* film about the disintegration of morale among

American troops in Vietnam was followed shortly afterwards by a profile of Conservative Prime Minister Edward Heath. With *The Truth Game*, the regulator for the first time demanded 'balance' *after* the production of a programme but *before* its transmission – and effectively dictated the content. In making this demand, the IBA extended its editorial control. (*The War About Peace*, presented by Max Hastings, who later became editor of the right-wing *Daily Telegraph*, was the 'complementary' programme, which argued the need for a nuclear deterrent.)

The IBA's and Channel Four's own truth games were soon under way, despite the new station's lawyer judging *Questions of Leadership* suitable for transmission. In July 1983, Paul Bonner, the channel's controller, told Central that the films would be screened in peak-time on successive Saturdays from 10 September, with an additional follow-up programme made by someone else. Loach and producer Roger James assumed this meant all four films, but Bonner later explained: 'Paul Madden did originally talk to me about a single documentary and, when it was clear that there was more material than for one programme, he brought Ken along to plead the case for more airtime. Ken, of whom I was, and am, a great admirer, was very persuasive, but I had to tell him that I would need to refer such a major change to Jeremy [Isaacs, the channel's chief executive]. I did so and Jeremy took over editorial supervision of the project at that point. Because we needed to allow extra airtime if the programme spread to two or more parts, I did indeed ask my planner to "pencil in" two further slots to the draft schedule – which would have gone to the IBA.'[8]

The IBA soon took a special interest in *Questions of Leadership*. 'The fourth programme, the discussion, was never scheduled formally but it would have been found a slot, by displacement of a "movable feast" item, at a point most relevant to the other programmes,' recalled Bonner. 'However, the IBA would certainly have known about the proposal as a result of the rather intensive dialogue that was going on about the project at all levels between Channel Four and the regulator.'[9]

Although Loach disputed the need for the 'follow-up' broacast, worse was to come when Bonner and Isaacs told him that a meeting between the IBA and Channel Four administrators had resulted in a new formula: one of his four films must be dropped. Isaacs explained it was simply 'a matter of quantity'[10] and said he did not mind which film was lost. In addition, each of the three remaining programmes would immediately be followed by another in which the union leaders who were criticised could reply, themselves or through their spokespeople, without any input from those involved in the original films. There would also be a further one-hour programme to which Loach might be allowed a small contribution.

Angry and determined to discover what the objections were to his films and who was responsible for demanding changes, the director telephoned David Glencross at the IBA. 'He was clear that Channel Four had submitted a package that contained only three of our original films,' recalled Loach, 'and that, if all four were submitted, the IBA would have to think again. He confirmed that no part of any film was banned in itself. There followed a further meeting with Paul Bonner, at which I reported my conversation with David Glencross. Bonner was adamant that all four pro-grammes had been submitted. He then left his office to have a private conversation with Glencross. On his return he said that his version was correct. As the atmosphere became more heated I spoke to Glencross myself in Bonner's presence, and Glencross said to me that only three programmes had been included in the package. The point in this wrangle was to make someone accept responsibility for what seemed to us a patently unfair decision. Clearly what had happened was that there had been a meeting between Channel Four and the IBA from which this formula had emerged. They were both responsible, but each pretended the onus lay with the other.'[11] Paul Madden, who was also present at the meeting in Bonner's office, confirmed this version of events.[12]

Following this meeting, Bonner wrote to Loach, 'David Glencross has . . . warned me that the IBA . . . might not feel that it could agree to the transmission of the programmes without replies from properly authoritative and knowledgeable sources within the trade union concerned. He would consult about the matter but in the meantime the IBA would not allow us to go ahead and bill the programmes. He will be speaking to the IBA during the course of today.'[13] Bonner added that Jeremy Isaacs 'is resolutely in agreement with you that censorship by non-appearance is unacceptable'.[14]

At about the same time, Loach heard that Frank Chapple had been making representations to Lord Thomson, the IBA's chairman. 'Some of what happened behind the scenes went on without the participants, like me and Ken, knowing,' recalled Paul Madden. 'I was told that Frank Chapple contacted the IBA, so the antennae were out early on. Then David Glencross contacted Channel Four. To me, that was when the shit started hitting the fan.'[15]

Several weeks passed, with no news about the 'balancing' programmes. So, in mid-September, Loach telephoned the office of Liz Forgan, Channel Four's commissioning editor for news and current affairs. 'I was told that everything was being done to get the programmes made as quickly as possible, and that a production company called Blackrod had been commissioned to do the work,' explained Loach. 'I then spoke to the producer at Blackrod. Far from working strenuously, all activity had ceased. This followed a letter from Liz Forgan on 6 September asking him to stop work on this project. Again I spoke to Liz Forgan's assistant. She apologised for giving me false information, and was as confused as I was. Moments later, Liz Forgan herself telephoned. Yes, it was true that Blackrod had been told to stop work. Eventually, it appeared that it was Liz Forgan herself, who, unknown even to her own assistant, was working flat out to make the arrangements. She admitted that no one else had yet been asked to appear because trade union leaders were difficult to contact. This was a few days after the TUC conference, where they were all eminently contactable, and appearing on television nightly. Significantly, I was then told that we "need an affirmative response", and that "the time is not yet right". The implication is clear: if the union leaders declined to appear, our films would not be transmitted.'[16]

Forgan resented this attack because she had been impressed by *Questions of Leadership* and was keen to ensure that it could be shown. 'It was, by miles, the best thing I had seen on the trade union movement – wonderful,' she explained. 'Ken is a brilliant filmmaker and it had the real feeling of the green canvas chairs and those dreary meetings. It was riveting! Just one problem: it went on for several hours, with rank-and-file members of various unions slagging off their leaders for selling out the members. But even Channel Four couldn't do that amount of time showing just one side of the argument; there was bound to be a row. Edmund Dell, the chairman of Channel Four, was a long-time former Communist of the Denis Healey variety and then became a right-wing Labour minister. He was interested in politics, particularly of the Left, and was deeply suspicious of everyone at Channel Four. He thought we were a bunch of Lefties and Ken Loach was beyond the pale. He said: "We cannot transmit it like this. We must have another programme in which we put these allegations to the trade union leadership." The programmes were deemed to be not transmittable in their present form.

'The next step was to get the trade union leadership to co-operate and agree to have the argument because, if they refused to participate, we would still be in trouble. The TUC conference was about to begin, so I took a train to Blackpool and spent a week there drinking more whisky than I've ever drunk in my life and sitting for hour upon hour persuading Moss Evans and others that it was their bounden duty to co-operate. I must have got them all to agree except Frank Chapple, who was holding out. He was very smart and knew that all he had to do was keep his mouth shut and we would be absolutely up a gum tree. So I had a long train journey back from Blackpool with Frank Chapple's right-hand man, who finally said yes. By the time I got back to London, I was triumphant. But I returned to Channel Four to find that Edmund Dell had persuaded the board to take the programmes and give them back to Central, declaring them "Untransmittable, return to sender". I was so disgusted. We were the publisher and, instead of doing our duty and getting them into a form in which they were transmittable, we sent them back. That was an absolute abdication of our duty. It was such an emblematic moment in Channel Four, a battle for free broadcasting, which we lost. The board was cowardly. Ken, understandably, hit the roof; he blamed everybody, including me.'[17]

In fact, the idea of sending *Questions of Leadership* back to Central came from Justin Dukes, Channel Four's managing director, at a board meeting. 'I could not see why we should, in addition to our other tasks, take on the role of "producers" of the group of programmes which we had paid Central to produce,' he explained. 'Their job was to deliver them in broadcastable form and I simply suggested we should get them to do their job to the satisfaction of ourselves and the IBA.'[18]

After the board meeting, Jeremy Isaacs wrote to Loach, 'The Board of the Company decided, as within the terms of its contract it was entitled to do, to ask Central Television to make itself responsible for the supply of a series of programmes that will, in its totality, be acceptable to the IBA. I regret that this is likely to cause a further delay in getting the programmes through on to the screen. However, I still hope very much that a way will be found. Please be patient.'[19]

Several days later, IBA chairman Lord Thomson wrote to Loach, in the same language he used to respond to *The Truth Game*, 'The issues raised in *Questions of Leadership* are quite properly matters of public interest which should be aired on television. They are, however, as you recognise, informed by a particular point of view about particular industrial disputes. The IBA's position is that these require opportunities for other views to be heard in order to fulfil our duty to ensure due impartiality. Channel Four have now asked Central to provide programmes to meet this requirement. I do not believe that this will weaken or dilute what your programmes say and I hope that a satisfactory outcome can be arrived at as soon as possible.'[20]

So responsibility for the series lay back at the door of Central, which had been satisfied with the programmes it had originally submitted. Richard Creasey, the company's controller of features, wrote to Loach, 'Central will now attempt to prepare a package of three hours and no more. This package must accord with the Broadcasting Act. Effectively this means *Questions of Leadership* must be reduced from four hours to two . . . If this package can be achieved Central will offer it to Channel Four. However, there are no guarantees that they will transmit it.'[21] Creasey, a much-liked executive who had helped to break down barriers to allow those in his department to produce the documentaries they wanted to make, offered two options: extracts from the four films could be edited into two one-hour documentaries, followed by an hour-long discussion; or each of the resulting one-hour documentaries could be followed by a half-hour discussion. 'I favour the second,' he added.[22]

Either side of Christmas 1983, Loach cut his films as requested. In February 1984, Frank Chapple and his solicitor viewed the edited programmes, along with Channel Four lawyer Don Christopher, Loach and producer Roger James. Chapple remained silent throughout the screening, but Central subsequently received a letter from his solicitor threatening legal action over 'defamatory' remarks about his 'undemocratic practices', censoring of members' opinions, punishing members who criticised his policies and the assertion that he was doing 'the job of employers for them to the detriment of his members'.[23] Seven days later, the same firm of solicitors wrote in defence of Terry Duffy, the engineers' leader, against similar allegations that he 'acted in an undemocratic manner', 'abused his position of power, broke union rules and disregarded the wishes of the majority of the members', '"betrayed" the interests of the union, collaborated with employers and the government to the detriment of the workers' and 'used deliberate delaying tactics, or was incompetent, thus weakening his members' bargaining position'.[24]

Don Christopher was unruffled. 'I'm convinced that what I saw at the end of the day was satisfactory,' he said. 'There have been many programmes that in-house lawyers cleared for television, suspecting that there will be a legal challenge to it. We don't suddenly say: "I'm going to change my mind about that." '[25]

Two months later, the 'balancing' discussion, chaired by Peter Sissons, the 'impartial' face of *Channel Four News*, was recorded at Molinaire Studios in London and a lawyer from Carter-Ruck, the London firm specialising in defamation law that was consulted by Central, pronounced *Questions of Leadership* a fair risk as long as one small deletion was made, to which Loach agreed. So it was with dismay that he subsequently heard Channel Four and Central announce that the films were still 'under discussion' because of 'legal difficulties'.[26] Almost twenty years later, Central director of programmes Charles Denton reflected, 'I don't think there were specific legal difficulties at all because the programmes had been cleared by the lawyers. I think it was a reference to the fact that there was the risk of writs.'[27]

When the Directors' Guild of Great Britain subsequently accused Central, Channel Four and the IBA of political censorship, there followed the extraordinary spectacle of its chief censorship officer, the right-wing Michael Winner, backing someone whose political views were the diametric opposite of his own. 'I am opposed politically to Ken Loach's philosophy,' he said. 'However, there have been many TV programmes suggesting lack of democracy in left-wing trade unions. Further, having investigated this matter fully I am drawn to the conclusion that Ken Loach's views are basically correct.'[28] Instead of this shaming the broadcasters into showing *Questions of Leadership*, the shutters were firmly brought down. Eight days after the Guild's intervention, Central's board announced that the company would not offer the programmes to Channel Four because they were 'defamatory and would have no adequate defence at law'.[29]

At the time, Loach responded, 'The films were edited under the guidance of an expert lawyer and we conceded to every request for changes. If there are elements in the two remaining films which are still thought to be libellous, then there is additional material which could be put in its place, so the argument simply doesn't stand up. The only explanation therefore is that this is not a legal but a political decision, and therefore of concern to anyone who is concerned with freedom of speech.'[30] Loach pointed out that the chairmen of the IBA and Channel Four, Lord Thomson and Edmund Dell, were both former right-wing Labour Party MPs and founding members of the SDP, and that Frank Chapple was a supporter of the new party. He saw a political conspiracy or, at best, those of a similar persuasion jumping to each other's defence.

For twenty years, until this author's investigations, the banning of *Questions of Leadership* remained clouded in a fog of secrecy – similar to the fifteen-year silence that followed the decision not to screen *The War Game*, when the BBC consulted the government on its views about the nuclear war film and gave in to political pressure, making it the worst case of censorship in the Corporation's history. The desire of those responsible to continue to hide the truth about Loach's documentaries being withdrawn – even from the programme-makers themselves – hinted at similarly sinister reasons.

In reality, it was obvious that the mystery lay in the reasons behind Central's decision not to re-submit the programmes to Channel Four and this was totally separate from the discussions about 'objectivity' that had previously taken place between the new channel and the IBA. The original dialogue between Channel Four and the regulator was simply a continuation of the discussions about 'impartiality' and 'balance' that those in ITV had been subject to for many years. In establishing its relationships with both the IBA and the ITV companies, the channel quickly learned that it could not be as innovative and 'alternative' as it wished to be seen at the time of its launch.

'Contrary to some people's views, Channel Four wasn't exempted from the terms of the Broadcasting Act,' reflected Jeremy Isaacs. 'It was subject to exactly the same terms in relation to the expression of political views as every other broadcasting channel. Of course, I made it my business to see that a great number of ideas and ideologies were discussed that were never getting near the screens of other channels. But, in the last resort, when the going got rough, we were up against the same law as everybody else. That was that the programmes had to preserve due impartiality on matters of political or industrial controversy.'[31]

Isaacs insisted that the original problems over *Questions of Leadership* lay in the fact that a documentary commissioned as a single programme had grown too big. 'I was thrown when what I thought started off as one programme ended up as four,' he explained. 'If it had been one programme, I would have broadcast it. The IBA would have said: "Four Ken Loach programmes? I think we had better have a chat." The board at Channel Four would then say: "What the hell are you on about, Jeremy?" There was an ongoing argument on the board of the channel, to which I answered, saying: "We are not going to take four programmes in a row on this theme from this programme-maker. We want some opportunity for other people to have a different point of view." '[32]

In his memoirs of those early years of Channel Four, Isaacs recounted his battles with Edmund Dell. He recalled 'struggling against the IBA and our own chairman' to keep *The Friday Alternative* on the air just six months after the channel's launch, when that weekly programme presented for the first time a regular view of news and current affairs different from that featured on mainstream television. Although he wanted to renew the producers' contract, he found that 'Edmund Dell, on this issue in agreement with George Thomson, was adamantly against', and the Channel Four board axed the programme. 'Liz Forgan's view was that editorial control of the channel had been wrested from the executive, hijacked by the board,' wrote Isaacs.[33]

He further revealed that, during the late spring and summer of 1983, when *Questions of Leadership* was clearly running into trouble at Channel Four, those who attended its board meetings believed 'the principal matter of concern was not political bias in our programmes, real though that concern was, but the behaviour of the chairman'. The chief executive ventured, 'Had he been urged by the IBA to be sure to hold the line? Or was it that he had opposed my appointment, was critical of my performance, wanted me out, and thought he saw a chance by forcing these issues to a vote against me, to have his way?'[34]

Whatever the battles on the Channel Four board, the manoeuvres that led to *Questions of Leadership* being banned took place in Birmingham among the directors of Central Independent Television after the programmes were returned. The ITV company had a unique board, which included only one programme-maker – Charles Denton – as a result of the formula demanded by the IBA in issuing a new franchise for the Midlands region. ATV, which had broadcast since the beginning of commercial television in the area, in 1956, as well as to London at weekends in the early days of ITV, was a major contributor to the network and known worldwide for 'transatlantic' series such as *The Saint*, but the IBA felt that it should have a stronger presence in the East Midlands and make more of an effort to reflect the region as a whole. (It had studios in Birmingham and, outside its area, in Elstree, Hertfordshire.)

In future, its parent company, Associated Communications Corporation, would be allowed to hold only 51 per cent of shares in a new contractor, with a new name, and the rest were to be taken by other companies or individuals from the region. The newly formed company would also have to operate bases in both the East and West Midlands. The result was that Central Independent Television was formed, but, with little local interest, the Ladbroke Group, D.C. Thomson and the British Printing Corporation were the only ones to take significant shareholdings. Sir Gordon Hobday was brought in as chairman after eight years in that position at Boots, the national chemist's chain with its head office in Nottingham. Unusually, two vice-chairmen, David Justham and John Madocks, were appointed to represent the West and East Midlands respectively. Responsibility for the day-to-day running of the company went to Bob Phillis as managing director, after three years in that position at Independent Television Publications, the publisher of ITV's programme journal, *TVTimes*. After a while, director John Jackson, of Ladbroke's, took the newly created position of deputy chairman.

Central went on air on 1 January 1982, but changes in its

shareholdings occurred after Australian media mogul Robert
Holmes à Court took control of ACC when its founding father,
Lew Grade, was reeling from the box-office disaster that befell his
$36,000,000 feature film *Raise the Titanic*. By the end of 1982,
Holmes à Court had disposed of ACC's Central shares. As a result,
Sears Holdings bought a stake in the company while Ladbroke,
D.C. Thomson and Robert Maxwell's British Printing Corpora-
tion, which he renamed the British Printing and Communications
Corporation, increased theirs. As a result, Maxwell and Sears's
Geoffrey Maitland Smith joined the board of Central.

Maxwell was a maverick media tycoon whose unfulfilled ambition and obsession was to own a national newspaper to add to his
empire, which he built from the profits of Pergamon Press, a hugely
successful publisher of scientific books and journals. Born Jan
Ludvik Hoch in Czechoslovakia in 1923, and brought up in a
Jewish community, he had fled the Nazis in 1939, won the Military
Cross for bravery while fighting with the British during the Second
World War and, in 1951, bought Pergamon. He was a Labour MP
for six years, from 1964, and made a failed bid for the *News of the
World*, losing out to Australian Rupert Murdoch. Then, after
agreeing a takeover of Pergamon in 1969 by the American financial
and data processing group Leasco, he was stung by three Department of Trade and Industry reports highlighting financial irregula-
rities in his business dealings. 'He is not in our opinion a person
who can be relied on to exercise proper stewardship of a publicly
quoted company,' reported the DTI.[35] Maxwell's acquisition of the
British Printing Corporation in 1980 was an important strategy in a
bid to reconstruct his tarnished character.

John Jackson recalled being asked by Central managing director
Bob Phillis about the idea of Maxwell joining the board of the
television company. 'I was slightly puzzled and remember saying I
wasn't very keen on Maxwell,' said Jackson. 'I had had business
dealings with him in 1969 when I was a director of Philips, the
electrical company. I had tentative discussions with Maxwell, who
owned Pergamon Press, and I broke off the negotiations because I
did not like his approach to the construction of profit-and-loss
accounts, and I recommended to my board colleagues that we did
not have business dealings with him. Therefore, I was a touch
surprised that Bob Phillis seemed to know Maxwell quite well and

was quite keen to have him as a shareholder in Central. It would not be unfair to say that he seemed to be facilitating Maxwell's involvement in Central. What baffled me was that, while Maxwell had undoubtedly done a good job in rescuing BPC, Central was in no need of any kind of rescue.'[36]

Phillis denied being 'keen' on Maxwell joining the board[37] but knew the businessman through his previous connections with the British Printing Corporation and Independent Television Publications. Phillis, who started his working life as an apprentice in the printing industry and member of the trade union SLADE (Society of Lithographic Artists, Designers and Engravers), and later gained a degree in industrial economics, had been personnel director, then managing director, of the BPC subsidiary Sun Printers, which had the lucrative contracts for *TVTimes* and *Radio Times*. In 1979, he joined Independent Television Publications as managing director.

'Bob Phillis had a very close relationship with BPC because he had worked for it and remained great friends with his old colleagues, and BPC continued to print *TVTimes*,' explained Bob Cole, who had been with the printer since 1962 and eventually became Maxwell's press representative after the businessman's takeover of the company. 'In those days, print was so competitive a business you had lots of printers with under-capacity, so they leaned over backwards to maintain good relationships with publishers. Maxwell would do everything he could to foster the best of relationships with BPC's two main clients, *TVTimes* and *Radio Times*.'[38] Indeed, Sun had secured a new, £125,000,000, seven-year deal with Independent Television Publications to continue printing *TVTimes*, overseen by managing director Bob Phillis, shortly before Maxwell took control of BPC.

Questions of Leadership came to the attention of the Central board when the four films were returned by Channel Four. While the programme-makers worked on editing these into a two-part documentary and making one hour of 'balancing' material, the board took an interest in its editorial content – much to the displeasure of director of programmes Charles Denton, who was also a director of the company. 'It was the board taking a position about the programme,' he recalled. 'I didn't think it was the job of the board to take a position. They don't necessarily act with full recognition of where their role lies and where the role of those they appoint lies. There were several such occasions with the Central board, which was very inexperienced and people brought in for all sorts of reasons to satisfy political requirements. I was constantly saying this was my job – it isn't a good idea for boards such as this to discuss programme content.

'I didn't think the chairman was fully apprised of the purposes of broadcasting. He was coming from a position as a retired chemist. He didn't even like programmes and very rarely watched them. He was one of nature's conservatives who found very late in his life, after retirement, that he was appointed chairman of a television company. I don't think he was suited to the role. "Why do we have to make these programmes that cause trouble?" he endlessly asked.'[39]

The first inkling of censorship came with the distribution of videotapes of *Questions of Leadership* to members of the board. 'All the non-executive directors were contacted by Bob Phillis, who said he would like us to look at a programme that had been made for Channel Four that he was concerned about,' recalled John Jackson. 'I said: "Why are you concerned about it? We won't be broadcasting it; we've made it for Channel Four." He responded: "Ah, yes, but it could affect our reputation." So we were given these videos.'[40]

Once again, Charles Denton was displeased. 'I do recall there was an argument about whether the board should ever have tapes and being quite cross about the fact that they should never see them,' he explained. 'Bob would have said the board has a right to see it. I think it provides all kinds of possibilities of trouble. Boards should under no account look at programmes, because that removes them from any possibility of arbitration towards the end or something dreadful, which should be pinned on me.'[41]

What occurred at the next board meeting set the tone for the censorship that was to follow, and alarmed two directors, Ellis Birk, who had previously been on the board of ATV and was an eminent lawyer in a City of London solicitors' practice, and John Jackson, himself a qualified barrister. 'Two non-executive directors – the chairman, Gordon Hobday, and one of the vice-chairmen, David Justham, who has since died – startled me by saying they didn't think it was good for the reputation of Central to give support to left-wing programme-makers of the nature of Ken Loach,' revealed Jackson. 'They were straightforward political remarks. Ellis Birk and I, supported to some extent by Leo Pliatzky, who is now dead, and, in a fairly muted way, by Charles Denton, who didn't really approve of the discussion anyway, said we were very unhappy to hear this, it sounded like censorship and surely, if we were to be concerned about anything, it would be why we couldn't make it available to a customer who seemed to want it. Bob Phillis, as I recall, did not participate in the discussion at all but was watching it with great interest, in a rather bird-like way. Ellis and I were left with the very uncomfortable impression that there was something at the back of all this that we just did not understand. I was absolutely astonished that we were discussing at all the politics of Ken Loach. Personally, I was a great admirer of Ken Loach as a programme-maker and had no interest in his politics whatsoever. I was very fond of Gordon Hobday, but his politics would not have been the same as Ken Loach's.'[42]

Charles Denton recalled of the chairman's remarks, 'I would have expected it from Gordon, whose prejudices were very visible. He put a view that programme-makers were rather dangerous people with heavy tendencies towards the Left. The board had an innate leaning towards the Right and hostility towards the Arthur Scargills of this world, and I assume they thought Ken was a sort of Arthur Scargill.'[43]

Although opposed to censorship, John Jackson had weighed in with his views on the editorial content of *Questions of Leadership*. 'I thought there was some very interesting material in the programmes and it was obviously controversial, but my main comment was that they were far too long and I was not alone in making that comment – it was a general feeling,' he explained. 'But it was a very strange discussion for any board to have about any programme. I said that I was puzzled that we were looking at the programmes because Channel Four wanted them. I can remember Ellis Birk really getting quite angry. He said: "The one thing I absolutely will not tolerate is any form of censorship. It is quite wrong." Ellis, who is a very nice man and pretty mild, obviously felt very strongly. It was one of those situations where people could sense that there was something up.'[44]

It was several board meetings later when the Maxwell factor kicked in. Maxwell had been invited to join the board in 1983 after increasing the British Printing and Communications Corporation's holding of voting shares from 9.2 per cent to 13.8 per cent. This came in the middle of a flurry of activity in his own business that included the acquisition of Oxford United football club and the loss-making Odhams magazine printers, but he rarely attended Central board meetings. 'Maxwell was the most terrible bully,' said John Jackson, 'and, the first board meeting he came to, he waited until we were about five minutes into the discussion on the first substantive item on the agenda and suddenly slapped the table and said: "Chairman, I think we've discussed this long enough. I move that we reject this proposal." Gordon Hobday, a polite man, had never been spoken to like that in his life. He looked across the table to me as if to say: "What should I do?" I said: "Chairman, I move that we don't." Maxwell looked very cross and, when we had a coffee break, he came across to me and said: "Have we met before?" So I said: "Yes, 1969, in connection with Pergamon Press." "Oh, yes," he said. "I remember. Jackson, Philips." I do not recall him coming to another board meeting; he sent his "alternate", Sam Silkin, instead. Every director had an "alternate".

'Maxwell had an extremely unpleasant habit of picking up able people with important connections who were short of money and turning them into economic slaves. Sam Silkin had not had a very strong practice before he became Attorney-General in the Labour government. After he stopped being Attorney-General, he was very hard-up – he had hardly any practice at all – and Maxwell took him on his board at BPC and paid him a lot of money.'[45]

Silkin was the brother of another Labour MP and Cabinet minister, John Silkin, who was a friend and political colleague of Maxwell. As solicitors, both acted for him during the Department of Trade and Industry inquiry into Pergamon's financial malpractices. Sam Silkin became a director of BPC in 1981 and deputy chairman a year later. He was to represent Maxwell once more when he was despatched to Birmingham to persuade the Central board that *Questions of Leadership* should not be sent back to Channel Four.

'The subject of the programmes came up again,' recalled John Jackson, 'by which stage they had been shortened and the balancing programmes made. Sam Silkin said that, in his view, the content of the programmes was clearly defamatory and a company like Central should not allow its name to be associated with defamatory programmes. So I asked Colin Campbell [Central's company secretary and legal officer]: "Are our insurers on risk? That is something essential for this board to know because programmes can be defamatory but a defence against defamation can be truth." There were two questions: one was the question of reputation; the other was the question of possible damages. Colin, who I think was made slightly uncomfortable by the question, didn't answer very fully. I said: "I do remind all of us that it is not we who will be transmitting these programmes – it is Channel Four."

'At the following board meeting, which I didn't attend because I was on holiday and Ellis didn't attend, the board discussed it and decided not to supply the programmes to Channel Four. When this came to my attention, I said to Colin Campbell: "Did you find out whether our insurers were on risk?" He said: "Yes, they were on risk. They had looked at the programmes and they were content to be on risk." Through discussions with Colin Campbell and Leo Pliatzky, another non-executive director, I learned that Sam Silkin, with the full weight of a former Attorney-General, had leant on all the directors and said the fact that the insurers were on risk was totally irrelevant; he was certain that we would be sued, the fact that the insurers would pick up the bill had nothing to do with it and, reputationally, we should have nothing to do with this. And that's how the programmes came to be suppressed. To refuse to put those programmes out because they were defamatory was ludicrous. Ellis Birk and I were both very unhappy that this decision was taken at a board meeting at which we were not present. I might not have known all the facts but, on the basis of the facts I did know, this was an appalling case of censorship, probably the worst I have ever come across.'[46]

The motivation for Maxwell's bid to ban *Questions of Leadership* was clear. After his acquisition of BPC in 1980, he mounted what he called a 'survival plan' that was dependent on co-operation from the unions. When the Loach documentaries became a hot potato with the Central board, he was preparing to make a bid for Mirror Group Newspapers and succeeded in his ambition just eighteen days before the programmes were finally dumped. Again, he would be dependent on the unions as he negotiated new deals to transform Fleet Street's notoriously archaic working practices.

'Changes in printing processes meant that the electricians played a key role in the printing industry,' explained Maxwell's then press spokesman, Bob Cole. 'While people think of the print unions, the printing industry couldn't run without electricians. They played an increasingly critical part in the technical side, on the machines. When Rupert Murdoch later moved out of Fleet Street to Wapping, it was the electricians who were to convince him and the News International organisation that it was then possible to run the machines without the printers in their traditional role. Maxwell always saw himself as a friend of the trade union leaders and, through his Labour MP days, had established himself on first-name terms with all of them. He had known Frank Chapple for years.'[47]

Cole described Maxwell's relationship with Chapple as 'very, very friendly, good bonhomie', adding, 'When union leaders in general came to the Mirror building, he would lunch with them in his private dining room, and Frank Chapple was a key union leader. He would have had his home telephone number.'[48]

Maintaining good industrial relations with the unions at BPC was essential to Maxwell. 'The two publications on which the survival of BPC was critical were *Radio Times* and *TVTimes*,' said Bob Cole. 'They were two major contracts and a major reason he acquired his control of BPC, representing work at Sun Printers in Watford and Waterlow at both Park Royal, in West London, and East Kilbride. To ensure he made a success of his acquisition of BPC, Maxwell had to make certain that the future printing contracts of *TVTimes* and *Radio Times* were set in concrete.'[49]

Although many printers' and electricians' jobs at BPC disappeared, Maxwell painted himself as the company's saviour. He would do the same at Mirror Group Newspapers, on which he swooped after its owner, Reed International, had planned a flotation on the Stock Exchange to guarantee no dominant owner of its Labour Party-supporting papers, the *Daily Mirror*, *Sunday Mirror* and *Sunday People*. Maxwell's successful £90,000,000 bid was a shock to those inside and outside the MGN offices. 'He had obviousy been talking to somebody, if not for months, then for a number of weeks,' said Bob Cole. 'You don't do a deal that big overnight – he had to line all his solidiers up in place and get his cash. Maxwell thought: "I shall need the electricians' co-operation when I get my feet under the table at the Mirror." The unions had done or were continuing to do favours, co-operate, in the survival of BPC and then Maxwell realised he would need them again at the

Mirror. He had a short-term and a long-term indebtedness to them.'[50]

The power of the electricians in the media was also familiar to Central managing director Bob Phillis. During the television company's first year on air, it had experienced industrial problems as a result of staff being relocated from the former ATV studios at Elstree, in Hertfordshire, to the new company's East Midlands studios at Lenton Lane, Nottingham. A dispute about overtime pay led to a brief electricians' strike and the loss of episodes of Central's new Saturday-evening game-show *The Price Is Right*, as well as the nightly news programme intended to satisfy viewers in that half of the region for the first time. This experience would also have cast Phillis's mind back to an electricians' strike at Sun Printers in the late 1970s. 'From then on, the electricians realised their power in the printing industry,' recalled Bob Cole, 'and Bob Phillis would have known all about their role and appreciated that power.'[51] Although leaving Independent Television Publications to join Central, Phillis – who lectured on industrial relations during the 1970s – remained a director of *TVTimes*'s publisher, which was then owned by all the regional ITV companies.

Twenty years after the *Questions of Leadership* saga, most of those who were on the Central board still refused to reveal the real reason for the censorship; Maxwell, of course, was dead, as was Sam Silkin (who had been elevated to the House of Lords in 1985). Bob Phillis's career had flourished and, after four years as deputy director-general of the BBC, he was chief executive of the Guardian Media Group; in 2003, he was appointed to chair an independent inquiry into the government's relations with the media – which became more significant when Lord Hutton was charged with heading another inquiry, into the death of weapons expert Dr David Kelly – and was knighted a year later. Central itself had been taken over in 1994 by Carlton Communications, which already had a stake in the television company and was by then the London weekday ITV franchise holder.

Some former Central directors said they could not recall an event that took place so long ago; some focused on other aspects of the programmes. 'The original series was too long for the subject-matter and these were not very interesting programmes,' said Bob Phillis. 'They were a bit boring and repetitive. There were people at Channel

Four who didn't want these programmes. We argued about the scheduling and we argued about the money. If you get commissioned to make four and then you're told they only want to take two, there's a price differential somewhere along the line.'[52] But such issues were clearly matters for Central's programme-makers and Phillis could not explain why the board would be so interested in them or why the directors would deprive Channel Four of the chance to show them for these reasons, especially when Central would have at least benefited from being paid for two programmes instead of getting nothing for supplying none.

Asked about the Maxwell–Silkin–electricians' union scenario, Phillis replied, 'Why would Central respond to issues between Maxwell and the electricians' union? We ran our own business; we had our own responsibility as broadcasters. Whilst we'd had some difficulties and differences of opinion with the electricians' union in 1982 and 1983, I don't recall having any in 1984. If you're telling me Maxwell might have had another agenda, well, you can't ask Robert Maxwell now. Central Television had a proud record of seriously independent programming. We often got ourselves in trouble with the IBA and with lawyers, and I cannot accept there was some sort of improper reason why these programmes weren't shown.'[53]

Colin Campbell, who as Central's lawyer had been satisfied with the programmes submitted to Channel Four, insisted, 'It would be inappropriate for me, in my capacity as the former company secretary of Central Independent Television plc, to comment on matters that were discussed and agreed by the board of directors of that company.'[54] Campbell was by then director of legal and business affairs at Britain's newest terrestrial channel, Five.

One board member of the time, talking off the record, recounted: 'Sam Silkin was a very distinguished lawyer and certainly would have had an opinion as to the legal issues. I recall him being involved in discussions about the matter, whether within or without board meetings. The Central board had a habit of the shareholders making decisions about things and telling the executive directors: "These are things we'd like to do." I can't recall whether that's what happened.'[55]

In the mind of chairman Sir Gordon Hobday, a determining issue was the inclusion of Arthur Scargill as a panellist in the programmes made to balance *Questions of Leadership* – although his recollection almost twenty years later was that Scargill chaired the discussion. 'A problem arose because what the board wanted to be an impartial programme was chaired by Arthur Scargill,' he said. 'I'm sure that's what finally caused the board to say drop them – that was the breaking point. There weren't any legal matters. It was thought to be incredulous that Arthur Scargill was going to chair it. He had a profound reputation as a very powerful left-winger who carried a lot of weight.'[56]

At the time, Scargill was Public Enemy No. 1 to anyone on the right of the political spectrum. The miners' strike had just begun, as a response to National Coal Board plans to lose 20,000 jobs, and, a month before the Central board's decision to ditch Loach's programmes, the bloody battle of Orgreave, in South Yorkshire, represented one of the most brutal confrontations between miners and police. The 1984–5 strike came while many people still had vivid memories of the Winter of Discontent, when widespread industrial action brought down the Labour government in 1979. 'Scargill wouldn't have been one of Gordon Hobday's favourite people,' said Charles Denton. 'That would have been a red rag to a bull as far as he was concerned. Anyone like that he would regard as completely beyond the pale.'[57]

Such conservative views had been displayed in another act of censorship five months before the dumping of *Questions of Leadership*. Central's Nottingham studios were due to be opened officially by the Duke of Edinburgh in the week after the first episode of the company's satirical puppet series, *Spitting Image*, was broadcast on ITV. Sir Gordon Hobday was to greet Prince Philip in two capacities: as chairman of Central and Lord-Lieutenant of Nottinghamshire, a title bestowed by the Queen as Her Majesty's representative in the county. Despite the programme being passed by Stephen Murphy of the IBA – a former film censor – the board instructed Charles Denton to ensure that all three Royal Family sketches included in it were taken out.[58]

Six weeks after giving his initial recollections of the *Questions of Leadership* saga, Bob Phillis was presented with this account of how Robert Maxwell's business interests were at the root of Central Independent Television's censorship of the programmes. In a one-thousand-word letter to the author, he did not expressly deny the central accusation but wrote, 'As a matter of personal principle I do not comment on the detail of the deliberations of any board meeting of any public company on which I have served.'[59]

Of the Maxwell–Silkin pressure, Phillis would only comment, 'Sam Silkin (later Lord Silkin), as Robert Maxwell's alternate director, would have been entitled to express his personal views and opinions as part of a Board discussion. The Board of Central Independent Television had no interest or position in any of Mr Maxwell's other business interests. These were never discussed by the Central Board and would not have influenced the deliberations or decisions of the Board in any way. I cannot speculate on what might have been in the minds of Mr Maxwell or Mr Silkin, but Mr Silkin was only one voice amongst many on the Central Board.'[60]

However, one of those board members, John Jackson, was clear about how Robert Maxwell had taken advantage of the political leanings of many directors to get *Questions of Leadership* banned. 'The only ones who tended to the Left were Ellis Birk, me, probably Charles Denton and perhaps Leo Pliatzky, who was certainly very liberal in his outlook,' he explained. 'Bob Phillis, despite his strong trade union background, was studiously neutral on political matters. The rest were a pretty solid conservative bunch, which coloured their initial approach to the programmes. It started off with political censorship and then undoubtedly turned into pressure from Maxwell for his own reasons. The two points of view came together and became one stream.'[61]

Not only did Central's decision have a damaging effect on Ken Loach's career, earmarking him as someone who made 'difficult' films, but it denied a voice to thousands of rank-and-file trade unionists who were never heard and to television viewers who were not given the opportunity to listen to them.

Loach was more successful with another Central documentary made for Channel Four shortly after *Questions of Leadership* was shot. In October 1982, weeks before the new channel went on air with its distinctive, multi-coloured '4' logo, he was filming a ninety-minute Central documentary about the Labour and Conservative parties' annual conferences. Screened during the following year's conference season, *The Red and the Blue*, subtitled 'Impressions of Two Political Conferences – Autumn 1982', would have caused a few blushes, opening with Margaret Thatcher's words, 'Let everyone be absolutely clear: the National Health Service is safe with us', at a time when nurses and health workers were battling for better pay; a Labour MP described factions in his party's leadership as 'dividing the party in the face of the enemy'; and a Young Conservative claimed that the Tories' conference was 'rigged from start to finish'. With egg on the face of both major parties, there was no uproar.

Lack of uproar was also guaranteed when Loach made *The View from the Woodpile*, another Central documentary – it was intended for ITV, never shown, taken by Channel Four and, after a long delay, eventually screened in its late-night 'Eleventh Hour' slot. Certainly, the film was topical, with members of a Black Country theatre group acting out a play in which they express their feelings about unemployment, homelessness, drugs and the lack of hope among many young people in Thatcher's Britain. Those in the Young Foundry Theatre Company, from Darlaston, outside Birmingham, also discussed with pensioners in their local community a bygone age of full employment. (The 'woodpile' was an area of wasteland on which a factory once stood.) Loach conceded that the documentary – which marked the first time he had filmed in his native industrial West Midlands – probably never fitted ITV's documentary slot. 'After Central said they wouldn't put it out,' he explained, 'Alan Fountain at Channel Four said he was interested, but he just sat on it for a year, until I wrote him an absolutely furious letter.'[62]

The View from the Woodpile was Loach's final documentary for Central. Despite his satisfaction with the director's work, Richard Creasey had no doubt that Loach saw his time at ATV and Central as a stop-gap. 'Ken was never going to be, or wanted to be, a mainstream documentaries producer for my department,' said Creasey. 'That's not what Ken was. He was making documentaries because, at that time, no one was commissioning feature films from him. All I was able to do was to keep some money coming into his bank account and keep people working with him for as long as I could. Central Television was never more than a temporary abode for Ken. He and I were absolutely clear that, as soon as he was able to find better pastures, he would go for those. In the meantime, any way I could keep him employed would enable him to get to those pastures.'[63]

One of those new pastures was a return to theatre after almost twenty-five years. When Jim Allen was commissioned by the Royal Court to write his first stage play, *Perdition*, Loach agreed to direct it. 'I had the time and I did it for Jim, really,' recalled Loach, ruefully. 'It was just six weeks' work for £100 a week.'[64] But this was another project that became the victim of censorship, cancelled by the theatre's management just thirty-six hours before the curtain was due to go up on a production starring Gabriel Byrne.

Perdition was the fictionalised account of a real-life libel trial in Israel. In 1953, a Hungarian Jew, Rudolph Kasztner, who was a member of the Zionist Relief and Rescue Council of Budapest during the Second World War, sued a journalist, Malkhiel Gruenvald, who accused him of collaborating with the Nazis. During the court case, it was established that a Zionist group in occupied Hungary did a deal with SS war criminal Adolf Eichmann in 1944, allowing 1,600 Jews of their choosing to leave for Palestine in return for silence over another 476,000 who were sent on death trains to the Auschwitz concentration camp. This was part of the Zionist plan to move Jews to Palestine to establish a claim to their biblical homeland.

In fictionalising this trial, Allen sought to destroy the Israeli government's long-promoted idea that equated Zionism with being a Jew. 'Most people, Jew or non-Jew, have this belief that if you're a Jew you're a Zionist,' he said. 'And this is the public relations job that the Israelis have been doing for the past forty-odd years . . . because they've been successful in that, anyone who attacks Zionism is seen as anti-Semitic. It's crap! Zionism is merely a political nationalist movement, nothing more than that. . . . The Zionists wanted the Jews out of Europe and back into Palestine and so did Hitler, so there was a basis for collaboration.'[65]

The Royal Court, a champion of artistic freedom and radical writing, commissioned *Perdition* eighteen months before it was due to be staged. Michael Hastings, the theatre's literary manager, worked with Allen and Loach to cut and edit the script; concerned to ensure historical accuracy, he also commissioned a report on it by Zionist historian David Cesarini. The theatre's artistic director, Max Stafford-Clark, did not hear about potential trouble until about two months before *Perdition* was due to open. After a meeting of the Royal Court's council, the theatre's advisory body, chairman Matthew Evans confided that millionaire publisher Lord Weidenfeld, an Austrian Jew who fled the Nazis, had told him the play would provoke opposition from the Jewish community, but Stafford-Clark saw no reason to take any action.

Loach became aware of potential trouble only during the final two weeks of rehearsals. 'About ten days before the play was due to open,' he recalled, 'I was asked if I would meet a man who was a Holocaust survivor who would just talk it through for accuracy. That was when I met the man who led the opposition to it.'[66]

Then the *Guardian* published an article containing lines that did not appear in the final script and backlash from leading Zionists.[67] Abusive letters to the paper followed, as did features by Zionist historian Martin Gilbert in the *Daily Telegraph*, Bernard Levin in *The Times*, Stephen Games in the *Independent* and Lord Goodman in London's *Evening Standard*. The final version of the script was not available to anyone outside the production, so their attacks were not supported by evidence from the play as it was to be performed. Allen and, to a lesser extent, Loach were accused of anti-Semitism.

Four days before the opening night, in January 1987, some members of the Royal Court's council met Lord Weidenfeld and Martin Gilbert. Then, at a formal meeting, the council discussed David Cesarini's report, which insisted there were historical inaccuracies. As the cast prepared for their dress rehearsal, Stafford-Clark told Loach that the play would not go ahead. The director responded that Stafford-Clark must be the one to tell the cast, which he did.

'His announcement was heard in silence,' recalled Loach. 'Then the questions rained down: Why have you suddenly found you cannot support the play, just before we open? Who has been getting at you? Is the "distress" you claim the play will cause genuine? What about the distress of the victims of the Holocaust, suppressed in life and now in death? Since we, the cast, know the play better than anyone, will you at least take *our* judgement into account?'[68] A request by the cast to perform the play in front of their agents and friends, so that they could judge it, was refused.

In a press release, Stafford-Clark declared, 'We have re-examined our position in the light of representations made to us and we do not accept that there are factual inaccuracies in Jim Allen's play and that the play is [in] any way anti-Semitic. We have the highest regard for Jim Allen's integrity, but we do accept that going ahead would cause great distress to sections of the community which finally outweighs our determination to proceed with the production.'[69]

In fact, it was Stafford-Clark's own decision finally to cancel the production – he was keen to do so before the Royal Court's council took the matter out of his hands. That body had voted eleven to four, with a few abstentions, to continue with *Perdition* on condition that the first preview be postponed for four days, another historian, Norman Stone, be allowed to read the play, as should a libel lawyer, and all members be provided with a script, which they still had not seen. But Stafford-Clark decided to abandon it at that point.[70]

'My main memories are the unprincipled way in which the play was misrepresented by people like Bernard Levin and Arnold Goodman,' said Loach. 'That really shocked me, along with the absolute failure of the Royal Court to defend its writers; they were worse than any television bureaucrats. Also, none of those old luminaries like Lindsay Anderson and Arnold Wesker, who owed their careers to the vision of the Royal Court, ever approached us or asked to read the play or sit through a rehearsal to see what it was really about. They absolutely refused to give us any support at all.'[71] Stafford-Clark himself viewed the experience with some regret. 'Ken is on record as saying *Perdition* was the most unpleasant incident of his professional life,' he recalled more than fifteen years later. 'My feelings are exactly the same.'[72]

But the Royal Court's artistic director took his unique decision to withdraw a production from that theatre for the equally unique reason that he had no confidence in the truth of the script that he was being asked to support. 'My first involvement was when I read a letter from David Cesarini warning how it would be construed as being possibly anti-Semitic and certainly inaccurate,' explained Stafford-Clark. 'It was a progressive disintegration of the relationship between me and Ken Loach that led to my withdrawal of support for the play. If a play purports to be in any way documentary and accurate, the normal rules of drama are suspended and a different set of rules come into play. Certainly, there were matters of interpretation, but there were also factual omissions.

'In a way, the play was a Trojan horse. It became clear that both Ken's and Jim's interest was in attacking Zionism today, using this 1953 incident to do so – it was an anti-Zionist play. If you are making accusations of this seriousness, you have to be very careful about the facts you choose to omit. One issue that became in question was about the number of trains that the Zionists had arranged for the Jews who could escape to Spain and Switzerland. There were several trains, which represented the efforts made by the Zionists to get Jews out, but Ken and Jim began to behave as if the Royal Court were the BBC, someone who could be negotiated with. They said: "We will include one train, but we are not going to include references to the others." This began to verge on the unacceptable and my belief in the overall project began to diminish.

'There were areas of disagreement between me and Ken, and it became a simple case of the trust and goodwill between us breaking down. At a subsequent council meeting, members were split on whether the play was anti-Semitic. My feeling was that I was being asked to defend a play that I no longer believed in and a breakdown had occurred between me and the director and that, if I didn't act myself, the Royal Court council would. I believed they were preparing to ban it and I wanted to take a decision myself, before they were able to do that. So I chose to withdraw the play, but I regretted being in a position where I had to make that decision.'[73]

Loach was emphatic that there was no compromise on historical detail, as claimed by Stafford-Clark. 'This is nonsense,' responded the director. 'We were only interested in accuracy. It made no difference if there were ten trains or one train. It didn't change the principle of keeping quiet about the vast majority going to their deaths.'[74]

After the ban, Allen consulted solicitors B.M. Birnberg & Co and provided books containing his source material: *The Black Book on the Martyrdom of Hungarian Jewry* by Eugene Levai, *Zionism in the Age of the Dictators* by Lenni Brenner, *Eichmann in Jerusalem* by Hannah Arendt, *Perfidy* by Ben Hecht, *Zionism: False Messiah* by Nathan Weinstock, *The Abandonment of the Jews: America and the Holocaust 1941–1945* by David S. Wyman and *The Holocaust Victims Accuse* by Rob Shonfeld.

It is clear that the case of Kasztner had been clouded in different historical interpretations, according to the agendas of different groups. What blurred the issue was the Israeli Supreme Court's subsequent reversal, on appeal, of the lower court's decision. However, the higher court accepted the essential facts and it became evident that at stake was something more important than Kasztner: Zionism itself, the movement to establish a separate homeland for the Jews. As a result, the Israeli government backed Kasztner, as a Zionist leader. 'I come here in this court to defend the representative of our national institutions,' said the Israeli Attorney-General at the appeal hearing.[75]

Benedict Birnberg eventually concluded, 'I am inclined to the view that if there were any proceedings there would be quite considerable scope for defending these by pleading justification and fair comment . . . I am strongly of the view that the play should be published and indeed performed and be judged on its merits rather than by so many critics who appear not to have read the text, but have rushed in to condemn.'[76]

Indeed, the public had a chance to judge for themselves when a shortened version of *Perdition* was performed for one night at the 1987 Edinburgh Festival, after an attempt by Loach and Allen to get it mounted at the Olympia Theatre, Dublin, failed. Twelve years later, shortly before Allen's death, he was able to witness a reworked production of the play at the Gate Theatre, Notting Hill, directed by actor Elliot Levey, the partner of Loach's younger daughter, Emma. There was no backlash and it was a fitting epitaph for Loach's long-time collaborator.

'Jim stood by every last detail,' said Loach of the *Perdition* controversy. 'There are conflicting accounts of some minor points which might possibly be argued, but the main argument was never questioned. Like *Questions of Leadership*, that is the irony. No one ever took us on regarding the central facts. To be banned when the principal facts are unchallenged is typical of Establishment hypocrisy. This applies to the Royal Court and its pretence of artistic integrity as much as to the bureaucrats who run broadcasting institutions.'[77]

15

WHICH SIDE ARE YOU ON?

KEN LOACH'S EXPERIENCE OF seeing *Perdition* banned by the Royal Court Theatre completed seven years of almost uninterrupted censorship of his work. Between the documentary series *Questions of Leadership* and that stage play, he found an urgent, contemporary political issue to tackle on television. The miners' strike of 1984–5 provided Prime Minister Margaret Thatcher with the chance to take on the miners, as she had wanted to do when they brought down the Heath government ten years earlier, and exact revenge. It was a bitter struggle by those in one of Britain's basic and longest-running industries to save tens of thousands of jobs against the threat of pit closures – and one that was lost. Again, lack of support from the upper echelons of the trade union movement, with talk of 'economic realities', helped the politicians in their work. Going for a different approach, Loach took *Which Side Are You On?* to London Weekend Television, where Melvyn Bragg was editor of ITV's flagship arts series, *The South Bank Show*.

'When the strike was on, I was trying to find a way of making a documentary about it,' explained the director. 'The left-wing papers were full of poems being written and there were charity concerts in support of the strike, so there was quite a cultural explosion. After *Questions of Leadership*, obviously I wasn't going to be allowed to do a straight industrial or political piece, so that seemed quite an imaginative way of making it and I put up the idea to Melvyn. I went to see him and suggested that we do a *South Bank Show* based on the songs and poems of the strike.'[1] Bragg was enthusiastic. 'Obviously, I was on the side of the miners and I was very excited by the idea that it was producing art,' he said. 'For me, it was echoes of the Ashington miners of the 1930s, who formed a painting group in Northumberland.'[2]

So, over five days during August 1984, Loach and his crew travelled the country to record the action from the picket lines and demonstrations; instead of joining the police, as most of the news media did, they stood with the striking miners. 'It was a really scary experience being on the picket line, facing the police and trunch-eons, helmets, batons and riot shields,' recalled Chris Menges, who shared the photography with Jimmy Dibling.[3] Loach also orga-nised gatherings of miners to perform their songs and read their poems. 'When people are so stirred, they become very eloquent,' he reflected. 'A lot of what they said was absolutely brimming with passion and eloquence. It just caught the mood.'[4] In addition, library footage was researched, including scenes of police beating miners with truncheons outside British Steel's coking plant at Orgreave, in South Yorkshire. 'We got together the material we had specially shot and library footage, and cut it to the music and poems,' explained Loach. 'It was very simple.'[5]

The first sign of trouble came when Melvyn Bragg was invited to see a rough cut of the one-hour documentary at an editing suite in London's West End. 'He appeared to be rather shocked and surprised at the film that Ken had made,' recalled film editor Jonathan Morris.[6] Although Bragg was anxious about the film, he was keen to get it screened, but LWT's controller of drama and arts, Nick Elliott, was not so amenable. (Elliott later insisted that his memory was 'not really enough to be a credible witness'.)[7]

'I don't think Melvyn was wholly delighted with it, but the critical showing was when Nick Elliott came,' recalled Loach. 'It boiled down to recutting it so that we cut out particularly the Orgreave footage – the attacks by the police – which had come mainly from students. News footage was taken behind the police lines, but what we had was amateur footage from students and film and television workshops. We were looking for anything that validated what the people themselves were saying and writing about, just as, if you were making a film in Pinochet's Chile, you would find evidence of the prisons because you're talking about the torture. Melvyn let Nick Elliott take the lead because he was in charge of the department. We argued pretty head-on at that meeting. I certainly didn't even consider doing what he was saying – to cut out some of the shots of the police hitting the miners – because it would have been a betrayal of the people I'd worked with. This is what they had experienced and were writing about, and it was my job to let people hear and see that. So I couldn't back down.'[8]

Bragg worked with Loach in an attempt to make *Which Side Are You On?* acceptable to Elliott. 'Ken made a terrific film, but it was more political than arts, as far as I was concerned,' said Bragg. 'I thought I would be getting a different sort of film: obviously, there would be a background of the miners' strike, but the foreground would be the art that came out of it. I just felt it was the wrong way round, a political film with poetry and songs attached. My job as editor of *The South Bank Show* is to edit a programme that keeps the parameters of what I set out to do.

'When I saw the first cut, I thought: "It's too political for *The South Bank Show*; we don't do that." I didn't want Ken to cut out the Orgreave footage, but just wanted the balance to be better. I started to work on it with him, as I would on any other film – and I've edited alongside Ken Russell and Karel Weiss. I told Ken that I thought there should be more poetry and songs. He and I dug in quite hard, but they were very well-mannered discussions and he changed the film somewhat. After a second rough cut, I still didn't think there was enough there, so he cut it again and, when we saw the third rough cut, Ken said: "This is as far as I'm going." So I came to a deal with him that that was the final cut.'[9]

When the film that was acceptable to Bragg was banned by his bosses from being screened on ITV, he worked hard to find another outlet. 'The hierarchy at LWT became very worried and got cold feet, perhaps because of the shadow of *Questions of Leadership*, and there was quite a strong board movement against it,' he recalled. 'Ken was a very worrying person to them at the time, but I said I was definitely going to show the film and felt it was in good nick. Nick Elliott went to see it again and said it wasn't an arts programme – it was too political. We had an argument in-house but then diverted the argument by getting it shown elsewhere. I thought: "If they are going to start to try to cut into the film, first, I'm not having that because I'm editor of *The South Bank Show* and, second, they are fucking up the film that I promised Ken was OK. How the fuck can I get this shown?" So I rang Channel Four, told them it was a terrific film and said I would sell it to them at cost so that they didn't have to take on any financial burden.'[10] Loach believed it was only 'too political' because it was 'about here', adding, 'If it had been about any other country – Chile, Poland or China after Tiananmen Square – there would have been no problem. Their arguments were quite hypocritical.'[11]

In the meantime, a fortuitous event, engineered by Loach, made *Whose Side Are You On?* particularly attractive to Channel Four. The director contacted Mario Simondi, organiser of the Italian Festival dei Popoli (Festival of Peoples), asking for the chance to have his film shown at the December 1984 event in Florence; it walked off with the gold medal. The following month, Channel Four screened *Which Side Are You On?*, whose title reflected that of the closing song, performed by folk musician Dick Gaughan. However, the channel insisted on transmitting a 'balancing' *Opinions* programme the following week in which miners' leader Arthur Scargill was attacked by Jimmy Reid, the Communist shop steward who led a 1971 sit-in that saved the Upper Clyde shipyards from closure but was more recently a columnist for the right-wing *Daily Express*.

Another repercussion was a complaint about Loach's film to the Channel Four viewer-feedback series *Right to Reply*. The Chief Constable of Northumbria, Stanley Bailey, claimed that the sound had been amplified in the scenes of police hitting miners with truncheons. Loach's response was humorously disarming. 'I simply asked him what the sound should be when a policeman hits someone over the head,' recalled the director, who appeared on the programme to answer the criticism. 'It was such an arcane complaint to make. He could see a crime being committed by a policeman but was objecting to the soundtrack.'[12]

After the screening of *Which Side Are You On?*, which was subtitled 'Songs, poems and experiences of the Miners' Strike, 1984', Loach was invited to be 'guest editor' for an episode of *Diverse Reports*, the weekly Channel Four current affairs series that replaced *The Friday Alternative*. As with his previous documentary, he had the chance to feature a view from the miners' side that had rarely been reported on the nightly television news. It drew on the theme that dominated his banned *Questions of Leadership* programmes – the rank-and-file members' feeling of betrayal by the wider trade union movement and Labour Party leadership – and explained how the Tories had broken the miners with well-laid plans to import coal from other European countries. Loach saw *End of the Battle . . . Not the End of the War* as an opportunity to 'keep the politics of the strike alive and show the mechanism by which the miners lost, because history was being rewritten'.[13]

Later, for the Channel Four series *Dispatches*, Loach tackled the vilification of miners' leader Arthur Scargill by Robert Maxwell's *Mirror* newspaper and ITV's *Cook Report* programme. An official inquiry chaired by Gavin Lightman, QC, cleared Scargill of using miners' funds at the time of the strike to pay off his mortgage, but the allegations had never been withdrawn. So in *The Arthur Legend*, with reporter-producer Lorraine Heggessey – later to become controller of BBC1 – Loach sought to unravel how such damaging claims had arisen. They turned the tables on burly television reporter Roger Cook by doorstepping him in a Birmingham hotel lounge and did the same to *Mirror* chief industrial correspondent Terry Pattinson after previous attempts to interview them had failed. Cook used the spurious argument of refusing to talk until he could be supplied with a transmission date for the programme and Pattinson's attitude to the unjustified attack on Scargill was, 'Why doesn't he sue us, then?' Questions about how much the *Mirror* and *The Cook Report* paid their sources and why Roger Cook did not check certain details went unanswered. Six years after the end of the strike, history was still being rewritten. Later, Roy Greenslade, the *Mirror* editor who ran the story, apologised publicly to Scargill, calling it 'a deplorable saga'.[14]

The miners had featured prominently in Loach's television work over the years, not because of his family background, but through the way they represented working-class struggle. 'I didn't know my uncles well on my father's side – they died young,' the director explained. 'However, as always, there was great warmth shown to us when we met people during the strike. It's easy to forget the extraordinary comradeship of those times.'[15]

In 1985, the songs and poems of the miners' strike segued into Loach's first feature film for five years, about an East German protest singer expelled to the West and discovering a society as repressive as the one he had left behind on the other side of the Iron Curtain. To those who had witnessed the suppression of British workers' voices and to Loach himself, who found his own forms of expression under attack, it was relevant to ask how more free a society the Free West really was. *Fatherland* was his first, and only, collaboration with socialist playwright Trevor Griffiths, who said at the time, 'I feel as if I'm living in a country which isn't mine any more. It's very hard to know how to belong to a society which is tearing itself to pieces, denying its best instincts and impulses.'[16] Loach also saw it as an opportunity to attack the Stalinist form of Communism that had hijacked Marx's socialist theories.

Unfortunately, the sombre and bleak result was probably the least pleasing of all of Loach's films; the director's Cold War myth-breaker failed to light any fires. As with David Mercer a generation earlier, Loach found Griffiths not the ideal professional partner. 'I thought Trevor and I would see the world in a similar way, which we did, but I didn't foresee some of the problems,' said Loach. 'Apart from David Mercer, I normally worked with people who were concerned with making something realistic; it was about the authenticity of what happened in front of the camera. Trevor had a similar attitude to David, about sticking to what was on the page, which is one way of working. He's more literary than I'm used to being; we are chalk and cheese. The big problem was that a lot of the script had to be in German, but Trevor's writing is quite dense and full of cross-references and precise use of words. It couldn't be translated precisely, word for word, because the whole thing would become completely unsayable. The Germans in the film kept telling me: "We can't say this." I couldn't judge it, so in the end I had to rely on them to find a way of saying it so that it was idiomatic. The challenge of making half the film in German was too great. Also, I don't think I got the right chemistry between the various performers.'[17]

Working with foreign actors who had limited knowledge of English was a new problem for Loach. Gerulf Pannach, as the German musician defecting to the West, was himself a songwriter who had been thrown out of East Berlin in the 1970s after serving nine months in prison, without trial, for 'state hostile agitation'. He and his partner, Christian Kunert, wrote the music for *Fatherland*. The original part of a Dutch journalist who helps the singer to track down his expatriate father in Britain, where a recording contract awaits, was taken by a French actress, Fabienne Babe, after some of the film's budget was pledged by France's Mk 2 Productions, which co-financed *Looks and Smiles*. The rest of the money came from Channel Four's theatrical arm, Film Four International, and Clasart Film of Germany. Executive producer Irving Teitelbaum spent eighteen months raising the £1,000,000 budget. He and Loach had founded Kestrel II Films following the departure to the United States of Tony Garnett, who kept the original Kestrel Films but agreed to the division of the company.

Shot in the autumn of 1985 over four-and-a-half weeks in Berlin and two-and-a-half in Cambridge, *Fatherland* was perhaps most significant for being Loach's last film with Chris Menges, before the director of photography himself started directing with the award-winning apartheid drama *A World Apart*. Loach's producer on *Fatherland* was Raymond Day, who had been assistant director on *Black Jack* and associate producer on *Looks and Smiles*. Loach's Cold War drama, made just four years before the Berlin Wall fell, ended with a twist – the singer's father was revealed to have betrayed Dutch resistance fighters to the Nazis during the Second World War and finally hanged himself – but it failed to have the impact of, for instance, Frederick Forsyth's thriller *The Odessa File*, whose feature-film ending was genuinely shocking.

With censorship of his work for television, the banning of the stage play *Perdition* and his most disappointing cinema film to date, Loach was facing the bleakest time in the quarter of a century since those adventurous days trying to set up theatre companies across the country. 'It was very dispiriting because I was endlessly battling on territory where the hostile forces were just too strong,' he reflected. 'There's some value in making films and censoring yourself; you get a *little* bit of what you want in the end and the broadcasters present themselves as liberal and tolerant. But I always resisted that.'[18]

Despite his frustrations, Loach refused to throw in the towel. 'Ken is an optimistic sort of person and very energetic,' said Lesley Loach. 'He got on with things and tried to find work. I can't say there was ever a time when he got depressed or fed up.'[19] But a large bank overdraft and the need to support a wife and four children led him to bury his principles. Having made only one commercial in his career, for potatoes in the mid-1960s, Loach had said, 'I'll never make another. Holding the views I do, it would be hypocritical.'[20] But hypocrisy was the price to pay for keeping food on the table and the mortgage paid. Martin Johnson, the production designer who had last worked with him on *Looks and Smiles*, had been working on commercials for a production company owned by Jan Roy and Tony Halton, who was assistant art director on *Days of Hope*, and put in a good word.

'It was a question of do some commercials or fade out of the business altogether,' confessed Loach. 'In the end, I did quite a few.'[21] They included ones for the *Glasgow Herald*, the *Guardian* and Tetley's bitter, as well as McDonald's. 'I should never have done that one, really,' he admitted. 'I checked with Greenpeace at the time and they didn't have a campaign against it, but I should not have done it, because McDonald's represents everything I've been campaigning against. If you do commercials, the production company you work for puts quite a lot of effort into letting people know that you're available. So I couldn't just walk away from doing them when it suited me.'[22]

Although he was grateful for the opportunity to earn money during a desperate period in his life, Loach took home with him the agony he felt. 'That was his most unhappy time professionally and it was something I wish he had never had to do,' Lesley recalled two decades later. 'It was very painful for him to make commercials because it was against all his principles. Then, when he got the flak from the press for doing them, it was doubly painful. If ever we get into an argument now, it always comes back to: "Of course, I had to do commercials." '[23]

Throughout this time, Loach was desperately trying to make a feature-film comeback. He also had the chance to make a television documentary on a controversial subject that did not end up on the cutting-room floor. For BBC2's 'Split Screen' series, produced by the Corporation's Community Programme Unit, he directed *Time to Go*, named after the retitled Troops Out movement, a thirteen-minute film arguing the case for British withdrawal from Northern Ireland. In the same programme, Belfast-born playwright Graham Reid argued the opposing case, providing the balance not just across a channel, but within one programme, of which the defenders of 'impartiality' would have been proud. Ironically, the most explosive subject on British television over two decades would provide Loach with his return to the cinema.

PART V

RENAISSANCE AND
INTERNATIONAL ACCLAIM

include another issue that had arisen in Northern Ireland over two decades of British occupation: the 'black propaganda' disseminated by the Ministry of Defence in Belfast to justify the continued presence of that occupying force. This was based on the experience of Colin Wallace, a County Antrim-born British Army press officer who eventually broke silence on the dirty-tricks campaign and was framed by the intelligence services when he went public on their alleged conspiracy to overthrow Harold Wilson's Labour government in 1974. (Wallace also recounted how evidence was falsified about the then Conservative Party leader Edward Heath's finances and personal life in an attempt to shift the Tories to the Right.)

Unfortunately, David Puttnam's enforced departure from Columbia after less than a year – the result of an outsider battling unsuccessfully against an ingrained Hollywood system – meant that the film giant's European production operation was closed down. For Loach, this might have seemed like another domino falling, but his new project was shaping up into a promising political thriller and he was keen to progress it. 'It was up to me to raise the money and then pay Columbia back for all the work they had put in,' he explained.[2]

In the meantime, another project arose – also set in Ireland, but during the war of independence of the early twentieth century. Working Title, a British film success story of the 1980s, with pictures such as *My Beautiful Laundrette*, *Wish You Were Here* and *A World Apart*, commissioned Loach to direct *Fools of Fortune*. With a screenplay already written by Michael Hirst, it was based on William Trevor's prize-winning novel about the disintegraton of a rural Anglo-Irish family, starting with the murder of one of their workers by a Republican, on suspicion of spying for the British forces, and the burning of their home by the 'Black-and-Tans', the much hated auxiliary police units drafted in from the British mainland, who also murdered the father and two of his three children.

Effectively taking on an 'outside' project, Loach found himself heading for another brick wall. 'I read the book and the adaptation, and there were various problems,' he explained. 'One was the fact that it was Anglo-Irish and I wanted to cast an Irishman, but I couldn't find anybody who was right. Working Title wanted to cast an American, Aidan Quinn, who was a nice enough guy, but he was from Chicago and nothing like an Anglo-Irish young man – just American with an Irish background. Also, something in the book that was kept in the adaptation was where the IRA were alleged to have carried out executions in a way they never did traditionally. I did some research in an attempt to find evidence that they had done it, but couldn't. So I said: "I don't think we should do this, because it's very politically charged. We are turning them into butchers, rather than simply people fighting a political cause." It fitted a British agenda. They were brutal enough; you don't have to exaggerate it. We didn't see eye to eye on that. Then I remember asking if Jim Allen could contribute to the screenplay and that wasn't well received.'[3]

However, Loach started work on the film and was teamed with producer Rebecca O'Brien, who had just made a Working Title television adaptation of Maeve Binchy's novel *Echoes*, set in 1950s Ireland and screened on Channel Four. They travelled to Ireland to research locations and cast roles for *Fools of Fortune*, but the project fell apart four weeks before shooting was due to start. 'Ken had wanted to take the script in a more political direction and put real life into it,' recalled O'Brien. 'He was absolutely right – it needed a context of the politics of the time. He had long discussions with William Trevor and Michael Hirst, but they weren't agreeing. Also, the production was going in a way that neither Ken nor I wanted, in being made to take an American lead actor. So the finance wasn't forthcoming and the whole thing collapsed.'[4] Working Title later returned to *Fools of Fortune* and made it with director Pat O'Connor, then a relative newcomer to feature films. Loach's departure, however, was amicable and the same company subsequently commissioned a three-part television series from him and Jim Allen, based on their idea for a Spanish Civil War story. Eventually, they bought it back and made it as the film *Land and Freedom*.

But in 1987, when everything he touched seemed to disintegrate, Loach was desperate to find a way back into feature films. Still suffering from the departure of Tony Garnett to the United States, he found in Rebecca O'Brien a potential producer partner. 'Ken and I decided that we actually quite liked working together,' she said. 'He was on his uppers and doing commercials, and I was on my uppers after leaving Working Title, although I did work with them later. Ken managed to get me some location manager work on his commercials. He also showed me Jim Allen's script, *In the Heel of the Hunt*, which became *Hidden Agenda*. There were two very lean years while we tried to get it off the ground. I had no experience of money-raising, having always had the comfort of a single funding source behind me such as Working Title or the British Film Institute. Eventually, we found Eric Fellner and his production company, Initial Film and Television, which had made *Sid and Nancy* – he was a "bright, young producer" and liked the idea. Then a girl who had been doing some research for us, Julia Kennedy, was at a pre-Christmas Dublin horse-set cocktail party and met John Daly, of Hemdale, told him Ken was trying to get this political thriller off the ground and his ears pricked up. Hemdale had a reputation for doing political thrillers like *Salvador*.'[5]

So Hemdale Film Corporation provided the entire £2,400,000 budget – making it Loach's most expensive film to date – with Fellner producing and O'Brien as co-producer. Although Hemdale did not interfere in any way, apart from stipulating that there should be at least one American actor in a leading role, there were lengthy discussions with solicitors about the content of the film and evidence had to be produced to corroborate some parts of the script, even the fact that the Chilean coup that unseated Salvador Allende took place on 11 September 1973. Having done initial research in Belfast in November and December 1988, Loach and O'Brien planned to shoot most of the picture there the following spring. Then Film Finances, the production's completion guarantors, insisted that relocation insurance must be obtained in case it became necessary to move from Belfast or a member of the cast was kidnapped. Failing to get this insurance meant that Loach had to make most of the film elsewhere, although Film Finances eventually agreed that some shooting could take place there, but not scenes with lengthy dialogue.

As a result, the shoot was delayed until the autumn of 1989 and relocated to London, with a base in a disused Victorian school at King's Cross, where most of the interiors were shot. However, this gave Loach and O'Brien the advantage that they could cast Brian Cox in the role of Peter Kerrigan, the Stalker-like police chief who investigates the killing of an American lawyer at a police road block. Cox was appearing nightly on the West End stage in *Frankie and Johnny in the Clair de Lune* but was able to work on the film during the day.

The lawyer, played by American actor Brad Dourif, was one of four members of an Amnesty International-style civil rights group investigating allegations of ill-treatment by British security forces.

One week before the start of filming, Dourif, Frances McDormand (the Oscar-winning actress who played his American girlfriend), French actor Bernard Bloch and Swedish actress Mai Zetterling (in her penultimate film) went to Northern Ireland to prepare for their roles with a mock investigation into civil liberties there. They heard stories of human-rights abuses from Irish Catholics and lawyers, and soaked up the unsettling atmosphere as they were surrounded by British soldiers in flak jackets and policemen armed with rifles while Army helicopters flew overhead. Dourif was stopped by the Royal Ulster Constabulary for taking a photograph of a police station. All of this gave the quartet stories to draw on for an improvised press conference early in the film.

One scene that had already been shot, in July 1989, was of the real-life Orange Day parades in Belfast. Although Hemdale had not finalised the deal, it agreed to finance one day's filming because such a sequence could not be authentically re-created. Three months later, Loach and his cast and crew started production for real and the director managed to squeeze in extra filming in Northern Ireland by shooting some 'rehearsals' there when his civil rights group flew over for their research and getting another ten days there at the end of the schedule by finishing early in London.

The film was far from a typical Loach picture in its style. By being a political thriller driven by a police investigation, the script was tighter and had to be adhered to much more strictly than usual. Actors such as Maurice Roëves, who played the Colin Wallace figure who colluded with the intelligence services to smear Edward Heath, recalled the shoot as 'standard film-making, but much more exciting in that a lot seemed to be hidden-camera work, documentary-style'.[6]

This did not stop Loach seeking authenticity by using non-professionals where possible – or from putting those whom he auditioned through improvised scenarios. Veteran actor Bernard Archard, who played a British politician clearly modelled on Airey Neave, the Conservative Northern Ireland Secretary assassinated by Republicans, likened this to being invited to take a 'ramble into the unknown while he sits back and watches'. He added, 'This, I – and I think most actors of a certain age – find extremely embarrassing, even giggle-making. It's like being pressed into party games with a group of complete strangers, but he handles it with great politeness and never lets on how pathetic he considered one's efforts.'[7]

Ivan Little, a long-time reporter with Ulster Television, ITV's regional station in Northern Ireland, appeared in *Hidden Agenda* in exactly that role – writing his own report five minutes before facing the camera – and Llew Gardner, a familiar face on current affairs programmes such as *This Week*, conducted a studio interview. (In 1982, Little had covered the shootings of three unarmed, young IRA members in County Armagh by a special RUC antiterrorist unit and its attack on two youths in a nearby hay shed less than a fortnight later: the events that formed the basis of the 'shoot to kill' inquiry.)

Other 'real' people in the film included Jim McAllister re-creating his real-life role of a Sinn Fein local councillor, and Belfast housewife and grandmother Maureen Bell as the widow of the murdered lawyer's driver, encouraged to improvise and voice her experiences of living under an army of occupation. Just as Colin Wallace had read the script and made valuable suggestions, another Army whistleblower, Fred Holroyd, put the 'British troops' in the film through a military drill.

Hidden Agenda's final scenes were shot in Dublin and, although Loach never worked again with Initial and producer Eric Fellner, the film marked a significant transitional phase in his career and the beginnings of a regular team that included editor Jonathan Morris and production designer Martin Johnson. With Chris Menges no longer available, Clive Tickner stepped in as director of photography, although in his subsequent films Loach used Barry Ackroyd, with whom he had worked at Central Independent Television.

The picture won the Jury Prize at the Cannes Film Festival and was predictably described by Conservative MP Ivor Stanbrook as 'the official IRA entry'.[8] At the South of France festival, film critic Alexander Walker, of the right-wing London *Evening Standard*, launched an attack on *Hidden Agenda* during a press conference with Loach. 'Alexander Walker was true to form – and more power to his voice,' said Loach. 'The more he huffs and puffs, the better it is for us.'[9] The award and wide cinema screenings in Britain and the United States, where it became his most successful film to date, ushered in a decade in which Loach could make films back-to-back for the first time and enjoy widespread acclaim, especially from audiences in mainland Europe.

alities colliding with those of their characters. These new films also harked back to the era of *Up the Junction* and *Cathy Come Home*, when Loach had a well-defined sense of purpose in giving a voice to the poor and dispossessed, those who survived on the margins of society, and projected their struggle with a distinctive visual rawness. As he was increasingly embraced by audiences outside Britain, the unassuming director assumed a mantle of greatness and even hero worship that might have seemed incomprehensible to many in his homeland – and would have done to *him* just a few years earlier. He also found a new home at Parallax Pictures, a company formed by producer Sally Hibbin, which was reconstituted as a co-operative comprising of producers Hibbin, Rebecca O'Brien and Sarah Curtis and directors Loach, Les Blair and Philip Davis.

Hidden Agenda had given Loach a path back after the dark years of the 1980s. Although he found a like-minded producer in Rebecca O'Brien, she took a back seat from film-making for a few years after the birth of her son. In the meantime, Loach approached Hibbin with another script that had gone into development during his short time at Columbia Pictures' London production base. The producer, whose film critic mother, Nina, had championed *Kes* in the *Morning Star* when it faced a difficult road to cinema release, was herself a journalist who switched from writing about films to making them. She had previously approached Loach about working on *A Very British Coup*, a television version of MP Chris Mullin's novel about the attempts by civil servants to unseat a left-wing Labour prime minister, but he simply introduced her to Alan Plater, who then adapted the book.

After making *Hidden Agenda*, he was keen to see *Riff-Raff*, written by Glaswegian Bill Jesse, go into production. Jesse had spent twenty years trying to make it as a writer, but achieved little beyond a couple of plays performed in fringe theatre and contributions to a Channel Four Hogmanay special. He earned his living by labouring on building sites and, while working on one in London's Marylebone Road and suffering a particularly stomach-churning encounter with rats, contacted Loach with the idea for a film; they had previously met through a friend of Loach's at Central Television who had read Jesse's unsolicited comedy scripts. 'After *A Very British Coup* was broadcast, Ken phoned and asked if I would like to have a look at *Riff-Raff*,' recalled Hibbin. 'I put the phone down, called my mum and said: "You will never guess who wants to make a film with me!" '[1]

Hibbin took *Riff-Raff* to Channel Four, which agreed to finance it fully on condition that it was made strictly as a television production for its *Film on Four* slot. This meant that it had a small budget of just £750,000 and was shot on 16mm film in a conventional 4:3 TV format, not Widescreen. Staying within the tight budget was made possible by working almost entirely on the building-site location in Tottenham, North London, with the Portakabins used as production offices.

Robert Carlyle and Emer McCourt in *Riff-Raff*
[Paul Chedlow/Parallax Pictures]

In Robert Carlyle, who had grown up living on the margins himself in Glasgow's tough Maryhill area after his mother walked out, leaving his father to bring him up, Loach found his ideal actor to play an unemployed former jailbird arriving in London from that city. 'Bobby had a real quality of being both very sharp and authentic,' said Loach, who saw about forty actors at the Central Hotel, Glasgow, accompanied by Sally Hibbin and Bill Jesse. 'I was looking for people who had experience of the building trade and he had some as a painter and decorator. Then I went to Liverpool to look for the others.'[2]

With Ernie Mack no longer working as an agent in Liverpool, Loach approached ART, a casting agency of mostly variety performers, run by Ricky Tomlinson, who had been jailed for two years for conspiracy to intimidate as one of the Shrewsbury Two pickets during a 1972 building strike. Unable to get work in that trade on his release, he performed a stand-up act in clubs and appeared in Jim Allen's 'Play for Today', *United Kingdom*, before gaining national fame as trade unionist Bobby Grant in the Channel Four soap opera *Brookside*. On his trip to Liverpool, Loach found two of his main building quartet through Tomlinson. He discovered George Moss, half of a comedy double-act called Plug and Socket, and was reminded of the talents of singer-guitarist Jimmy Coleman, who had appeared in *The Rank and File*, *After a Lifetime* and *Days of Hope*, and had just finished a one-year building contract in Turkey. 'They're not only both very realistic, but also very funny and their timing is so good,' said Loach.[3]

At the end of lengthy auditions, the director had still not cast one of the four leading building workers, then realised that he had already met the perfect person – Ricky Tomlinson. In putting him into a leading role, Loach found a performer who would ad-lib with lines that contributed greatly to the film's humour and anti-Thatcher political message. 'Bill Jesse's script was very easy in that he used to write good scenes,' said Loach, 'but he wasn't a master of narrative, so we constructed the story out of those he told me.'[4]

The time spent making *Riff-Raff* and the friendships built were memorable to all who took part. 'You were on that building site all day long,' recalled Robert Carlyle. 'So, when you went on to do your scene, it was only like going to a different part of the building and you got so used to that environment and the people surrounding you. Clearly, the reason was to create a camaraderie between us. There's a kind of triangle: Glasgow, Belfast and Liverpool. The people from these places are basically the same people – Glaswegians are always going to get on with Scousers, especially when you find someone else with that background.'[5]

As filming progressed, Loach sought advice from his actors who were familiar with the tricks and conventions of the building trade, such as the use of false names. At the same time, the director, returning to his style of filming in script sequence, used the element of surprise throughout to elicit natural reactions and banter from the fictional group of building workers. One unnerving instance of this came when a motor was thrown from the top of the building – and Carlyle and Tomlinson found the results a bit too close for comfort. 'The guys had to throw it over and into the skip,' recalled Carlyle, 'but, on the third take, it missed and hit the bonnet and windscreen of a car. Ricky and I were in shock and shouting up at them: "You fucking wankers! What do you think you've done?" It wasn't until we finished the take we realised it was a prop car. Those sort of reactions you cannot buy.'[6] Another scene had a labourer falling to his death off unsafe scaffolding. 'That's almost the norm in the building trade,' said Tomlinson. 'Although it's horrific, it's something you would see or hear about most weeks; someone died almost every day. The fatality rate was as high as those lads who got killed in the mines.'[7]

In contrast, the most memorable comic moment featured Tomlinson being 'caught short', climbing scaffolding and entering a show home. 'Ken told me to look round, maybe take an apple, then have a bath,' he recalled. 'So I got in, saw the bowl of fruit and went to pick up an apple, but it was false! Then I got into the bath and I was in the nude, the door opened and three Muslim women appeared. I stood up with a hard hat over my privates and they screamed and ran away. So I ad-libbed: "I'm checking the plumbing." I wasn't expecting that, as they weren't.'[8]

A moment of black humour, in which Carlyle's character returns to Scotland for the cremation of his mother and a gust blows the ashes all over the guests, was added to the script after Loach and Bill Jesse searched for a Glasgow cemetery in which to film and were told that such an event had actually happened there. A wind machine gave Carlyle an idea that another surprise was around the corner, but he was totally unprepared for a telephone call on camera back at the building site – with his real-life girlfriend in Scotland on the end of the line instead of a fictional friend or relative.

More shocking for Carlyle was when he walked into a room and saw his screen girlfriend, Emer McCourt, injecting heroin. 'That was kept from me,' he revealed. 'I had an inkling that something was going to happen, though, and I was a bit hyped up and a wee bit scared. I thought I was going to walk in and get a beating, but finding Emer doing that changed the scene completely. Things like that make Ken a puppet master.'[9]

Irish actress McCourt, playing a struggling club singer, had the advantage of a complete script in her possession. 'So I knew about the junkie bit,' she recalled. 'It's a central part of the character, which is perhaps why Ken wanted me to have the script. Sally Hibbin took me to a methadone centre to talk to some drug addicts about the effects of taking heroin. Bobby was really shocked when he walked in.'[10]

Riff-Raff proved to be a landmark for Loach, defining the style of his films for the future – and ensuring that there *was* a future. But that happened only after Hibbin demonstrated her tenacity in making an international success out of a domestic television film. 'We showed it to British distributors and had quite a bad reception,' she explained. 'One of them stomped out and said he had had enough of British realism. Then we were invited to the Directors' Fortnight at the 1991 Cannes Film Festival. Channel Four said it could not afford to send us there because they believed it wouldn't sell. So I told their head of drama, David Aukin, that we had some money left in the budget and asked if we could spend it on getting us to Cannes. He said yes, we went and the film received the most extraordinary standing ovation.'[11]

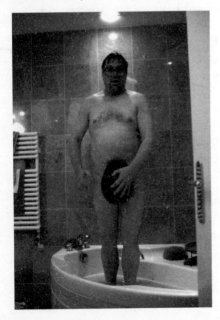

Ricky Tomlinson brought his barefaced cheek to *Riff-Raff*
[Paul Chedlow/Parallax Pictures]

It also took the international critics' FIPRESCI Award there, was bought by a French distributor, and Channel Four agreed to hold back the British television screening to allow a limited cinema release after an initial run at the National Film Theatre. *Riff-Raff* finished the year by winning the Best Film honour at the European Film Awards in Germany, where it subsequently went on general release, as it did successfully in countries such as Sweden and Finland. 'There was just a sense that the tide had turned,' said Loach.[12] Tragically, Bill Jesse never lived to see his Cannes triumph, drowning in his bath at the age of forty-eight, six months earlier. Having spent his life in manual labour, a promising writing future was denied him. By the time of the film's release, Margaret Thatcher had gone, too, after being forced by her own party to resign from her job as Prime Minister.

As with *Up the Junction*, *The Big Flame* and *The Rank and File*, *Riff-Raff* was about working people – an unpopular subject among film-makers. Hot on its heels came *Raining Stones*, Jim Allen's story of people's struggles to survive *without* work, as the gap between the 'haves' and 'have-nots' had widened over the previous decade under Thatcher. It was set on the Langley Estate in Middleton, north of Manchester, where Allen had spent fifteen years of his life. 'That's where the slum-dwellers used to get rehoused,' he said. 'Nowadays, victims of Thatcherism are just left to rot – there's even a place around here called "valium hill". When someone can't cope any more, they're just fed tranquillisers. Mind you, I'll always stay in Manchester. I like Northerners; they're good people. That's what the film's really about.'[13]

Raining Stones, originally with a working title of *The Estate*, was the story of Bob Williams, an unemployed Catholic who supplements his dole money with various scams and cash-in-hand jobs, and is determined to raise the money to buy his seven-year-old daughter a new dress for her first communion. When he borrows money and cannot pay it back, his wife is threatened by thugs, with the result that Bob explodes into a fit of violence that ends with the loan shark dead. Like Reg in *Cathy Come Home*, Bob exudes a spirit of optimism through most of this, despite the reality that he and his family are on a downward spiral.

After auditioning around the Manchester area, Loach found his Bob in a performer with whom he had previously worked on a commercial – Bruce Jones. A former pipe-fitter and fireman from Stockport, Jones was working by day as a boilerman in a dairy and by night as half of the club act Clark and Jones; he had appeared as an extra in *Brookside* and Alan Bleasdale's drama series *G.B.H.* 'He was very funny, committed and full of energy,' recalled Loach. 'He was clearly the best one for the role.'[14] Bob's wife was played by another variety entertainer, Julie Brown, who worked as a singer, under the name Roxanne, at Northern venues such as Bernard Manning's Embassy Club, in Manchester.

Casting Ricky Tomlinson as Bob's friend, Tommy, was guaranteed to bring comic moments to the film, following his impromptu contributions to *Riff-Raff*. The pair's escapades included sheep rustling and stealing turf from a Conservative club. But finding Tomlinson to offer him the role was a problem that was solved only by advertising in a newspaper for him to come forward. On top of his marriage break-up of several years earlier, he had suffered further setbacks. 'I had gone through a really bad patch,' he said. 'I'd been divorced, lost my house and the agency had gone by then. Someone who knew where I was staying came round and showed me the advert in the paper, with a picture of me in the bath in *Riff-Raff*.'[15]

The sheep-stealing scene was particularly memorable for Tomlinson. 'No one expected us to catch a sheep, which we did – on camera,' he said. 'Running up and running down the moors, it was so slippery that I must have fallen over thirty or forty times. When we got back to the road, the farmer who had been there rounding the sheep up with his dog said: "You film fellows, you don't 'arf know how to fall!" I was black and red, and full of aches and pains.'[16] The turf-digging sequence, which included Jimmy Coleman and George Moss from *Riff-Raff*, was embellished by Tomlinson's impromptu decision to pull his woolly hat over his face on the last take, as he waved from the back of a truck to an irate witness.

The filming of *Raining Stones*, with a £950,000 budget fully financed by Channel Four, took place over six weeks during the autumn of 1992 on the real-life Middleton estate, with the production office based in a disused school. Locations used included pubs, shops and flats, and locals became extras and, in some cases, even took bit-parts. Sound recordist Ray Beckett worked

with Loach for the first time and became an important member of
his regular team. Shooting was done with a lightweight Super-16
camera by Barry Ackroyd, establishing his place in the Loach line-
up as director of photography after working on *Riff-Raff*; his
documentary background enabled him to follow the action in a
way that gave it gritty realism. 'For the first three films I did with
Ken, I was like the apprentice watching how he wanted it done,'
said Ackroyd. 'There's a technique in that the camera is very
discreet, on a tripod and watches like an observer. You know
what you have to cover and the camera is free to shoot the reactions
at the same time or to let the action happen and be ready to capture
it as if it were only ever going to happen once, as in a documentary.'[17]

Loach was up to his tricks once more for a scene in which Bruce
Jones had to rod out a drain, which gushed fake excrement over
him. But one actor who went through a much more bruising
experience was Antony Audenshaw – later to play lingerie sales-
man-turned-barman Bob Hope in *Emmerdale* – after passing
Ecstasy to one of the girls from the estate in a rave club, in reality
the Hippodrome in Middleton, with locals as extras. He was
confronted by Jones at the top of a staircase and a tussle followed
in which both rolled down the steps. 'We did it time and time
again,' recalled Audenshaw, 'and Ken covered it with one camera
from every conceivable angle. It was quite rough and Bruce is a big
lad. We finished at about eleven-thirty that night and I had only
about five pounds on me. I thought I'd finish earlier and get a bus
back, so I went to Sally Hibbin and said I'd missed the last bus and
could I have some money for a taxi. She said: "It's a very low-
budget film and we don't have money for that." I lifted my shirt and
said: "I wasn't expecting *this*." I had a massive carpet burn all
down my back; all the skin had flailed off. So she dipped into a tin
and gave me twenty pounds. I didn't mind the carpet burn, though
– I enjoyed it! I could say: "Look, I've been in a Ken Loach
film!" '[18] The tables were turned on Loach when, after the club
scene, he discovered his trademark leather jacket had been stolen.

The film's other violent incident was that in which Bob confronts
the debt collector who has terrorised his wife and child, a scene that
Bruce Jones was not allowed to witness as it was being filmed. 'In
the afternoon,' he explained, 'Ken took me to one side and played

the soundtrack of that scene for me and it was so bloody powerful I wanted to kill that bloke there and then. Ken did such a good job that when it came for me to have a go at him I was really psyched up for it.'[19] Julie Brown, as Jones's wife, had shared the original scene of terror with a singer she knew from the club circuit, Jonathan James, who played Tansey, the loan shark. 'We're good friends,' said Brown, 'but he scared me to death. After every take, he would give me a hug!'[20]

The Bishop of Salford's refusal to allow filming to take place in the local church meant travelling to another in Warrington. This was, perhaps, a response to the attitude expressed by the priest in the film following the death of Tansey, when Bob causes him to crash by smashing his car windscreen. 'Fuck Tansey!' says Father Barry after listening to Bob's explanation. 'I tackled Jim on this and we discussed it extensively,' Loach recalled. 'The local priest he modelled him on was very down-to-earth and Jim used to go and have a drink with him in a pub there, and he said he could imagine him saying that – in extremis, really. Theologically speaking, anyway, the priest isn't answerable to temporal authority, but spiritual authority – if that's the right thing to do, it's the right thing to do. So I think he could justify it theologically.'[21]

Irish actor Tom Hickey, who played Father Barry, had previously been cast as a defrocked priest by Loach in his unmade drama Fools of Fortune and kept the role when the film was finally made by Pat O'Connor; he also acted priests in My Left Foot and Nuns on the Run. When he arrived to film Raining Stones, Allen introduced him to the real-life parish priest. 'Reading the script, I had thought this might be a radical priest,' said Hickey. 'He was Irish, but quite a conservative man. He told me the Church didn't publicly want to have anything to do with the film. I think they were upset by the unorthodox methods used by the priest. But this man agreed to talk to me about parish work on the estate, which was helpful. The reaction I got back in Ireland was that there was absolutely no problem, despite how unusual it was. When I played the character, I had in mind Michael Harding, a playwright I worked with who was a priest. He was quite a radical guy and always talking about the worker priests in Central America who became the heart of the community. That's the way this priest saw himself, as suffering with those people on the estate. Ever since the film, a friend of mine, the Irish singer Christy Moore, has often shouted at me: "Fuck Tansey!" He has never forgotten that.'[22]

The film's title came from a line spoken by one of the characters, 'When you're out of work, it rains stones seven days a week.' For those like Bob, it was one long battering. On receiving its premiere at the Cannes Film Festival, *Raining Stones* won the Jury Prize. Loach knew he was on a roll when his next film, *Ladybird Ladybird*, took an award at the Berlin Film Festival – the Prize of the Ecumenical Jury. In featuring the questionable practices of social workers, it was another picture that bore comparisons with *Cathy Come Home*. If Loach thought that Jeremy Sandford's 1966 drama was 'a very dramatic story to make your toes curl',[23] the new one was enough to make them shrivel up. It was based on the true story of a woman, a victim of abuse in childhood, who had four children – by four different fathers in abusive relationships – who are all taken from her by social services after one nearly died in a fire when left alone. The injustice highlighted is the taking away of her two subsequent children by a new boyfriend, a gentle Paraguayan political refugee, apparently for no reason other than the fact that she is branded an 'unfit' mother. The second is whisked from her in hospital shortly after birth.

Loach was approached by a social worker who had been present when one of the babies was seized and was assigned to take charge of the woman's case after all six children had gone. She felt that a family had been 'crushed in the most shameful manner' by a system that seemed to protect the professionals, who would use the courts, other child-care professionals and the medical profession, rather than the children.[24] The social worker listed a catalogue of questionable assertions and distorted evidence in the case.

Sally Hibbin suggested that the screenplay might be written by Rona Munro, after seeing one of her stage plays. Although she had never scripted for the cinema, Munro had some television experience – Hibbin was intrigued by the fact that she had written for *Doctor Who* – and an impressive track record in the theatre. She had won a 1991 London *Evening Standard* Award as Most Promising Playwright for *Bold Girls*, about the wives and girlfriends of three Belfast men killed or imprisoned for their political activities. Together, Loach and Munro talked to the social worker, then to the woman and her South American partner – named

Maggie and Jorge in the film – and decided that the script should focus on the cycle of abuse in her life and how that and her pent-up anger, sometimes reflected in violent behaviour, led to the loss of her first four children, before the injustices took over. The story was told, in the present and in flashback, through the ups and downs of the loving relationship she finally found.

Loach faced his greatest challenge ever in casting the role of Maggie, a Londoner, and eventually looked further. 'I thought I would never find someone who would be credible as a working-class woman and have the range of emotions that would do justice to the cataclysmic things that happened in her life,' he explained. 'I went all over, to Glasgow, Newcastle, Sheffield and Liverpool – places where there was a really strong working-class culture and I had contacts. It was Ricky Tomlinson who I have to thank for finding Crissy Rock.'[25]

Tomlinson's wife-to-be, Rita Cumiskey, had experience as a social worker manager, but he himself knew entertainers on the club scene who might fit the bill. 'Ken explained the background of the person he was looking for,' explained the actor, 'and I asked him: "How many do you want?" Before he did auditions at the Dockers' Club in Liverpool, I wrote down two names of who I thought he would pick. One was Crissy Rock and the other was Sandie Lavelle. When he finished, he said: "I can't make my mind up." I asked him who he was considering and I had picked the same two names. After another three auditions, he gave the main part to Crissy and that of the sister to Sandie. I had them down the other way round!'[26]

Rock, who was married for a second time and lived in a council house in the Huyton district of Liverpool, had performed as a stand-up comedian on the Northern club circuit for several years. That ability to think on her feet, combined with a harrowing background, made her the perfect Maggie. She grew up in poverty-stricken Toxteth, attempted to hang herself at the age of eleven in the belief that she could join her dead grandmother in Heaven, and was abused by her grandfather and battered by her first husband after marrying at the age of sixteen.

She spent some time sitting around at Liverpool's Dockers' Club, before walking upstairs to a room for her audition. 'There was a man sitting there in denim shirt and trousers and a belt,' she recalled. 'He was dead meek and mild. I said: "I suppose I've been sent up here as well. I've heard all about acting and actresses. I hope there's no casting couch because I'm crap in bed! I bet he'll come in in a minute and say, 'Hello, duckie,' and he'll have a blue rinse." I was just babbling on to this man and there was a little smile on his face. Next thing, this woman came in and said: "I would like to introduce you to Ken Loach." I told him I was sorry and so ashamed, but he just asked if I'd like to go for the screen test in London.'[27]

Loach's other find for *Ladybird Ladybird* was Vladimir Vega, who played Jorge. Like his character, Vega was a political refugee, from General Pinochet's Chile. Since moving to London in 1978, he had worked as a professional musician, playing mostly guitar, in Grand Union, a jazz band, Antara, which performed mostly folk music from the Andes, and Alianza, a Chilean–English 'alliance' of musicians and music from South America and Britain, which also included some Irish music in its repertoire and listed the Royal Albert Hall among the venues at which it had performed. Those who played social workers in the film were given a flavour of what the job involved by meeting a real-life professional and attending cases in London's Family Court, in Marylebone; one of the actors, Tom Keller, had some social work experience after leaving university.

Fully funded by Channel Four with an £850,000 budget, *Ladybird Ladybird* was shot in Acton, West London, during the autumn of 1993. Throughout, Loach guided Rock through her role, as if she were living it. 'I felt like a duck out of water,' she said. 'But there's something in Ken that is like a dad. He will hold your hand and say: "I'm going to take you across this plank and there's a massive drop down there but, if you trust me to take you across, I promise you will get to the other end." He has so much compassion for actors and actresses and the crew. Sometimes, it was like a big adventure. He would say: "This doesn't look good, does it? What would you do in this situation? Go back on the set and go with it." '[28]

The chilling final scene of *Cathy Come Home*, in which Carol White had her children taken away from her, found a new in-carnation in *Ladybird Ladybird* when social workers and police arrived at a hospital to part an unsuspecting Crissy Rock and Vladimir Vega from their newborn screen baby. 'All hell broke loose,' recalled Tom Keller, who played the leading social worker in the scene. 'When Crissy realised what was happening, she just let go all the emotions and launched into an attack on a policeman.'[29] Vega, too, could not control his emotions. 'I really couldn't handle it,' he admitted. 'We knew these two social workers were coming in, but we didn't know about the police.'[30] Another scene, showing Maggie's former partner, played by screen hard man Ray Winstone, beating her up in front of the children, recalled memories of Carol White and John Bindon in *Poor Cow*; the youngsters did not witness the most brutal takes but saw a toned-down version still shocking enough to elicit authentic reactions.

Echoes of the old argument, dating back to 'The Wednesday Play', about where fact ended and fiction began resurfaced when journalist Carol Sarler wrote a scathing feature in the *Sunday Times Magazine* alleging that *Ladybird Ladybird* had been selective in its use of the facts from the real-life case. In making herself a voice of that publication after researching the case, she wrote, 'We are wholly satisfied, now, that there were good, serious reasons for removing the children; much better reasons than those that appear in Loach's film.'[31] The article included the views of an unnamed legal adviser, social worker and court-appointed guardian who were not involved in the case. Perhaps Loach's message of social disharmony and a society split so savagely into the 'haves' and 'have-nots', as so eloquently demonstrated in his two previous films, was now a threat to the established order. A decade earlier, Loach's messages were no threat once they were censored; now, his films were getting screenings – and acclaim – worldwide.

Peter Smith, the solicitor who advised Loach and Hibbin on *Ladybird Ladybird*, subsequently wrote in the *Sunday Times* that he 'didn't recognise the film' as described in Sarler's article, adding, 'My advice was that a true story – as *Ladybird* is – should be filmed without any facts being changed. Ken Loach and Sally Hibbin accepted that without question, asking me to ensure that the script was as true to the real story as the law allowed.' After outlining the real-life details and their depiction on screen, as well as inaccuracies in Sarler's feature, Smith concluded, 'Sarler accuses us of "glossing over" the case against Maggie. Wrong. It is all in the film, and if she had shaken a little of the acidity from her pen, she may have taken a more balanced view of the research effort that went into it.'[32]

Inevitably, with such a harrowing saga, there was little humour in this Loach film, which the director regarded as essentially a story about grief. But, in addition to winning the Prize of the Ecumenical Jury at the Berlin Film Festival, *Ladybird Ladybird* landed Crissy Rock the Best Actress award there. Like Rock, the real Maggie had finally found a loving relationship – and had another three children who were not taken away from her.

Three years after the film's release, an interesting postscript appeared in a national newspaper. The *Observer* reported that police had offered the real-life Maggie, whose identity it concealed behind the name 'Someone', £4,000 for allegedly beating her up, without admitting liability. This related to their final visit to her house, when they broke down the door, dragged her away in front of the three children and, she alleged, injured her wrist and neck, before locking her in a cell for the night. The children were put into care until she was released the following morning.

'In the years that have followed the film,' wrote Nick Cohen, 'Someone's credibility has risen. Her social worker, who has since retired from Camden to St Albans, describes Someone's treatment as shameful and says her colleagues were hysterical.'[33]

18

LAST GREAT CAUSES

MORE THAN HALF A CENTURY after blood was spilled on the streets and battlefields of Spain in defence of democracy, the sound of guns and fighting returned to a country that endured two generations of Fascism and dictatorship once the newly established Republic had been defeated. Men and women lay wounded and screaming on a hillside, burning under the scorching sun, as a nurse picked shrapnel from a Scotsman's leg and stretcher bearers rushed to and fro.

Ken Loach could be spotted on a nearby hill literally calling the shots as the action unfolded in this Spanish Civil War drama. It seemed a long way from the London and Lancashire locations of his three previous films. But their international success paved the way for Loach and Jim Allen to realise their long-held ambition to bring a watershed in modern history to the screen. It was the director's biggest and most ambitious production, with the need for a large cast, shooting on remote locations in a foreign country – and a £2,750,000 budget. The landscape and epic story also signalled a move from 16mm to 35mm film.

The Spanish Civil War was a *cause célèbre* for socialists. Good-versus-evil has rarely been so clearly demonstrated as when supporters of the democratically elected Republican government fought against Franco's Fascists, who sought to reimpose the old order in which privilege reigned over poverty. People travelled from all over the world to take up arms for the Republic in the hope of wiping out centuries of feudalism and corruption, upheld by the monarchy, Army, Church and powerful landowners, and the Spanish revolution of the 1930s is still looked back on as 'the last great cause'. Loach saw it as that but was determined to tell a more complex story that might explain the defeat of those who stood up for democracy. This meant revealing the bitter truth that the Spanish Communists, under Stalin's influence, had betrayed and repressed other groups on the Republican side, particularly the anarchists and the revolutionary militias of the POUM (Workers' Marxist Unity Party); the cracks in the unholy Republican alliance were as significant a cause for defeat as the failure of Britain and France to support it while Hitler and Mussolini gave aid and troops to Franco. (Loach's Marxist analysis of history cast Stalin as a brutal dictator who hijacked Communist principles and purged all opposition, just as Britain's left-wing Labour governments had betrayed socialism.)

'There have been several great opportunities in this century for the people to inherit the Earth and that was one of them,' said Loach. 'The reason it didn't happen is the interesting story to tell because it's a remarkable story that I think not many people know, just as a story of people who went to fight and how they were sold out. Simply to make a film where the Fascists were the bad guys and everybody else was the good guys is, in the end, uninteresting because it's too easy and it hides the villainies that went on on the Republican side. That's the tragedy.'[1]

Although intellectuals such as George Orwell and Stephen Spender had joined the crusade, Loach and Allen were determined to reflect the fight as it really was, with mostly ordinary people fighting in the militias. But *Land and Freedom*, subtitled 'A story from the Spanish Revolution', was not just a lesson in history. Loach and Allen saw contemporary significance in attacks on ethnic minorities throughout Europe, growing anti-Semitism and the rise of Fascist politicians once more. Among his many noted, and prize-winning, films of the 1990s, *Land and Freedom* stood out as a masterpiece. In the manner of George Orwell's book *Homage to Catalonia*, it told the story of the Spanish Civil War from the defeated Republicans' viewpoint and highlighted the rifts that split them in those early, revolutionary days.

The budget needed for a film of such magnitude was much more than could be secured from Channel Four. In 1991, the idea was bought back from Working Title, which originally commissioned it as a three-part television series, and Sally Hibbin sought new forms of funding. 'A number of people had asked how we made films so low-budget,' she explained. 'The idea is to plonk yourself down in one base and not travel more than a mile; you have to adjust the story to the location you find. Then we had three films in development, all slightly higher-budget, including *Land and Freedom*. We knew we had to start to do something different.'[2]

British Screen provided money to enable Parallax to put the Loach picture into development. Then Hibbin attended the Valladolid International Film Festival in Spain with the express intention of seeking companies of a similar size who might be interested in co-production. After finding a Spanish distributor, Messidor Films, she was introduced to German producer Ulrich Felsberg, who ran Road Movies, a company set up with director Wim Wenders. The result was that Parallax provided half of *Land and Freedom*'s budget, with Messidor and Road Movies funding 40 per cent between them and Eurimages, a European film support body, supplying the final 10 per cent. Each co-producer raised money in its own counry through pre-sales to television and theatrical distributors. With Channel Four not keen on the script, Parallax eventually pre-sold British television rights to the BBC and BSkyB.

Hibbin was working on another Parallax film, *I.D.*, so she became executive producer while Rebecca O'Brien took on the task of producing her second picture with Loach. 'We went to Spain, dug a few trenches and set up the Spanish Revolution!' said O'Brien, with the enthusiasm that was to become a hallmark of the production.[3] *Land and Freedom* itself featured actors from Britain, Ireland, Spain, Germany, France, Italy and the United States, and was three years in development before cast and crew travelled to the Maestrazgo, a highland area spanning the border of Aragon and Castellon in a region of fierce civil war battles still remembered by locals. A Catalan location manager found a suitable village for filming in Mirambel, whose plaza, church, streets and landowner's house had remained relatively unspoiled. It was a four-hour drive from Barcelona.

In the months before shooting began, Loach called on an old friend from his early 'Wednesday Play' days, Roger Smith, to work on Jim Allen's screenplay. 'The storyline had been very slow to evolve and was constantly being reworked,' said Loach. 'There were some magnificent scenes, but the narrative wasn't very coherent.'[4] The reunion was prompted by a failed project, when Loach was commissioned by Palace Pictures to develop an idea for a Channel Four soap opera set on the shop floor of a car factory. Smith was hired as script editor and episodes were written, some by Allen, but the proposed television serial failed to gel. 'It foundered because I couldn't put a team of writers together who had the same perspective as we had,' said Loach. 'The scripts they turned in were oddities about individual circumstances, but had no sense of the underlying struggle.'[5]

Smith then looked at the *Land and Freedom* script. 'I suggested that the real crisis, when the main character, David, discovers what the Communist Party was doing, would be much stronger if he were a member of that party,' he said. 'So it was a total turning-point and it is that that sends him back to the front. Then it was a question of setting it up as a love story, which wasn't there to begin with. The other point was how to connect those events with today and out of that came the beginning, with the old boy dying in Liverpool. It was the story of his experiences in Spain, the betrayal and his relationship with Blanca.'[6] Allen's original idea of featuring a German as David's love interest – to bring Hitler's Fascism into the story – was quashed on realising that neither of the two leads would be Spanish.

When Loach travelled to Barcelona to cast the Spanish roles in the film, he telephoned Smith with the news that he had found Icíar Bollaín, an award-winning actress, who was not right for the role of Blanca, but was impressive enough to have another part created for her. As a result, Smith went to Spain for ten days and did a final rewrite to include her as fiery guerrilla fighter Maite. Loach was adamant that all of his cast must have political views reflecting those of their characters.

For the two leads, unemployed British Communist David and idealistic anarchist Blanca, Loach chose Liverpudlian actor Ian Hart, who had previously starred as John Lennon in the television film *Backbeat*, and Spanish actress Rosana Pastor, a familiar face in films and TV dramas in her own country. 'Ian's part was the hardest to cast,' said Loach. 'All the characters are politicised, particularly the volunteers; they are there out of their commitment. I auditioned hundreds for that role; it was a question of finding a young man who was working-class and had a sense of politics.'[7]

Others among those playing foreign volunteers in Spain to support the Republican cause were Tom Gilroy as American Gene

Lawrence and Frédéric Pierrot as French militiaman Bernard. During the filming, Loach succeeded in building up among the cast a camaraderie that reflected that shown by those on the Republican side during the Civil War. 'It was one of those extraordinarily passionate films that affected everybody,' recalled Rebecca O'Brien.[8]

When Loach's troops arrived in the Maestrazgo, they were given two weeks' training by two serving sergeants in the Spanish Army, the same training as the militia would have had. 'We had our own kit and guns,' recalled Eoin McCarthy, who played an Irishman in the militia. 'I realised that maybe I was one of the leaders because I kept on having to drill the guys myself in Spanish. We learned how to shoot and how to strip down the guns. It was a bit like being in the Scouts, but cooler because there were really tasty girls there and it was sunny and great fun. At five o'clock we would walk into the local taverna with our guns and get a couple of beers in. After an hour, we would go back to the hotel for dinner, where the actors, Ken and the crew all ate together – the first time I have ever done that on a film. In the evenings, we met the veterans of the Civil War and learned a lot of militia songs.'[9] In the village of Mirambel, a digger excavated trenches and Loach's militia built the sets themselves as part of an exercise in making them feel a unit all in it together.

Throughout the six-week shoot, interpreters were used and everyone spoke in their own language, which meant the film combined English with Spanish and Catalan. Loach kept the film crew – all Spanish except for director of photography Barry Ackroyd, sound recordist Ray Beckett, designer Martin Johnson, script supervisor Susanna Lenton and a handful of others – as far away from the action as possible, hoping to elicit responses from the cast as if in a real war scenario. True to his style, he issued to actors and actresses only the minimum script needed to play their parts. 'We have a contract, so we know more or less how many days we have to be here,' explained Icíar Bollaín, 'but I don't know what is going to happen to me. I don't know if I'm going to die or if I'm just going to leave the trenches and go away . . . We had a big battle in Mirambel, so we all knew that someone was going to die because it's a battle and there are shots and grenades, and everybody was so frightened because nobody wanted to die, because to die means to leave the

movie. But no one was saying: "I don't want to leave the movie."
Everybody was saying: "I don't want to die." '[10]

When Eoin McCarthy's Irish militiaman was shot dead, it proved
an emotional wrench for the actor. He recalled, 'They put a plastic
explosive on my back and a mattress down on a roof, and said:
"You're going to get shot here." Then Ken sent me back to the hotel,
packed my stuff and had me off to London within eight hours. They
filmed my funeral three days later. I felt fucking awful. He wanted the
group to feel the loss of one of their own, he said. Back in London, I
was thinking about them all out there in Spain and, at the end of
filming, I flew out to say goodbye. While we were filming, we all knew
we were doing something truly, truly amazing.'[11]

Just as Jim Allen had incorporated portrayals of workers
eloquently discussing their grievances and political ideologies in
The Big Flame, *Land and Freedom* featured a scene in which the
militia members and locals – many found in a nearby town –
discuss whether to collectivise a former landowner's estate. At
twelve minutes, it was the longest scene in the film, with the basic
script launching the group into ad-lib and improvisation. 'I remember Ken being quite nervous as we set off to film the scene
about collectivisation,' recalled Barry Ackroyd. 'He said: "I want
this to feel like a real debate about real politics: should you take a
socialist view of the world or a self-interested view?" He really felt
this debate would happen on camera and it wasn't a foregone
conclusion what they would say at the end, although the characters
were stacked heavily in favour of the film's view.'[12]

To shoot the 'real' debate, Loach used two cameras and filmed
for two days. Editor Jonathan Morris recalled being 'surrounded
by film' when Loach arrived in a London editing suite. Morris was
a master of dealing with the director's habit of shooting scenes
endlessly. 'I have always likened it to the painting of the Forth
Bridge – by the time you get to the end of it, you forget what you
have seen,' he said. 'But Ken is very good and makes notes and
knows what he is doing. It took at least a week to cut the
collectivisation sequence.'[13]

Loach's militia provided unexpected reactions as they prepared
for the filming of a scene following their retreat from a bloody
battle when promised reinforcements failed to materialise. 'Right,'
the director told his cast, 'you've been expecting some help from the

Popular Army in the struggle you've been engaged in and you see three lorries full of soldiers get here . . . In the first instant you should respond as you think you would in the situation . . . But remember, you do share a certain discipline, and you would take notice of what your commander tells you. OK. Here we go then.'[14]

So the militia sat in a field, tending their wounded, with shouts of '*agua*' and '*medico*', before three trucks arrived. 'We hadn't told them that the Communists were going to come out and point their guns at them,' recalled Rebecca O'Brien. 'We had two cameras running and wanted to get the militia's reaction. The guns were pointed and they disappeared behind the terracing in the fields! Later, we hooted with laughter at what had happened.'[15] Loach talked to the cast about what had been expected, gave out an instruction for the guns to be kept down and prepared for a second take of this, one of the final scenes in Spain, when the Communists' commanding officer declared that the POUM had been outlawed for 'collaborating' with Franco and, in the fracas that followed, shot Blanca dead.

To relate the Spanish war to modern-day Europe, *Land and Freedom* began and ended with scenes of David's death and funeral, shot in Britain in one week. His granddaughter is seen finding letters and mementoes, including a photograph of Blanca. Suzanne Maddock, who played the granddaughter, Kim, recalled, 'Ken said: "This is your grandfather. You see him every day. He is on the couch, saying, 'You have to get somebody to help me.' "' The crew kept themselves very much to themselves. They were very aware that the actors are in the skin of their characters. I remember doing take after take and feeling like it was real. There were real tears; it wasn't acting, but *re*acting.'[16]

The reactions of critics and public to Loach's first successful 'foreign' film were extraordinary. At the Cannes Film Festival in May 1995, with Loach's full militia in attendance, it won both the international critics' FIPRESCI Award and the Prize of the Ecumenical Jury. Among other honours, it was named Best Film at the European Film Awards. One of the greatest compliments paid to *Land and Freedom* came from the Spanish newspaper *El País*, whose critic wrote, 'It is a work of great moral sculpture and brilliance . . . It contains the most beautiful tribute that cinema has given to the memory of free Spain.'[17]

Loach and Allen's epic was most successful with audiences in Spain, France and Italy, where the director subsequently retained a loyal following. In Barcelona, so many people flocked to its first cinema screening that Loach and O'Brien had to sit on the floor. 'It was like bringing it home,' recalled O'Brien. 'It was very scary for us because here we were rewriting Spanish history. It was hailed to the rafters and the most moving experience.'[18] As Spaniards rushed to cinemas, many young people learned a secret history that they had never been taught at school; even after Franco's death, in 1975, Spanish historians had failed to chronicle the true story of the revolution. Now it had taken a foreigner to combine the romance, heroism and struggle of the Civil War with the bitter truth of the Communists' betrayal. 'The most amazing thing is, I didn't know that that happened with the POUM, with the Republican band, that their own Republicans killed POUM people,' said Icíar Bollaín of an event that occurred in her own country.[19]

However, Loach's Spanish epic was not praised by everyone, especially some who had travelled from foreign countries to support the fight against fascism. The great American reporter Martha Gellhorn, who in Spain became the world's first accredited female war correspondent, complained that she did not recognise the country and camaraderie that she had experienced.[20] Despite its partisanship, there is no doubt that Gellhorn's reporting of the war from the Republican side ranked among the most vivid and honest, and it did not suffer from the outright bias contained in the dispatches of her husband-to-be, Ernest Hemingway, and in the propagandist documentary film *The Spanish Earth*, for which he wrote the narration. But Gellhorn arrived in Madrid in March 1937 and began travelling to the war's major battlefronts the following month. Much of the bitter infighting between different Republican factions had already taken place and led to the Communists' attack on the POUM in May 1937, events covered by Loach in *Land and Freedom* and by George Orwell, who left London for Spain in December 1936 specifically to fight for the Republican cause. As Loach explained, 'Most people fought as part of the International Brigade [volunteers raised by Communist Parties around the world], but they didn't go through the earlier critical period – the struggle for leadership on the Republican side.'[21]

Orwell's reporting of the battles around Barcelona and his subsequent book, *Homage to Catalonia*, made clear his sympathies for that side but spared no criticism for the bitter rifts within it. Indeed, just as *Land and Freedom* would be criticised, the book was condemned by some at the time as a defence of 'Trotskyites and anarchists' who 'betrayed' the Republican cause. Like Loach, Orwell identified the threat to socialism as coming from within its own legions. Later, the historian Raymond Carr observed, 'It was a bitter irony of the Civil War that it ended in a civil war within the Republican camp.'[22]

Author Phillip Knightley concluded in his definitive account of war reporting, *The First Casualty*, 'The drawback of reporting with heart as well as mind is that if the cause is basically just, as the Republican one undoubtedly was, the correspondent tends to write in terms of heroic endeavour, rather than face unpalatable facts, and to mislead his readers with unjustified optimism. Few resisted the temptation.'[23]

Loach's Republican militia in *Land and Freedom*
[Paul Chedlow/Parallax Pictures-Messidor Films-Road Movies]

The experience of working with Loach left such an impression on the Spanish cast that one of them, Icíar Bollaín, shadowed him as he made his next film in Glasgow and Nicaragua, and wrote a book, *Ken Loach – Un Observador Solidario* ('A Sympathetic Observer'), which was published in Spain.[24] She also followed to Britain and

Central America Paul Laverty, who was drafted in to play one of the militia in *Land and Freedom* but was actually a writer who scripted the new drama. He eventually made his home with Bollaín in Madrid, from where he became Loach's regular collaborator.

This new, partly Spanish-speaking epic grew out of Laverty's travels to Nicaragua in the 1980s, a politically explosive time of modern-day interference in Central America by the United States government. Getting itchy feet and wanting to see the world, he was interested in what was happening in Nicaragua, whose revolution had seen the Sandinistas overthrow the American-backed dictator Somoza. Without the approval of Congress, President Ronald Reagan sanctioned the financing and training of the Contra rebels in an attempt to destabilise the new regime, which had been backed by a decisive majority in democratic elections in 1984. For many on the Left, the Sandinistas' health care and education advances, along with land reform, represented an ideal echoing that of the Spanish revolution.

'I was fascinated by that country, which had taught its population to read and write and had wiped out polio and won prizes from international health organisations and UNESCO, and was doing all these incredible things to transform society,' said Laverty, who gave up work as a lawyer in criminal courts in his native Glasgow. 'Nicaragua had a population that was less than the Strathclyde region of Scotland.'[25]

On his first, six-month visit to Central America in 1984, Laverty worked in a farming co-operative in the north of Nicaragua and travelled to both Guatemala and El Salvador, whose American-backed regime was responsible for death squads murdering thousands of its citizens. Returning to Scotland, he worked with solidarity campaigns organised by students and trade unions, and with Scottish Medical Aid to Nicaragua. This resulted in his going back to the country in 1986 with the medical charity – and his partner, a nurse – although he ended up working for a Nicaraguan human rights organisation. 'I interviewed people in the countryside, spoke to delegations arriving in the country and did an analysis of other organisations,' explained Laverty. 'We also used to get reports and details of attacks by the Contras. What I saw was the most systematic campaign to tear the country apart.'[26]

With no intention of practising law again, Laverty returned to Scotland, continued to do solidarity work and aspired to write a story based on his experiences. He came up with a treatment for a film and sent it to various producers and directors, including Loach. On receiving a call from the director registering his interest, Laverty jumped on a bus to London. After several meetings, Loach encouraged him to script several scenes, even though he had no experience of writing dialogue. An approach to the Glasgow Film Fund with the treatment and some pages of the script led to a screenplay being commissioned. Laverty's original idea was set entirely in Nicaragua, but he developed it with Loach so that the first half was in Britain. The result was the story of a love affair between a Glasgow bus driver, George, and a traumatised Nicaraguan dancer and refugee, Carla, in 1987, at the height of war in her own country. After the shock of her suicide attempt, George travels to Carla's homeland with her to exorcise the painful demons of her past by seeking to track down her boyfriend, who was captured by the Contras. While there, they come under attack from the Contras and George is horrified to learn of the CIA's involvement. Carla finally finds Antonio, discovering that his spine was crushed and tongue cut out; George returns home alone.

With the need to film abroad again, Loach travelled to Nicaragua several times with Laverty to meet the writer's contacts, get a feel for a country he had never visited and find locations for filming. 'There's no film industry there at all,' said Laverty. 'We went to the Minister of Culture and he started off talking about French New Wave cinema! Then there was this big bitch on heat, running around us, and a tiny dog jumping up and licking its fanny. This was followed by the little dog jumping up on the back of the bitch, trying to shag it, then sitting up on one leg and swinging round. It was quite surreal and Ken and I were like two schoolboys, desperately trying not to laugh.'[27]

Because no trade agreement existed between Nicaragua and Britain, a deal was struck whereby the government there would not impose tax on anything bought by Parallax in the country as long as it was left behind. This included typewriters and 'short ends' of film stock, which were used by Nicaraguan film-makers to produce two- or three-minute shorts that were put together and won a prize at the Berlin Film Festival.

To tackle the difficult task of casting his leading lady and others, Loach held open auditions in the capital, Managua, to which even a man in drag turned up. He discovered that his usual practice of putting performers into improvised scenarios involving conflict did not suit the Nicaraguan sensibility; they were too polite! But, as with *Ladybird Ladybird*, he succeeded in finding a woman he believed would be convincing in the title role. In fact, he was so impressed with Oyanka Cabezas, a dancer with some acting experience, that Parallax enrolled her on a language course in London to develop her non-existent English before filming started. Easier to cast was George, played by *Riff-Raff* star Robert Carlyle, hot from shooting *Trainspotting*, the film that was to make him famous in Britain – but not until after shooting was completed on *Carla's Song*. American actor Scott Glenn, who had appeared in Hollywood blockbusters such as *Apocalypse Now* and *The Silence of the Lambs*, took the role of a CIA agent-turned-human rights activist.

Sally Hibbin, returning to her role as producer for *Carla's Song* while Rebecca O'Brien was working on the film *Bean*, also made trips to Nicaragua to help in the logistics of setting up the picture, then the decision was made to shoot *Land and Freedom* first. For *Carla's Song*, which had a £3,000,000 budget, Hibbin built on the co-production arrangements made for *Land and Freedom*, with Parallax and Road Movies being joined by Tornasol Films of Spain in making it for Channel Four Films; it also had support from Spain's Alta Films and television channel TVE, and Germany's Degeto Films and Filmstiftung Nordrhein-Westfalen, in addition to sponsorship from the Glasgow Film Fund, the European Script Fund and the Nicaraguan State Institute of Culture.

Writer Paul Laverty
[Joss Barratt/Sixteen Films-Road
Movies-Tornasol/Alta Films]

Shortly after *Land and Freedom* was released in British cinemas, Loach was ready to film *Carla's Song*. To stick to his ritual of shooting in chronological order, this involved two shoots in Nicaragua, the first for flashback scenes, then another for the trip undertaken by George and Carla. In total, there were four weeks spent in Nicaragua and four in Scotland. Both countries presented a challenge, with sub-zero temperatures around Glasgow and in the mountains near Loch Lomond, where the December days drew in early and restricted filming time, then some of the cast and crew fell sick as a result of consuming unfamiliar food and water in the tropical heat of Nicaragua. Having worked in documentaries, Barry Ackroyd was used to filming in such environments. 'You know that, technically, you can cope with everything and you are used to the difference in the light,' he said, 'but it is hot and you have to be able to get up early in the morning and survive a whole day of hard graft, then get up and do it again the next day.'[28]

Carlyle, offered his part in a phone call from Loach, also had to learn to drive a bus, which meant taking an intensive, one-week course, with a test on the Friday. 'I have no fucking idea how I passed that,' he recalled, 'but I had to because I was carrying nine or ten people on a double-decker. There was no pressure put on me to do it, though.'[29] After his experience in *Riff-Raff*, the actor was ready for Loach-style surprises. Whereas he was unaware of his girlfriend's drug habit in that film until he walked in on her injecting heroin, here he discovered Carla floating in a bath of blood after attempting suicide. 'That was as big a shock to me as if it had really happened,' said Carlyle. 'It was completely out of the fucking blue. Then, in Nicaragua, the next big shock was that Carla had a baby. I didn't see that coming. The scene where she has the baby in her arms is my favourite that I've done with Ken because the emotion is so raw; it transcends acting.'[30]

During the second shoot in Nicaragua, filming took place in Managua and in Estelí and Ducale in the north, requiring a road trip along the Pan American Highway, which was still bandit country. Some critics complained that the second half of the film was less coherent than what had gone before, but it still won the President of the Italian Senate's Gold Medal at the Venice Film Festival and the Coral award at the Havana Film Festival.

By the time of *Carla's Song*, the Nicaraguan revolution was no longer even a flickering flame. Years of American sanctions had worn down the people, some of whom regarded the Sandinistas as having become too arrogant. In 1990 elections, the Sandinistas narrowly won more votes than any other single party, but a new government was formed by a coalition led by the American-backed candidate, Violeta Chamorro, who represented the power and privilege of the old Nicaragua. Within a decade, the country's achievements of the 1980s had disappeared and it sank to become the second poorest country in the region, after Haiti.

Closer to home, another light going out was the ability of workers to unite and protect their jobs, as they attempted in *The Big Flame*. Loach returned to documentary-making in 1996 to give a voice to 329 Liverpool dockers who had been sacked the previous year after refusing to cross a picket line; their jobs had been taken by non-union labour. *The Flickering Flame* was screened twenty-seven years after *The Big Flame* and reflected the weakened position of workers after the onslaught of Thatcherism, mass unemployment and anti-union laws. It told a story that had been largely ignored by the media and, in highlighting the betrayal of the dockers by national union leaders, was familiar to those who followed Loach's work.

Parallax made the documentary, with Rebecca O'Brien producing 'by fax' while still working on *Bean* in Los Angeles. Turned down by Channel Four, *The Flickering Flame*, subtitled 'A Story of Contemporary Morality', was screened in BBC2's 'Modern Times' series, becoming Loach's first documentary for the Corporation, where he had started his television career. Times had certainly changed over three decades but, in the dockers, Loach recognised the fire he had witnessed previously in Liverpool people. He also followed their wives, who united in the Women of the Waterfront support group, standing up like those in the miners' strike, as they travelled to the TUC conference in Blackpool and confronted Transport and General Workers' Union general secretary Bill Morris, who had refused to make the dispute official.

'It's such a strong culture and they're very conscious of their industrial heritage,' said Loach. 'The spirit of the times was very different. The unions and militant trade unionism were seen as out of date and coming from a position of weakness. In the early Eighties, it looked as if Thatcher was going to win the day; in the mid-Nineties, it was almost all over and people had the sense that they were going to lose. I hope the film was a record of those people at that time and what was at stake with the introduction of agency working and casualised and deregulated labour.'[31]

Loach's disappointment with the Labour Party, in which he had put his faith back in 1964, had already led him to leave after thirty years. 'I joined Labour to be part of the Left of the party,' he explained. 'I kept paying the subs and went through various periods of activity. But now it was a question of where those left-wing politics were going to be articulated.'[32] Shortly after his membership lapsed, Loach made a last-ditch effort to re-ignite socialism by directing a twenty-two-minute film for the Clause IV Campaign Group. *A Contemporary Case for Common Ownership*, released in February 1995, was an attempt to stop new Labour leader Tony Blair's plans to abandon the party's constitutional commitment to nationalisation of basic industries.

Blair's victory, along with so-called New Labour's increasing alignment with the business community and free-market economic policies, led some members to desert and join the Socialist Labour Party, founded by Arthur Scargill in 1996. Although Loach never threw in his lot with that party, he directed a political broadcast for Socialist Labour in the following year's General Election. After Labour's win, a return to power after eighteen years in the wilderness, Loach was one of the arts community approached by the Foreign Office to be included on a Planet Britain CD-Rom and website promoting the country's 'Cool Britannia' culture. Unfortunately, the civil servants did not take kindly to the witty, slightly tongue-in-cheek mini-biography that Loach submitted. A reference to his recurring theme of exposing 'the two curses of the labour movement: Stalinism and Social Democracy, the latter exemplified by the Blairite project of trying to give a radical gloss to hard-line capitalist politics' was, presumably, what offended them; it was not used.[33] (In 2004, Loach unsuccessfully stood in London as a Euro MP for Respect, the new political party that was formed out of the Stop the War Coalition group, which he had supported since it began protesting against any planned invasion of Iraq by the United States and Britain.)

One non-political cause close to Loach's own heart, Bath City Football Club, became slightly more political when, in 1998, he became a director. The majority shareholder installed a new board made up of supporters from the terraces when the club was in financial difficulties. Ricky Tomlinson travelled from Liverpool to perform a stand-up comedy fundraiser, and Loach even made a half-hour documentary for his regional ITV station, screened in the HTV West area only. *Another City: A Week in the Life of Bath's Football Club* followed the team on and off the pitch, and Loach organised a gathering of former players and managers, some of whom had gone on to find success in the Football League, including Malcolm Allison and Tony Book. The unending admiration for Loach in France was confirmed by the screening of the film on television there, too. Back in Bath, the supporters' participation in the business had an air of the dockers taking over the port of Liverpool in *The Big Flame*.

19

ATLANTIC CROSSING

AS WITH THE LIVERPOOL dockers, the resolve of the human spirit to fight back shines through in *My Name Is Joe*, the story of an alcoholic's attempts to escape his past and create a new life through his relationship with a health visitor. Paul Laverty's second script for Ken Loach was, like *Riff-Raff*, *Raining Stones* and *Ladybird Ladybird*, a reminder of forgotten areas of British society in the 1990s. 'At the end of the shoot for *Carla's Song* in Nicaragua, we were absolutely drained,' recalled Laverty. 'On the last day, Ken said: "Maybe we should do a little film back home." He wanted to do a story set in Glasgow and I had an idea of writing something very intimate, a complicated love story. So I went to a wee, quiet place in the south of Nicaragua, a fishing village called San Juan del Sur, and came up with the characters of Joe and Sarah.'[1]

Joe was another person exorcising demons, surrounded by inner-city housing estates, unemployment, drug-taking and crime. A romance develops with Sarah through her involvement with his friends Liam, just out of jail for drug-dealing, and Sabine, who is a drug addict and on the game; they have a baby boy and are in debt. Joe ends up helping Liam, who is in the football team of unemployed men that he coaches, by transporting drugs for the local dealer, jeopardising his own romance if he is found out. Before the shock of Liam's suicide – he jumps from a window rather than face the wrath of the drug king's mob – Joe remonstrates with Sarah but finds their class differences too wide to unite them: 'Ah'm really sorry, but you know I don't live in this nice, tidy, wee world of yours. You know, some of us cannae go tae the polis, some of us cannae go tae the bank for a loan, some of us cannae just move hoose and fuck off out of here. Some of us don't have a choice. I didnae have a fuckin' choice.'

In presenting Joe as a sympathetic character, Laverty takes up a Loach theme of not imposing middle-class values and moral judgements, as in *Ladybird Ladybird* and, further back, *Cathy Come Home*, *Kes* and *Family Life*, but he also succeeds in eliciting some sympathy for Sarah as the caring professional, which makes for a rich drama with real-life shades of grey and no black-and-white answers.

Once he had created his two main characters and was given the go-ahead by Loach, Laverty returned to Scotland and, with no current home there, rented a room in a church house in Glasgow's Ruchill district. The writer regarded the city as his home, having moved there as a child after being born in Calcutta; he had actually studied for the priesthood before deciding on law as a career. To research his new story, Laverty trudged the streets for several months, speaking to community workers, current and former drug addicts, and ex-prostitutes, before writing the script. 'Paul's writing is always very good, but it's more instinctive when he is writing in his own idiom,' said Loach.[2]

Peter Mullan, who played Joe and was born in Peterhead but raised in Glasgow, had previously acted Robert Carlyle's brother in the cremation scene of *Riff-Raff*. 'I clocked him then,' said Loach, 'and he was at the back of our minds when we were casting Joe, but I felt I should see everybody, so I did go through lots of other people, but Peter had a really special quality we couldn't find in anyone else.'[3] Similarly, in casting Louise Goodall as Sarah, Loach, attracted by her 'authenticity and warmth',[4] opted for an actress who had taken a small role, as Robert Carlyle's dumped girlfriend, in *Carla's Song*. Others in the cast included Lorraine McIntosh, a former singer with the Scottish group Deacon Blue, as Maggie, Sarah's colleague at the health centre, and David Hayman, an actor known for tough, gritty roles on stage and screen, as McGowan, the gangland boss.

With *My Name Is Joe*, the partnership of Loach, Laverty and producer Rebecca O'Brien was cemented. 'Paul became a very important person in the whole mix,' said O'Brien. 'He is so overtly political and so full of energy – an energy that matches Ken's very well. If you get a combination of people right, it's a joy working together, so you do more. There's always a desire to work with other writers as well, but Jim Allen was on the wane then and we were developing a project with him that never saw the light of day. Jim was a wonderful writer with a very good ear and very funny.'[5] O'Brien built on the foundations of Sally Hibbin's methods of financing and succeeded in achieving further pre-sales abroad. 'You raise lots of bits of funding, so no one has overall control,' she explained.[6] Channel Four paid for initial development and British television rights, then Parallax and Road Movies funded the £2,700,000 production and raised money through a string of pre-sales, as well as £500,000 of Scottish Lottery money and £100,000 from the Glasgow Film Fund.

After several drafts, with valuable input from Roger Smith, who took on the regular role of script consultant, Laverty's screenplay was ready. Some of the amendments were made after checking facts and procedures with local community worker John Hamill, who chairs the Alcoholics Anonymous meeting that opens the film, and Stef McBride, a rehabilitated heroin addict who advised on the props needed and injecting methods for the drug scenes. A former prostitute took David McKay and AnneMarie Kennedy, who played Liam and Sabine, to Anderson, Glasgow's red-light district. 'Film-makers often forget to talk to real people and not many films about the drug culture bother to get it right,' she said.[7] Loach's critics continued to accuse him of making the same films as he was thirty years earlier, but My Name Is Joe, while still portraying the underbelly of British society, was right up to date, a story of the 1990s.

Yet it proved difficult to secure the services of Peter Mullan, who had previously appeared in the cult hit Trainspotting, another drug-culture film set in Scotland. He was directing his own film, Orphans, for Channel Four and still had editing work to do on it. Eventually, Parallax paid the costs of putting the editing on hold and he prepared himself for My Name Is Joe by meeting Alcoholics Anonymous members. 'My father was an alcoholic – and various memories came back,' revealed the actor.[8] Goodall could draw on her husband's experience as a psychiatric nurse who 'detoxed' drug addicts and alcoholics, and she shadowed a health visitor from Drumchapel Health Centre, near Ruchill, for four weeks. 'It opened my eyes up about poverty and people who haven't been educated very well and are trapped within poverty, people who didn't have all the support that I had when I had my kids or the knowledge of what to do,' she said.[9]

Another part of Goodall's preparation was taking driving lessons. 'I'm the worst driver in the world,' she said. 'I had thirty lessons and I still wasn't ready for my test.' This restricted filming of a scene in which Sarah drives off from the health centre car park. The actress recalled, 'Ken told me: "Just get in the car with Peter, drive off and, once you're out, with the pavement next to you, stop because you haven't passed your test." I got in, turned on the ignition and drove badly, then got out of the car and never switched anything off. So the car kept going and I started chasing after the car and it almost got hit by a bus. Then it crashed into a woman's car outside her house and she came out screaming. I was crying and laughing at the same time! I thought: "I can't look back. Ken will be so angry." But I looked back and he was absolutely in stitches.'[10]

Realism collided with reality on the streets of Glasgow several times. During the first week of the six-week shoot, camera equipment worth several thousand pounds was stolen from a crew van. Within hours, it was recovered by a burly security guard hired from the local community who knew where to ask about it. 'You can't blame us,' said one youngster. 'We saw an opportunity and we took it.'[11]

When it came to some of the screen characters themselves indulging in robbery, taking football shirts from a sports depot, with the film crew well out of sight, there was a *déjà vu* shock for Gordon McMurray, a former heroin addict who played one of the team members. 'Ken had told most of us what was going to happen and gave us a basic script,' recalled Simon Macallum, another of the gang. 'Peter Mullan didn't know. His brief was that we were going to go for a drive, so he was taken by surprise on the first take of that scene when we were breaking into the warehouse. An old woman and her son were wandering back and thought a real robbery was taking place. Ken kept the camera rolling and shot her reaction, although in the end he didn't use it. Then he did the same scene with Gordon as a lookout for the robbery. We were supposed to stop and pick him up, but Ken told us to drive off. Suddenly, a police car appeared and they hauled Gordon, who was well known about those parts, into the back.'[12] The officers, unable to see signs of Hollywood-style activity, were not swayed by McMurray's pleas that he was acting in a film, but an assistant director moved swiftly to back up his story.

Filming ended in the autumn of 1997 and *My Name Is Joe* was edited in time to receive its premiere at the following year's Cannes Film Festival, where Peter Mullan won the Best Actor award. He subsequently gained respect not just as an actor, but as a director of films such as *The Magdalene Sisters*. Among a dozen international prizes, *My Name Is Joe* swept the board at the British Independent Film Awards, taking the Best Director, Best British Film and Best Original Screenplay honours.

Peter Mullan in
My Name Is Joe
[Barry Ackroyd/
Parallax Pictures-Road
Movies-Tornasol/Alta
Films]

The Loach–Laverty–O'Brien bandwagon rolled on, with another trip abroad – in spitting distance of Hollywood. As with *Land and Freedom*, it took a British director to tell the story of those in another land to its own people. Forty-five per cent of the Los Angeles population was Hispanic, but this was never reflected in Tinseltown. *Bread and Roses* celebrated the struggles of immigrant workers, in a story based on the Justice for Janitors campaign, when cleaners finally stood up for their rights. Making a film showing the other side of Beverly Hills glamour and riches, Loach also took to the city a method of filming that was the antithesis of Hollywood practice.

Just as, two decades earlier, he had turned down a request to make television programmes about the American labour movement because he was unfamiliar with that environment, Loach rejected an offer from celebrated director Robert Duvall to make a film there after finishing work on *Carla's Song*. 'I had some offers from America after making *Poor Cow* and *Kes*, but I couldn't see any way of going there and doing the kind of work I wanted to do,' he said. '*Bread and Roses* was a serious challenge, and a challenge I just felt I couldn't duck. Once I'd met the janitors and we found one or two of the actors, I started to feel a loyalty to them, but it was hard work.'[13]

The cleaners' story might never have found its way to a world-wide audience but for Paul Laverty taking up a Fulbright writing scholarship at the University of California, Los Angeles, after scripting *Carla's Song* and waiting for that film to go into production. Living in the city's downtown area, he rented a room in a house just off MacArthur Park, living alongside some illegal Mexican immigrants. At two-thirty one morning, as he stood at a bus stop, Laverty found himself surrounded by people, mostly women, speaking Spanish and dressed in the uniforms of their job. As he began talking to them in their own language, he discovered a hidden population that provided a necessary service to enable large corporations to continue making billions of dollars while they remained on starvation wages. These workers had taken on the might of American corporate power in the Justice for Janitors campaign. It was started by the service employees' union in 1985 and gained nationwide awareness five years later when demonstrations and pickets in Los Angeles spread across the country. Gradually, the union won victories: better wages, holiday pay, health insurance and job security.

'In my first draft, it was set ten years back, to coincide with a huge Justice for Janitors march in which the police attacked the unions and the workers,' said Laverty. 'We contemplated building up to that march and having a huge riot at the end, but that would have made the film much more expensive and maybe lopsided. In the end, we made it contemporary, but we looked back to that march and showed footage of it. That made it much more manageable and it probably works better.'[14] The footage, showing police wielding truncheons and injuring dozens of demonstrators, was reminiscent of that in Loach's miners documentary, *Which Side Are You On?*, and news film of the Sharpeville massacre in apartheid South Africa. Laverty called the film *Bread and Roses*, after an old strikers' refrain, 'We want bread and roses, too', bread being a metaphor for wages and roses for respect.

Compared with the rate of his film-making during the 1990s, an unusual gap preceded the *Bread and Roses* shoot; setting it up took a long time, with Loach travelling to and from Los Angeles for more than a year. 'I knew *Bread and Roses* was on the cards when I agreed to produce *Bean*, which was shot in LA,' said Rebecca O'Brien. 'So I used *Bean* as a training ground for how to work there and learned about the very industrialised nature of film-making there and the fact that every blade of grass has a lawyer. It's a very obstructive system. I said to Ken: "Brace yourself!" *Bread and Roses* was the most difficult film to make and, ironically, for a film about unions, it cost too much because we had to make it under Hollywood union rules. I had to convince the Screen Actors Guild that we couldn't find all the cast by using actors and we needed some of the real janitors. In the end, they came round to it.'[15]

Astonishingly, for a picture with a large cast needed each day, most of them Spanish-speaking, and some scenes that took time to organise, *Bread and Roses* was shot in thirty days – six five-day weeks – which was several days fewer than for more straightfor-ward Loach productions. Also, the director was working with an American crew – 50 per cent bigger than his usual ones – that found his methods and practices totally foreign to them. 'It was com-pletely different from working in Spain,' explained Loach. 'They are set in their ways, very bureaucratic and hierarchical, and quite timid in not questioning the way they do things. They've learned not to be interested in the film; they are just hired to do their job and go home. But there were a dozen or more who were really brilliant, committed, hardworking and talented.'[16]

Loach and his regular creative team of Barry Ackroyd, Ray Beckett and Martin Johnson held firmly to their principles and indoctrinated the Los Angeles crew into their way of working. The first idea that the technicians found anathema was shooting in sequence. Some recalled that the last director to do this was John

Cassavetes, and the one before that Charlie Chaplin. First assistant director Ricardo Méndez Matta, who, after fifteen years of learning established Hollywood practices, was responsible for relaying to the crew what Loach wanted, recalled, 'I threw everything I knew out of the window and got ready for a new learning experience.'[17] Loach showed from the start how he worked by leaving most of the technicians in Los Angeles on the first day of filming while he travelled to the Mexican border to shoot the opening scene of immigrants being driven across illegally; Ackroyd, with his shaky, handheld camera recalling those pioneering days of 'The Wednesday Play', was just one of six crew members used. Although Loach had left behind that method of filming, it provided the suspense necessary to portray the desperate desire of many to earn money in the United States to send back to their families in Central and South America.

The story centres on two Mexican sisters. Maya makes it across the border to follow in the big adventure undertaken by Rosa, who is already settled in Los Angeles with a husband and children. After getting a job at the office block in which Rosa works, Maya shows her fiery, rebellious spirit by joining a union organiser's campaign to win better pay and conditions for the cleaners: by putting pressure on the wealthy businesses that rent the offices, they hope to win over their own employers.

Casting the largely Spanish-speaking roles was a daunting task, and Loach put actors alongside real-life cleaners. He was helped by Pablo Cruz, who spent almost a year with the Justice for Janitors campaigners, identifying individuals who might be suitable. Cruz also found Jornaleros del Norte, a group that provides the music at a party on the union's premises in the film.

Through auditions, Loach was able to cast American-based Mexican actress Elpidia Carrillo as elder sister Rosa; she had appeared in dozens of Hollywood films, including *The Border* and *Salvador*. But he had greater difficulty in filling the critical role of Maya. 'I couldn't find anyone in Los Angeles who didn't look as if they had been Americanised,' recalled Loach, 'so Paul and I went to Mexico City and saw thirty people. On the third day, we were doing call-backs and we asked a girl we liked, but whose English wasn't very good, to do a scenario opposite the others we had shortlisted and she was so much better than anyone else.'[18] As a result, Mexican stage actress Pilar Padilla attended an intensive, two-month English course in San Francisco before filming began in October 1999. Union organiser Sam was another role difficult to cast. Loach saw hundreds of actors but was eventually drawn to the mischievous air exuded by Adrien Brody, who was building up an impressive CV, having acted in films for directors such as Spike Lee, Barry Levinson, Terrence Malick and Steven Soderbergh. (Four years later, he won a Best Actor Oscar for *The Pianist*.) To prepare himself for the role, Brody met union members, took part in marches and attended a weekend course in union organisation.

In Los Angeles, when Loach was approached by Soderbergh with a request for permission to use clips from *Poor Cow* in his film *The Limey*, the American director also helped the Englishman abroad to assemble the crew for *Bread and Roses*. While there, Loach was able to visit one of his *Hidden Agenda* stars, Frances McDormand, and borrow her ironing board. The familiar leather jacket disappeared for this shoot in the California heat and he wore shirts with sleeves rolled up – and, sometimes, a sun hat.

With his army of cleaners, Loach once more gathered a group who established a camaraderie throughout filming, as in the story. The American crew were immediately introduced to his egalitarian practices when a parking space was designated for him and marked, 'Director Ken Loach'. 'The first thing Ken said when he saw it,' recalled Barry Ackroyd, 'was: "I don't think we can do that." Five minutes later, everybody's names had gone off the parking spaces. He said: "We will share the parking spaces. Whoever gets here will have them." The Americans quite like the hierarchy, but we prefer to break that down a bit.'[19]

Two major setpieces required meticulous planning. One was a scene in which a party to celebrate the merger of two Hollywood talent agencies was disrupted by the cleaners as part of their protest campaign. Real actors such as Benicio Del Toro, Chris Penn, Ron Perlman, Tim Roth and Sam West appeared as themselves and mayhem erupted when the cleaners brought their equipment out. 'We just rang around to find friends of friends,' said Loach, 'but I really screwed that up. We were in a location that just wasn't big enough. It really needed more scale to make it a bigger do, but we had run out of money.'[20] The other feat of organisation came with the re-creation of a Justice for Janitors demonstration in a street in

Los Angeles' financial district, before the marching cleaners stormed the office block. Two hundred extras took part and a German television crew covering the making of the film were themselves cast as a local news team.

For such scenes with large numbers of people, a second unit was needed for filming. Barry Ackroyd asked documentary-maker Nick Broomfield's camera operator, Joan Churchill, to join the crew, but she sprained a muscle at the last minute. 'She then told me she had asked her friend Haskell Wexler to do it,' recalled Ackroyd. 'I said: "Haskell Wexler?" He is one of the greatest directors of photography in America, who shot *One Flew Over the Cuckoo's Nest* and worked on *American Graffiti*. She said he was really keen. He brought along a laser disc of *Ladybird Ladybird*, asked me to sign it and said: "You and Ken are my heroes. How you do this, I don't know." '[21]

Bread and Roses was recognised on both sides of the Atlantic for the case it was putting, although it is not one of Loach's greatest films, perhaps partly a reflection of working in a foreign land whose dominant culture is anathema to his own sensibilities; he later acknowledged that his work on the picture 'wasn't quite sharp enough'.[22] Certainly, the film sits alongside his television plays *The Big Flame* and *The Rank and File* as a document showing the spirit that makes workers unite in an attempt to improve their lot. Once more, though, the optimism is combined with a very un-Hollywood ending. Maya is deported as an illegal immigrant involved in the demonstration, after Rosa shockingly reveals the depths to which she has sunk in the land of the American Dream: she worked as a prostitute to pay for Maya's education and maintain her own family, and slept with the supervisor to get her sister the job in the office block.

Just as Loach and Laverty had taken *Carla's Song* back to Nicaragua for people to see the results of their filming in that country, they organised the American premiere at a cinema in the Avenue of the Stars, Century City, on 16 June 2000, ten years to the day after the first famous Justice for Janitors march had taken place there, outside office blocks that house large media companies, Hollywood agents and other major businesses. Many who had lived through that decade attended the screening, providing an afternoon of laughs and cheers, before going to their night shifts.

Bread and Roses went on to win the Best Foreign Film award at the Rio de Janeiro Film Festival and the Phoenix Prize at the Santa Barbara International Film Festival, and Elpidia Carrillo was named Outstanding Supporting Actress in the ALMA (American Latino Media Arts) Awards.

In the meantime, Loach was on the move back in his own country, making his home in London again after twenty-six years in Bath; domestic issues such as having children and grandchildren there were just as important as the fact that he was busier than ever in the capital. Leaving their Georgian house in Bath, Loach and his wife returned to the same Georgian terrace in Kentish Town where they had previously lived and sold the nearby flat they had maintained in London. 'We'd always had a passion for old houses, repairing the fabric as well as possible,' said Loach. 'Luckily, we got on the ladder with the money from *Poor Cow* and borrowed from then on!'[23]

By the time of the Loaches' move back to London, their son Jim had, without encouragement, followed his father's career path. After working as a researcher at the BBC, he directed television serials such as *Coronation Street* and *Hollyoaks* and the popular drama series *Bad Girls*. Younger daughter Emma trod a similar route, becoming a producer and researcher of documentaries, while Stephen was a solicitor and Hannah a musician.

There was a return of other sorts when Loach headed for South Yorkshire to make his next film. After the rigours of shooting in Los Angeles with a large crew, he was keen to work on a small-scale production. In fact, *The Navigators* was set up in a similar way to *Riff-Raff*, commissioned as a television film by Channel Four in Britain but distributed in cinemas abroad. Like that previous picture, it was a social comedy featuring a group of workers, this time railwaymen working on track maintenance. *The Navigators* also proved very timely: just as Loach was staging a derailment in South Yorkshire, a real-life tragedy was unfolding just north of London, when a train travelling at 115mph careered off the track as a rail shattered into 300 pieces at Hatfield; four people died.

This followed Britain's worst rail disaster of recent times, exactly a year earlier. Two trains collided near Paddington station, in London, after one had gone through a red signal; thirty-one people died. Railtrack, which had been responsible for the line since the privatisation of British Rail, was blamed, having failed to respond to warnings that at least eight previous trains had gone through red lights on the route. Similarly, a cracked rail resulting from Rail-track's poor maintenance was cited as the cause of the Hatfield crash. In October 2001, the government stopped funding Railtrack and later replaced it with the not-for-profit company Network Rail. Later, manslaughter charges were brought against the engineering contractor, Balfour Beatty.

The railways fiasco followed the 1996 privatisation, when British Rail was effectively replaced by more than 100 different companies. Railtrack was in charge of track maintenance, train operating companies ran the services and leasing companies were responsible for rolling stock. By 1997, the number of railway workers fell from 159,000 to 92,000 and track maintenance staff from 31,000 to fewer than 20,000.

One South Yorkshire rail worker, Rob Dawber, wanted to tell the horror story of privatisation from the point of view of those working under the new system. He had long been an activist in the National Union of Railwaymen and vented the anger of many through his Fat Controller column in its journal, *Off the Rails*. 'Rob wrote in,' explained Loach, 'and he was very persistent, saying: "You have to do this." It was carrying on the idea from *The Flickering Flame*, about how work was changing and the confidence trick of how they had been persuaded to vote for their own destruction or go along with it. I like stories with a group, a team of actors, and a very specific location, rooted in one place.'[24] Also like *The Flickering Flame*, the resulting film showed the move away from secure jobs to casual labour, without holiday or sick pay, or a guaranteed regular income.

Dawber had been a track worker for eighteen years, until privatisation arrived and he was made redundant. Eleven days after receiving the screenplay commission, he was diagnosed with mesothelioma, an incurable cancer caused by exposure to asbestos in his job. Doctors gave him six months to live, but he survived a further two years. During that time, Loach and producer Rebecca O'Brien gave evidence in court about his likely future earnings as a writer that helped to win him £450,000 in compensation.

Loach and Roger Smith worked with Dawber on the script for *The Navigators*, a title not just reflecting the way in which track workers 'navigated' through the new problems, but also paying tribute to the navvies who constructed the railways in the nine-teenth century. The subtitle 'Tales from the trackside' indicated the mosaic of stories and experiences encapsulated in the film. Barry Hines, credited as script editor, was also on hand in Yorkshire to give useful advice to Dawber.

In line with his casting for *Kes* and *The Price of Coal*, both written by Hines, Loach teamed professional actors with Northern club entertainers to form his main group of modern-day navvies. Steve Huison's face was already known to worldwide audiences through his role in *The Full Monty*, a more romanticised take on unemployment, and Tom Craig played a paper factory owner in the feelgood television series *Where the Heart Is*, but, at the time, Joe Duttine was less well known on screen. To these Yorkshire actors Loach added Dean Andrews, Venn Tracey, Sean Glenn and Charlie Brown, whose instant wit added to the humour in the script.

Preparations were made for the five-week shoot in the autumn of 2000. As his own life ebbed away, Dawber saw new life breathed into the depot near Doncaster where he once worked. Loach's 'navvies' also prepared for their roles by taking a course that would earn each of them a Personal Track Safety card. 'A week before filming started, we had five days in Doncaster, learning to do the safety exam to work on the tracks,' recalled Tom Craig. 'That was doing our background without realising we were doing it, as we chatted with the lads there. We were surprised how easy it is to have an accident on the trains; so many who work on it die each year. Those 125 trains sneak up behind you and you don't hear them. We saw videos about how easy it is to have a fatal accident on the railways. Anybody can get the ticket that we got in a week and work on the railways.'[25]

Agonisingly for Loach, he had to shoot scenes of his gang working on the line out of sequence because access and use of rolling stock was limited. The usual Loach 'surprises' came thick and fast, though. As one train went speeding past, the men were sprayed with excrement from the toilet – not the real thing, but a mix that still caused them to disperse in all directions. Sean Glenn, a theatrical agent who performed in clubs and had television experi-ence in bit-parts and as an extra, immediately found his authority role as the depot supervisor being lampooned. 'I went in with my clipboard to tell the men about the break-up of British Rail and that they were now working for a different company,' he recalled. 'But Ken hadn't warned me that he told them to react like a rabble. I thought they would jump to attention, but they were cat-calling and sending me up. The hardest thing was to deliver the line: "We must keep deaths to an acceptable level." I don't know how I said it with a straight face.'[26]

It was equally a surprise for Charlie Brown, whose club act as a singer-comedian was as clean as a whistle, to be cast in the role of a foul-mouthed cleaner. 'Most of my action took place in the canteen,' he said. 'The others wouldn't know what I was going to say and I would come in, F-ing and blinding. They were all gobsmacked and, eventually, all laughing their heads off. I was cleaning up the canteen and there were a lot of extras there sitting at the tables. Ken came up to me and said: "The guy in the check shirt – when you are sweeping up, whack him on the ankle with your brush." I looked at him. "It will be all right," he said. I did, and he got the reaction he wanted.'[27]

Filming Tom Craig and Angela Saville in bed provided more impromptu entertainment. 'There was a scene with me and my wife trying to have sex when my mate's in the other room and she's not on for it,' recalled Craig. 'The camera was in the bedroom, but Ken was round the corner in the corridor. He doesn't like to bring film terms to the set, like "Action!" or "Cut!" He just says: "And away you go." When everything was ready, Ken said: "Away you go!" He then realised what he'd said and chuckled a bit. Before the scene, he had whispered to me: "Unbutton her top and start kissing her breasts." I said: "Have you told her?" And he said: "No!" She was all right, though!'[28]

Like Craig, who had six years' experience as a plumber, Steve Huison had a background in manual labour, having worked as a plasterer on leaving school. He observed the director in action, getting the best from his cast. 'I was talking to one of the other characters who was played by a comedian and over time, with each take, his reply was becoming more wooden and you could tell he wasn't listening to what I was saying,' recalled Huison. 'Ken doesn't watch a lot of the takes but listens to them and can hear the truth in the performance. Just before the fifth take, he said to me: "When he says the line to you, pretend you can't hear him and get him to repeat it." So I said: "Sorry, what did you say?"

It shocked him into realising he wasn't listening. I employed that technique afterwards with an actor on television, in *Peak Practice*.'[29]

Rob Dawber, who had a cameo as a track worker at the scene of the derailment, never lived to see *The Navigators*' release, but he enjoyed sitting alongside Loach in the editing room. Most of the track gang from the film visited, too – a practice that had begun with *Land and Freedom*. 'There were short bits of film hanging up all over the place,' said Sean Glenn.[30] Film editor Jonathan Morris revealed, 'I usually edit on a computer. The only time I don't is when I work with Ken and we edit in the old-fashioned way, handling the film, splicing it, marking it up with a Chinagraph pen and joining it together with tape. When we are cutting bits, we peg them in the film bin and can find any frame in seconds.'[31] Dawber viewed an early cut of the edited film shortly before his death, in February 2001.

The picture, which Parallax co-produced with Road Movies and Spanish companies Tornasol and Alta, did particularly well in France, where Loach continued to have a loyal following, almost thirty years after *Family Life* was so well received there. Before its Channel Four screening, it won the Children and Cinema Award at the Venice Film Festival.

20

A CHANGING WORLD

KEN LOACH'S NEXT excursion was to Scotland. Like *My Name Is Joe*, *Sweet Sixteen* was a gritty drama written by Paul Laverty, set in streets where children are prey to the lure of drug barons. The sharp focus on a central character and the dilemmas he has to face made it one of Loach's strongest films. More than thirty years after David Bradley embodied the hopes and unrecognised talents of a Yorkshire schoolboy in *Kes*, young Martin Compston lived the role of Liam, a youngster approaching his sixteenth birthday and the release from prison of his drug-addicted mother. He longs for a family life again and wants to buy a caravan on the coast, where he can live with his mother and sister. Again, optimism and resourcefulness were demonstrated, but the Clydeside location of *Sweet Sixteen* reflected a crueller world, where drugs are the currency – more readily available than jobs. Liam's admirable plans are dependent on money, so he sells drugs and sinks deeper into the mire.

'It was a development of *My Name Is Joe*,' explained Loach. 'It was the kids in the football team that sparked it. We had met a lot of them in various anti-drugs projects. In a way, they were demanding attention then and we couldn't explore their situation at the time because we were concerned with Joe.'[1] Laverty was aware of the problems confronting young people in that region of Scotland. 'I was very interested in the choices teenagers were facing and making,' he said, 'especially in that area, because jobs were crap – either service industries or retail, like McDonald's. I heard there were kids who were not using drugs, but dealing in drugs and making fortunes; there was the story of a girl who bought her own house. It says a lot about society when we only have the freedom to do that and take that risk.'[2]

Loach was attracted not just to Laverty's story, but to the landscape in Greenock, with the contradiction of poor housing looking out over the River Clyde and to the hills and mountains. It was a view familiar to Laverty, who had lived there while studying law. Over the years, he saw the prospects for young people in the area change dramatically. 'Fifty years ago, people were having apprenticeships,' he explained. 'They had money at the end of the week, the discipline of working with colleagues – a shape to their lives. Now, you go there and it's call centres or kids working on one-day contracts. I spent a lot of time there and talked and talked to kids who were selling drugs, before writing the first draft.'[3] As he visited schools, boxing clubs and children's homes, Laverty found a very receptive audience. Many told him that they had seen *My Name Is Joe* on video, despite its 15 certificate, and they found that the characters spoke like them.

Loach with Martin Compston on the set of *Sweet Sixteen*
[Joss Barratt/Sixteen Films-Road Movies-Tornasol/Alta Films]

The 'kids in the football team' idea followed through in the casting of *Sweet Sixteen*. After seeing hundreds of teenagers over several weeks, Loach found his Liam. Seventeen-year-old Martin Compston was in a school team in the town and an apprentice with the local Scottish League side, Greenock Morton, having joined it at the age of twelve. He had no experience of the close-to-the-edge existence endured by Liam, but had grown up surrounded by people who had. 'I come from a very nice family and have never really struggled for anything,' he said. 'I'd never been in Liam's position but, living in Greenock, you can't avoid people like that and you can relate to it. It makes you realise how easy it could be for anyone without strong family support to go wayward.'[4]

Compston was also familiar with some of Loach's work, if not the director himself. 'I loved films like *Kes* and *My Name Is Joe*,' he said. 'But I was terrified going to the audition. I walked in and saw this old man sitting behind a table, but he is such a quality guy. He chatted away to us about our football and school, and asked us to do improvisations. I knew they were looking for streetwise, working-class lads. I did about five auditions before I was offered the part, but I was thinking about my football. I said I'd just earned my full-time contract with Morton and I didn't want to do anything to disrupt it. Ken said he would sort it out with the club. He did that and I was still able to sign my contract.'[5]

Liam's mother was a role that was even more difficult to cast, but Loach eventually found Michelle Coulter, who had never previously acted but had experience of helping to rehabilitate women with drugs problems. Jon Morrison, an actor with a reputation for playing hard men on screen, with roles in films such as *Nil By Mouth*, played the drugs baron.

As Loach called the cast together for a week's rehearsals before shooting over six very rainy weeks in the autumn of 2001, his mother, Vivien, died at the age of ninety-three. She had lived for twenty-eight years after the death of his father, Jack, who encouraged his son to take advantage of the educational opportunities that he himself had been denied. Now they were both gone. Rehearsals were called off, but filming went ahead as planned. Despite his own sadness, Loach gave a guiding hand to his young cast in his usual caring way. 'Ken made me feel really at ease,' recalled Compston. 'He took all the pressure off.'[6]

But the teenager felt all the pressure on when he had to perform a scene in a nightclub. Liam, acting as a runner for the drugs king, is told to kill a man in a toilet with a lethal knife. 'I had been working all day with Ken and a stuntman on how I was going to stab him,' explained Compston. 'So I was all psyched up. Then Ken said:

"One minute – we've got a camera problem." Unknown to me, all the gangsters were smuggled into the cubicle. As I went in, these guys started running at me. I started to crap myself, but it got the desired effect. All day, I had thought I was going to stab the guy, until they jumped out. It got to the point in filming where I didn't have a clue what I was doing a lot of the time, but I just went with the flow.'[7]

Gary McCormack, an actor who had left behind a previous career as a bass guitarist in punk bands, was warned that he had an experience of a lifetime ahead of him as he set off at the beginning of filming to play Liam's mother's drug-dealing boyfriend, who ends up being stabbed by the boy – on Liam's sixteenth birthday. 'I bumped into Peter Mullan, who starred in *My Name Is Joe*,' recalled McCormack. 'He said: "You will never work with a guy like that again. He is just fantastic." I had prepared for it by spending a day in Greenock, speaking to an ex-dealer, a junkie. Greenock does have a serious heroin problem and he told me he didn't want to do it if the film was going to glorify heroin.'[8]

Sweet Sixteen proved to be tough and, at times, painful to watch, a drama in the mould of *Raining Stones*, *Ladybird Ladybird* and *My Name Is Joe*. During the editing stages, a decision was made that laid itself open to criticism from all sides. Any cries that *Kes* should have featured subtitles were resurrected with *Sweet Sixteen* and there were long discussions about whether to use them to clarify the strong Scottish accents. The British distributor, Icon, was not keen to use subtitles, which can alienate mainstream cinemagoers, but Loach was equally keen to ensure that they understood what they were hearing, so it was eventually decided to subtitle the first reel – the opening fifteen minutes – to allow audiences to acclimatise themselves before being left to their own, attuned devices. (In the United States, subtitles appeared throughout.)

Subtitled or not, there was one word that the British Board of Film Classification did not like. Clearly, the very strong language made the film as authentic as walking the streets of real-life Greenock, but Loach, Laverty and Rebecca O'Brien did not believe that frequent use of the word 'cunt' warranted the issue of an 18 certificate. 'It was ridiculous,' said the producer. 'My son, who was eleven at the time, saw the film and said there was nothing that he had not heard in the school playground when he was eight. I'd never had dealings with the BBFC before. It was purely to satisfy Middle England. One of the great things about working with Ken is that there's always new territory, a new dilemma, a new issue.'[9] In a rare move, Inverclyde Council invoked its right as a local authority to overturn the decision in its area, reclassifying *Sweet Sixteen* with a 15 certificate so that those who were most prominently represented on screen could see the film in cinemas. Bristol, showing itself to be more liberal than other English authorities, made the same reclassification.

Abroad, there were no such problems. Indeed, at the film's Cannes premiere, *Sweet Sixteen* won Paul Laverty the Best Screenplay award. A string of honours followed, including the Golden Spike at the Valladolid International Film Festival, the international critics' FIPRESCI at the European Film Awards and the Best British Film prize at the British Independent Film Awards, at which Martin Compston was named Most Promising Newcomer. For Compston, the film was a life-changing event. Once work finished on *Sweet Sixteen*, he returned to play football for Morton but, after eight months and a trip to Cannes, decided that acting was his future. As a result, he transferred his on-pitch talents to the semi-professional Greenock Juniors and accepted offers of roles in television series.

It was also a time of change for Loach; *Sweet Sixteen* signalled his departure from Parallax Pictures. He and producer Rebecca O'Brien had evolved an exclusive working partnership together while Sally Hibbin was working on other films, so they left to set up their own company, which they called Sixteen Films. 'We had drifted apart and were working on our own projects,' said O'Brien.[10] Hibbin thought her own partnership with Loach, which had re-established his name in the first half of the 1990s, had exhausted itself. 'Ken and I had a very competitive relationship, which can be very stimulating or very draining,' she said. 'I remember we had a row in Glasgow, while doing *Carla's Song*, about where the production secretary should sit in the production office. When I saw *My Name Is Joe*, I knew that I couldn't have done another. It would have been treading the same ground, from a production point of view. But I felt Ken was now on a secure footing, as was Parallax.'[11]

A move around the corner from Parallax's Denmark Street offices in London's West End meant that Sixteen Films, with a handful of staff, was based in Wardour Street. It was the summer of 2002 and, with another Paul Laverty script already in development, there was a more immediate idea to go into production. An offer had come to make a short film that was part of a much bigger project allowing directors to respond to the events of the previous September the Eleventh. In the days and months following the attacks on New York's Twin Towers, the United States looked for wars to fight in revenge, and only a brave minority spoke out about the terror it had wreaked around the world over fifty years itself. Not surprisingly, Loach found himself in the firing line of right-wing critics for illuminating this hypocrisy. Alexander Walker, of the London *Evening Standard*, who had so vociferously labelled *Hidden Agenda* as pro-IRA, felt it 'brings shame on this country'.[12]

French producer Alain Brigand asked film-makers in eleven different countries to contribute a short, of exactly eleven minutes, nine seconds and one frame in length, to a compilation with the title *11′09″01 – September 11*. Each had a budget of 400,000 euros. Alexander Walker aside, Loach's 'United Kingdom' contribution was singled out by many critics as the standout film among a varied bunch.

After being approached, Loach remembered pages of manuscript he had received from Vladimir Vega, the Chilean exile who had starred with Crissy Rock in *Ladybird Ladybird*. Vega had begun writing a book about his terrifying experiences in his homeland after democratically elected president Salvador Allende was unseated in General Pinochet's coup, carried out with CIA backing on . . . September the Eleventh 1973. Here was an immediately relevant indictment of American foreign policy that explained resentment abroad, without condoning the horrors in New York.

Vega's experiences were conveyed in the form of a letter. As a victim of September the Eleventh in Chile, he writes to the victims of September the Eleventh in New York, saying they have something in common. Archive news film was used, so, for the only time on a Loach production, editor Jonathan Morris carried out his job on a computer, instead of cutting film manually.

The memories remained very real for Vega, who still had a knee injury sustained when he was shot in a gun battle with police on the day of the coup; he was just twenty. 'I was a member of the Socialist Party in Chile, young and idealistic,' he explained. 'I spent eleven or twelve days in hospital, with a guard. I was in horrible pain, but the nurses had orders not to approach us, although I was chained to the bed. Fortunately, I wasn't subjected to the worst of the torture, with electric shocks, but it was more psychological. They didn't allow me to sleep and there were constant threats every day. Finally, I was taken to a prison and put in a room with no windows for thirty or forty days, in solitary confinement. I was interrogated a couple of times, but it wasn't too bad.'[13] He was in prison for five years, until Pinochet declared an amnesty effectively making himself immune from prosecution for his crimes. Vega was given a visa to travel to Britain and settled in London in 1978.

Paul Laverty drafted a script based on his experiences, before Loach and Vega himself contributed to subsequent drafts. The Chilean also performed two of his songs, 'Missing' and 'Voices of Freedom'. 'After the filming, I was in a downward spiral emotionally because it really affected me a lot to live the situation again and what happened to me and my country,' he said. 'I found a piece of wood about thirty centimetres long and three centimetres wide and carved a face at the top, then an arm and a hand, and the lower part of a face with a spike through it and someone shouting in pain, then a broken skull, a broken guitar, a dead dove and an aboriginal person from the south of Chile with a nail through the hand. It described pain and torture, and the dove meant the peaceful country was destroyed. All my pain had to come out in some way. I put this on a wood platform so that it stood up and gave it to Ken. After that, I felt a lot better.'[14]

Meanwhile, Laverty produced the first draft script for Loach's next feature film, a modern-day *Romeo and Juliet* story set in Glasgow and influenced by events after September the Eleventh in New York. It told the story of a Catholic woman's relationship with a Pakistani man whose parents were born in Scotland. 'After September the Eleventh, there was so much Islamophobia, problems about asylum seekers and a tremendous sectarian atmosphere of condemning people,' explained Laverty. 'In the middle of all that, a friend of mine who is Scottish but Pakistani, with a Muslim background, born in England but having lived most of her life in

Scotland, said: "I will never feel at home here. I will always be a stranger here because of my colour and roots." This was someone I knew so well who loved this part of Glasgow the way I did but, because of her colour, she felt isolated. Many like her felt under threat.'[15]

Eva Birthistle and Atta Yaqub in *Ae Fond Kiss . . .*
[Sixteen Films-Bianca Film-EMC-Tornasol Films]

Originally titled *Our Own Kind*, the film was renamed *Ae Fond Kiss . . .* – after the Robert Burns song about the pain and pleasure of love – several months before shooting was due to start, in the summer of 2003. Like *Carla's Song*, it featured a cross-cultural relationship. For the role of Catholic music teacher Roisin, Loach found Dublin-born actress Eva Birthistle, who began her screen career in the Irish television soap opera *Glenroe*, before graduating to feature films in her homeland, then appearing as Robson Green's young trainee assistant in the British television legal drama *Trust*. 'I'm not very musical,' admitted Birthistle, 'so I had thirteen piano lessons before shooting started. It was very daunting, although I had done a year of piano when I was a kid, so it wasn't totally starting from scratch.'[16] Birthistle did some of the piano-playing in the film herself but mimed to the more difficult music.

A non-actor, Atta Yaqub, landed the role of disc jockey Casim, who meets Roisin through his sister Tara, one of her pupils. Yaqub was completing an MA in information management at the time, had worked part-time as a model for six years and related completely to the cultural dilemmas faced by Casim, including the Muslim tradition of arranged marriages. 'I went through scenarios like this a few years ago,' he explained during filming, 'but Casim is more powerful and has more passion. It's bringing out a new aspect of me that I didn't have before.'[17] Like many other Loach protégés before him, Yaqub had no plans to change his career plan. After shooting finished, he took up a job as a counsellor to young people with drugs and alcohol problems in Glasgow and simply waited to see whether the release of the film would bring him offers of more acting work.

Moments of comedy and farce contributed to a particularly good-humoured shoot, buoyed up by an unusually sunny Glasgow summer. As Loach and Barry Ackroyd were lining up a shot outside the district court, a drunk came out through the front doors, rocking on his heels, pointed directly at them and said, 'The editor's going to batter you!' Loach roared with laughter.

One of the main locations used for *Ae Fond Kiss . . .*, Holyrood Secondary School, in Glasgow, enabled the director once again to give children opportunities to display their talents, just as he had with David Bradley in *Kes*, Stephen Hirst and Louise Cooper in *Black Jack* and Martin Compston in *Sweet Sixteen* – the sort of chances his own father had been denied. Head of music Brian Marshall, who was on hand to advise Eva Birthistle during scenes shot at the school, put forward groups of pupils when Loach was looking for a singer to perform 'Ae Fond Kiss' and a drummer for another sequence. Seventeen-year-old Jacqueline Bett and Jamie Quinn, two years her junior, rose to the occasion and Loach dealt with them in the gentle, encouraging manner for which he was known.

Such empathy with his performers belied the determination and refusal to compromise that had always formed part of Loach's make-up, as revealed by Jim Allen's remark, 'His innocence is lethal. He's got a steel spine going up his back. He knows what he wants and he gets it.'[18] Loach's willingness to stretch authenticity to include scenes of upset children in *Cathy Come Home*, *Kes* and *Ladybird Ladybird* was part of that determination and continued to be questioned quietly by some who worked with him, but he was not immune to the criticism and apparently agonised over such sequences.

The release of *Ae Fond Kiss . . .*, in 2004, marked the fortieth anniversary of Loach's first screen work. Although the middle decades had been frustrating and yielded few triumphs, the boy from Nuneaton could lay claim to being Britain's most successful director of recent times, although he would be the last to make such a claim. Just as Tony Garnett had returned to Britain in the 1990s to mark out a new chapter as an independent producer of television series such as *Between the Lines*, *Cardiac Arrest*, *This Life* and *The Cops*, Loach's revival was remarkable for bringing him greater plaudits than ever before.

Working with Garnett and other regular collaborators was important to him. Jim Allen, Barry Hines and Paul Laverty were like-minded writers who could engage with the director in a shared vision. But David Mercer and Trevor Griffiths, while displaying a similar socialist outlook, were writers of a different kind, less prepared for their words to be modified, and it was not surprising that their brief partnerships with Loach resulted in creative tensions. After drifting through the 1980s, the director finally found successors to Garnett in producers Sally Hibbin and Rebecca O'Brien. With Parallax Pictures, then Sixteen Films, he established a permanent base that gave him the means to make a film almost every year, with financing deals that ensured him complete independence. Building a rapport with other key members of his production team was also significant. Successively, cameramen Tony Imi, Chris Menges and Barry Ackroyd forged long-running relationships with Loach, as did designer Martin Johnson (who died of cancer in October 2003), film editor Jonathan Morris, sound recordist Ray Beckett, script supervisor Susanna Lenton and, since 1994, composer George Fenton. (Loach insisted on music soundtracks that were not intrusive, in line with his practice of putting a story on screen unadorned by melodramatic techniques.)

Although the director found new life in the 1990s, international success did not bring universal acknowledgement of his achievements in his own country. Indeed, the marked differences in attitude by professional critics in Britain over the merits of his film-making contrasted with the acclaim he reaped abroad, especially in countries such as France, Spain and Italy. Undoubtedly, part of the reason was cultural: the disdain for the Hollywood studio system felt by so many directors on the European mainland, something shared by Loach, who regarded a film's content as more important than its form. At the same time, the mainstream press in Britain has been largely supportive of Hollywood values.

One appreciative British critic who witnessed Loach's development as a film-maker down the years, Derek Malcolm, said, 'If you look at his work film by film, there are no inalienable masterpieces, though I would certainly maintain that *Kes* is one of the best films about education ever made. But, in Loach's case, the whole is undoubtedly greater than the parts. His achievement, apart from being a film-maker skilful enough to make you laugh in one sequence and shed tears in the next, is that he has never lost faith in his initial belief that film can help to change attitudes, that ordinary people deserve a fairer deal and that there is no adequate substitute for the humane form of socialism he espouses. If some think he is naïve in this, it is astonishing how much he is admired throughout the world – almost venerated, in fact – partly because he refuses to be deflected from his political and social concerns, and because he can create characters everyone can believe in.

'His personal modesty and determination to serve his material sometimes prevents him showing his film-making talent to the best advantage. He would, it seems, rather not draw too much attention to himself as a director and some of his films are weaker as a consequence, especially when the material isn't as good as he is. But there is never a Loach film which doesn't have exceptionally true performances, which is as much a tribute to him as to his casts and, while no one would call him as sophisticated a film-maker as some other British directors, there are few others who are so admired and whose films are so fondly remembered. The pity is that the people for whom they are made have often not been allowed to see them, at least in his own country, because of an American-dominated distribution and exhibition system.'[19]

The views of professional critics have never, in fact, weighed strongly in the Loach psyche. This attitude is perhaps reflected in the greeting that one of his collaborators, Paul Laverty, gave a journalist interviewing him about *Sweet Sixteen*. 'Are you a film critic?' he asked. Fiona Morrow subsequently wrote, 'The defensiveness is understandable. Laverty and Loach are coming from a political position increasingly marginalised; always vehemently anti-capitalist, that now pits them against the modern incarnation of the Labour movement, too.'[20]

Whether this marginalisation was true or just a reflection of politicians growing increasingly apart from their electorate, Loach had firmly mapped out his own constituency. As he approached seventy, he showed no sign of slowing down, despite two warnings: a brush with prostate cancer in the summer of 2002 and an operation for a detached retina the following spring. 'That did dent his confidence and knock him more than anything because I think he believed he was invincible,' said Lesley Loach. 'But I don't think he will ever stop working – he *is* his work. It would be killing if he had to stop. I don't like him going away, but it's what he does. Of course, I get fed up sometimes and we have arguments and I say: "You're just swanning off to make a ruddy film." It was bloody hard work bringing up four kids and I did find it hard in the aftermath of the accident.'[21]

In a new century and a new millennium, Loach was continuing to plough his own furrow, untainted by fashion. His astonishing output since 1990, appreciation from audiences all over the world and dozens of international awards proved that maintaining his own, independent voice transcended fashion; holding on to the principle of portraying social realism and maintaining an uncompromising political stand had served him well – and, he hoped, served those who were not usually given a voice on screen.

'It just grows ever more apparent,' said Loach, 'that there are two classes in society, that their interests are irreconcilable, and that one survives at the expense of the other.'[22]

NOTES

1. 'An Eagle for an Emperor . . . a Kestrel for a Knave'

The title for this chapter comes from the quote used as a preface to Barry Hines's novel *A Kestrel for a Knave*, first published by Michael Joseph, 1968. The full quote, selected from the Boke of St Albans, 1486, and a Harleian manuscript, is, 'An Eagle for an Emperor, a Gyrfalcon for a King; a Peregrine for a Prince, a Saker for a Knight, a Merlin for a Lady; a Goshawk for a Yeoman, a Sparrowhawk for a Priest, a Musket for a Holy water Clerk, a Kestrel for a Knave'.

1. Cited by Ken Loach in an interview with the author, 31 October 2002.
2–24. Ken Loach interview, 31 October 2002.
25, 26. Roger Smith, interviewed by the author, 18 December 2002.
27. Ken Loach interview, 31 October 2002.
28. Gordon Honeycombe, interviewed by the author, 10 April 2003.
29. Ken Loach interview, 31 October 2002.

2. Living Theatre

1–4. Ken Loach, interviewed by the author, 31 October 2002.
5. *Loach on Loach*, ed. Graham Fuller, Faber and Faber, 1998.
6–9. Ken Loach interview, 31 October 2002.
10. Lesley Loach, interviewed by the author, 10 September 2003.
11, 12. Ken Loach interview, 31 October 2002.
13. Patricia Leventon, interviewed by the author, 13 August 2002.
14. Ken Loach interview, 31 October 2002.
15. Lesley Loach interview, 10 September 2003.
16. Ken Loach interview, 31 October 2002.
17. Lesley Loach interview, 10 September 2003.

3. Angry Young Men

1. *Loach on Loach*, ed. Graham Fuller, Faber and Faber, 1998.
2. Roger Smith, interviewed by the author, 18 December 2002.
3. Ken Loach, interviewed by the author, 31 October 2002.
4. Roger Smith interview, 18 December 2002.
5. *Radio Times*, 18–24 January 1964.

6. Roger Smith interview, 18 December 2002.
7. Geoffrey Whitehead, interviewed by the author, 10 August 2002.
8. Tony Garnett, interviewed by the author, 1 November 2002.
9. Troy Kennedy Martin, interviewed by the author, 10 January 2003.
10. Colin Welland, interviewed by the author, 10 September 2002.
11. George Layton, interviewed by the author, 16 January 2003.
12. Frank Windsor, interviewed by the author, 11 February 2003.
13, 14. Ken Loach interview, 31 October 2002.
15. *Encore*, March–April 1964.
16. Troy Kennedy Martin interview, 10 January 2003.
17. Ken Loach interview, 31 October 2002.
18. *Radio Times*, 22–28 August 1964.
19, 20. Nerys Hughes, interviewed by the author, 6 August 2002.
21. Ann Mitchell, interviewed by the author, 29 July 2002.
22. Frank Williams, interviewed by the author, 15 October 2002.
23. Ken Loach interview, 31 October 2002.
24, 25. Glynn Edwards, interviewed by the author, 6 August 2002.
26. Ken Loach interview, 31 October 2002.
27. Frank Williams interview, 15 October 2002.
28, 29. *Daily Herald*, 8 September 1964.

4. 'The Wednesday Play'

1. BBC press release, 24 November 1965.
2. Letter from Lord Normanbrook to Sir Burke Trend, 7 September 1965, cited by Michael Tracey in *Sanity Broadsheet* no 6, 1980.
3. Ken Loach, interviewed by the author, 31 October 2002.
4. Tony Garnett, interviewed by the author, 1 November 2002.
5. Ken Loach interview, 31 October 2002.
6. *Encore*, May–June 1964.
7. Tony Garnett interview, 1 November 2002.
8. Troy Kennedy Martin, interviewed by the author, 5 September 2003.
9. Roger Smith, interviewed by the author, 18 December 2002.
10, 11. Ken Loach interview, 31 October 2002.
12. Lee Montague, interviewed by the author, 10 August 2002.
13. Ken Loach interview, 31 October 2002.
14. *Radio Times*, 2–8 January 1965.
15. Tony Imi, interviewed by the author, 28 October 2002.
16. Ken Loach interview, 31 October 2002.
17. Glynn Edwards, interviewed by the author, 6 August 2002.
18. Lyn Lockwood, *Daily Telegraph*, 23 December 1965.
19. George Sewell, interviewed by the author, 13 May 2003.
20. Ken Loach interview, 31 October 2002.
21. *The Times*, 18 February 1965.
22. Ken Loach interview, 31 October 2002.
23. Christopher Logue, interviewed by the author, 27 May 2003.

24. Joanna Dunham, interviewed by the author, 19 January 2003.
25. Tony Garnett interview, 1 November 2002.

5. Up the Junction

1. Letter from Mary Whitehouse to Kenneth Robinson, Health Minister, cited in the *Sun*, 5 November 1965.
2. *New Statesman*, 18 May 1962, 28 December 1962 and 5 April 1963.
3. *Radio Times*, 30 October–5 November 1965.
4. Tony Garnett, interviewed by the author, 1 November 2002.
5. Ken Loach, interviewed by the author, 31 October 2002.
6–9. Tony Garnett interview, 1 November 2002.
10. Ken Loach interview, 31 October 2002.
11. Tony Imi, interviewed by the author, 28 October 2002.
12. Tony Garnett interview, 1 November 2002.
13, 14. *New York Times*, 10 February 1968.
15. Tony Garnett interview, 1 November 2002.
16. Letter to the author from Anna Wing, 26 August 2002.
17. Anna Wing, interviewed by the author, 16 September 2002.
18. Tony Garnett interview, 1 November 2002.
19. Ken Loach interview, 31 October 2002.
20. *Financial Times*, 10 November 1965.
21. Tony Garnett interview, 1 November 2002.
22. *Sun*, 5 November 1965.
23. *Daily Mail*, 6 November 1965.
24. Letter from Mary Whitehouse to Kenneth Robinson, op. cit.
25. *Sun*, 5 November 1965.
26. Piers Paul Read, *Daily Mail*, 15 July 1993.
27. George Orwell, 'Looking Back on the Spanish Civil War', *England Your England*, Martin Secker & Warburg, 1953.
28, 29. Tony Garnett interview, 1 November 2002.
30. Ken Loach interview, 31 October 2002.
31. Roger Smith, interviewed by the author, 1 April 2003.
32. Ken Loach, interviewed by the author, 1 November 2002.

6. Cathy Come Home

1. *Guardian*, 14 July 1973.
2. *Morning Star*, 3 December 1966.
3. Cited by Irene Shubik in *Play for Today: The Evolution of Television Drama*, second edition, Manchester University Press, 2000.
4. Tony Garnett, interviewed by the author, 1 November 2002.
5. Ken Loach, interviewed by the author, 31 October 2002.
6. Carol White, *Carol Comes Home*, New English Library, 1982.

7, 8. Ken Loach interview, 31 October 2002.

9. Tony Imi, interviewed by the author, 28 October 2002.

10. Tony Garnett interview, 1 November 2002.

11. Ruth Kettlewell, interviewed by the author, 29 July 2002.

12. Barry Jackson, interviewed by the author, 3 October 2002.

13. Gabrielle Hamilton, interviewed by the author, 30 July 2002.

14. Tony Imi interview, 28 October 2002.

15. Ken Loach interview, 31 October 2002.

16. *Today*, 25 November 1986.

17. *Loach on Loach*, ed. Graham Fuller, Faber and Faber, 1998.

18. Tony Imi interview, 28 October 2002.

19. Tony Garnett interview, 1 November 2002.

20. Ken Loach interview, 31 October 2002.

21, 22. *Today*, 25 November 1986.

23. Memo from Tony Garnett to Sydney Newman, head of drama, copied to Gerald Savory, head of plays and drama, 1 December 1966.

24. London *Evening Standard*, 12 August 1976.

25. Ken Loach interview, 31 October 2002.

26. *Loach on Loach*, op. cit.

27. *The Times*, 17 November 1966.

28. *Sunday Telegraph*, 15 January 1967.

29. *Sunday Telegraph*, 8 January 1967.

30. Memo from Tony Garnett to Gerald Savory, 26 October 1966.

31. *Cathy Come Home* screenplay, Children's Book Press, 1976.

32. Ken Loach interview, 31 October 2002.

33. *Cathy Where Are You Now?* ('Byline'), 9 July 1990.

34. Tony Garnett interview, 1 November 2002.

35. Ken Loach interview, 31 October 2002.

36. Ken Loach interviewed by the author, 1 November 2002.

37. Ken Loach interview, 31 October 2002.

38. Ken Loach interview, 1 November 2002.

39. *Theatre Quarterly*, January–March 1973.

40. Tony Imi interview, 28 October 2002.

41. *Sun*, 3 March 1967.

42. Neville Smith, interviewed by the author, 11 March 2003.

43. Gordon Honeycombe, interviewed by the author, 10 April 2003.

44. Ken Loach interview, 1 November 2002.

45. Neville Smith interview, 11 March 2003.

46. Tony Imi interview, 28 October 2002.

47. Neville Smith interview, 11 March 2003.

7. Poor Cow

1. *The Times*, 20 March 1970.

2. *New York Times*, 10 February 1968.

3, 4. Ken Loach, interviewed by the author, 1 November 2002.

5. *Morning Star*, 26 March 1968.
6. Ken Loach interview, 1 November 2002.
7, 8. Billy Murray, interviewed by the author, 28 April 2003.
9. Ken Loach interview, 1 November 2002.
10. Kate Williams, interviewed by the author, 8 August 2002.
11. Ken Loach interview, 1 November 2002.
12. Lesley Loach, interviewed by the author, 10 September 2003.
13. Billy Murray interview, 28 April 2003.
14. Carol White, *Carol Comes Home*, New English Library, 1982.
15. *New York Times*, 10 February 1968.
16. Billy Murray interview, 28 April 2003.
17, 18. *New York Times*, 10 February 1968.
19. Kate Williams interview, 8 August 2002.
20. John Halstead, interviewed by the author, 10 August 2002.
21. Kate Williams interview, 8 August 2002.
22. John Halstead interview, 10 August 2002.
23, 24. Kate Williams interview, 8 August 2002.
25. Ken Campbell, interviewed by the author, 15 August 2002.
26. Ken Loach interview, 1 November 2002.
27. *Carol Comes Home*, op. cit.
28. Ken Loach interview, 1 November 2002.
29. *Sunday Times*, 10 December 1967.
30, 31. *Carol Comes Home*, op. cit.
32. Ken Loach interview, 1 November 2002.
33. *Sight and Sound*, Winter 1968/69.

8. A Wet Summer in Barnsley

1. *The Times*, 20 March 1970.
2, 3. Tony Garnett, interviewed by the author, 1 November 2002.
4–7. Barry Hines, interviewed by the author, 13 December 2002.
8. Richard Hines, interviewed by the author, 22 May 2003.
9, 10. Ken Loach, interviewed by the author, 1 November 2002.
11. David Bradley, interviewed by the author, 8 May 2003.
12. Ken Loach interview, 1 November 2002.
13. *Sunday Express*, 7 May 1974.
14. David Bradley interview, 8 May 2003.
15. Barry Hines interview, 13 December 2002.
16. Ken Loach interview, 1 November 2002.
17. Colin Welland, interviewed by the author, 10 September 2002.
18. *Independent on Sunday*, 26 September 1999.
19, 20. Tony Garnett interview, 1 November 2002.
21–23. *Sunday Express*, 7 May 1994.
24. *Independent on Sunday*, 26 September 1999.
25. David Bradley interview, 8 May 2003.
26. *Sunday Express*, 7 May 1994.

27. Ken Loach interview, 1 November 2002.
28. Chris Menges, interviewed by the author, 2 May 2003.
29. Ken Loach interview, 1 November 2002.
30. Colin Welland interview, 10 September 2002.
31. Tony Garnett interviewed by the author, 14 January 2003.
32, 33. Barry Hines interview, 13 December 2002.
34. Chris Menges interview, 2 May 2003.
35. Ken Loach interview, 1 November 2002.
36. David Bradley interview, 8 May 2003.
37. Barry Hines interview, 13 December 2002.
38. Richard Hines interview, 22 May 2003.
39. David Bradley interview, 8 May 2003.
40. Barry Hines interview, 13 December 2002.
41. Richard Hines interview, 22 May 2003.
42. Tony Garnett interview, 1 November 2002.
43. *Guardian*, 28 September 1999.

9. The Rank and File

1. Socialist Labour League constitution as amended at the June 1968 congress.
2. Ken Loach, interviewed by the author, 28 April 2003.
3, 4. *Daily Mail*, 10 February 1969.
5. Ken Loach, interviewed by the author, 31 October 2002.
6. Tony Garnett, interviewed by the author, 14 January 2003.
7. Ken Loach interviewed by the author, 1 November 2002.
8. Granada Television press release, December 1973.
9, 10. Tony Garnett interview, 14 January 2003.
11. Ken Loach interview, 1 November 2002.
12. Tony Garnett interview, 14 January 2003.
13. Ken Campbell, interviewed by the author, 15 August 2002.
14. Neville Smith, interviewed by the author, 11 March 2003.
15. *Radio Times*, 15–21 February 1969.
16. Nancy Banks-Smith, *Sun*, 20 February 1969.
17. Ken Loach, interviewed by the author, 16 January 2003.
18, 19. Johnny Gee, interviewed by the author, 22 May 2003.
20. Jimmy Coleman, interviewed by the author, 12 November 2002.
21, 22. Neville Smith interview, 11 March 2003.
23. *Morning Star*, 20 March 1971.
24. *Guardian*, 19 March 1971.
25. Ken Loach interview, 28 April 2003.
26. *City Close-up*, Allen Lane, 1971.
27. Ken Loach interview, 16 January 2003.
28. Irving Teitelbaum, interviewed by the author, 19 May 2003.
29. Ken Loach interview, 16 January 2003.

10. Family Life

1. Tony Garnett, interviewed by the author, 14 January 2003.
2, 3. Ken Loach, interviewed by the author, 16 January 2003.
4, 5. Sandy Ratcliff, interviewed by the author, 28 May 2003.
6. Ken Loach interview, 16 January 2003.
7, 8. Malcolm Tierney, interviewed by the author, 16 August 2002.
9. Sandy Ratcliff interview, 28 May 2003.
10. *Daily Telegraph*, 3 February 1972.
11. Malcolm Tierney interview, 16 August 2002.
12. Ivan Strasburg, interviewed by the author, 1 May 2003.
13. Malcolm Tierney interview, 16 August 2002.
14. Chris Webb, interviewed by the author, 29 July 2002.
15. Letter from Ann Penfold to the author, 27 July 2002.
16. Doremy Vernon, interviewed by the author, 9 September 2002.
17. Tony Garnett interview, 14 January 2003.
18–20. Sandy Ratcliff interview, 28 May 2003.
21, 22. Lesley Loach, interviewed by the author, 10 September 2003.
23. Tony Garnett interview, 14 January 2003.
24. Ivan Strasburg interview, 1 May 2003.
25, 26. Lesley Loach interview, 10 September 2003.
27. *Observer*, 8 February 1976.
28. Lesley Loach interview, 10 September 2003.
29. Ken Loach interview, 16 January 2003.

11. Days of Hope

1. Ken Loach, interviewed by the author, 16 January 2003.
2, 3. Melvyn Bragg, interviewed by the author, 7 May 2003.
4. Lucy Fleming, interviewed by the author, 29 October 2002.
5. Peter Eyre, interviewed by the author, 15 August 2002.
6. Ken Loach interview, 16 January 2003.
7, 8. *Radio Times*, 6–12 September 1975.
9. Interview with Jim Allen, 1995, published on the World Socialist Web Site on 11 August, 1999: *http://www.wsws.org/articles/1999/aug1999/alle-a11.shtml*.
10. Tony Garnett, interviewed by the author, 14 January 2003.
11, 12. From Ken Loach's personal archive.
13–15. Letter to the author from Paul Copley, 13 August 2002.
16. Ken Loach interview, 16 January 2003.
17. Paul Copley letter, 13 August 2002.
18. From Ken Loach's personal archive.
19. Jimmy Coleman, interviewed by the author, 12 November 2002.
20, 21. Paul Copley letter, 13 August 2002.
22. Stephen Rea, interviewed by the author, 14 November 2002.
23. Tony Garnett interview, 14 January 2003.

24. *Daily Telegraph*, 25 September 1975.
25. *Tonight*, BBC1, 2 October 1975.
26. *Daily Mail*, 23 September 1975.
27, 28. Tony Garnett interview, 14 January 2003.
29. Ken Loach interview, 16 January 2003.
30. Both cited in *Stills*, May/June 1986.
31. Letter to Elsa Rassbach from Ken Loach, 26 August 1976, from his personal archive.
32. Ken Loach, interviewed by the author, 28 April 2003.
33. Tony Garnett interview, 14 January 2003.
34. Barry Hines, interviewed by the author, 13 December 2002.
35, 36. Stan Richards, interviewed by the author, 20 May 2003.
37. Barry Hines interview, 13 December 2002.
38. Tony Garnett interview, 14 January 2003.
39. Ken Loach interview, 16 January 2003.
40. Undated draft of letter from Ken Loach to Kenneth Stowe at 10 Downing Street, in response to a letter of 18 May 1977, both from Ken Loach's personal archive.

12. End of an Era

1. *The Times*, 21 February 1980.
2. *Films Illustrated*, December 1978.
3. Ken Loach, interviewed by the author, 16 January 2003.
4. *Films Illustrated*, December 1978.
5. Chris Menges, interviewed by the author, 2 May 2003.
6. Ken Loach, interviewed by the author, 28 April 2003.
7. Letter from Kneale Pearce to the author, 16 July 2002.
8. Margaret Crosfield, interviewed by the author, 16 July 2002.
9–11. Bob Pegg, interviewed by the author, 2 May 2003.
12. Ken Loach interview, 28 April 2003.
13. *The Times*, 21 February 1980.
14. Tony Garnett, interviewed by the author, 14 January 2003.
15. Ken Loach interview, 28 April 2003.
16. Tony Garnett interview, 14 January 2003.
17. Ken Loach interview, 28 April 2003.
18. Lewis Rudd, interviewed by the author, 20 May 2003.
19. Ken Loach interview, 28 April 2003.

13. Pastures New and Old

1. Ken Loach, interviewed by the author, 28 April 2003.
2. Richard Creasey, interviewed by the author, 12 March 2003.
3. *Monthly Film Bulletin*, January 1983.
4. Barry Hines, interviewed by the author, 13 December 2002.
5. ATV press release, December 1980.

6, 7. Ken Loach interview, 28 April 2003.
8. Irving Teitelbaum, interviewed by the author, 19 May 2003.
9, 10. *TVTimes*, 15–21 May 1982.
11, 12. Tony Pitts, interviewed by the author, 10 August 2002.
13. Ken Loach interview, 28 April 2003.

14. Questions of Censorship

1. Ken Loach, interviewed by the author, 28 April 2003.
2, 3. Charles Denton, interviewed by the author, 17 June 2003.
4. *The Times*, 13 November 1981.
5. Letter from Frank Chapple to Roger James, 14 June 1982; letter from Roger James to Frank Chapple, 21 June 1982; letter from Lawford & Co to The Secretary, Central Independent Television, 25 June 1982.
6. Letter from Don Christopher, Channel Four's solicitor for programme acquisition, to Roger James, 15 June 1983.
7. Don Christopher, interviewed by the author, 19 June 2003.
8. Paul Bonner, interviewed by the author, 18 August 2003.
9. Paul Bonner, interviewed by the author, 19 August 2003.
10, 11. Cited by Ken Loach in *Tribune*, 25 November 1983.
12. Paul Madden, interviewed by the author, 16 June 2003.
13, 14. Letter from Paul Bonner to Ken Loach, 24 August 1983.
15. Paul Madden interview, 16 June 2003.
16. *Tribune*, 25 November 1983.
17. Liz Forgan, interviewed by the author, 21 August 2003.
18. Justin Dukes, interviewed by the author, 3 September 2003.
19. Letter from Jeremy Isaacs to Ken Loach, 22 September 1983.
20. Letter from Lord Thomson of Monifieth to Ken Loach, 26 September 1983.
21, 22. Letter from Richard Creasey to Ken Loach, 3 November 1983.
23. Letter from Lawford & Co to Colin Campbell, Central Television's company secretary and legal officer, 14 February 1984.
24. Letter from Lawford & Co to Colin Campbell, Central Television's company secretary and legal officer, 21 February 1984.
25. Don Christopher interview, 19 June 2003.
26. Cited in a Directors Guild of Great Britain press release, 23 July 1984.
27. Charles Denton interview, 17 June 2003.
28. Directors Guild of Great Britain press release, 23 July 1984.
29. Central Independent Television press release, 31 July 1984.
30. Ken Loach, interviewed by the author for an article originally published in *Screen International*, 4 August 1984.
31, 32. Jeremy Isaacs, interviewed by the author, 19 June 2003.
33, 34. Jeremy Isaacs, *Storm Over 4: A Personal Account*, Weidenfeld and Nicolson, 1989.
35. Department of Trade and Industry, International Learning Systems Corporation Limited; Pergamon Press Limited (interim report), London, HMSO, 1971.

36. John Jackson, interviewed by the author, 23 August 2003.
37. Letter to the author from Bob Phillis, 9 October 2003.
38. Bob Cole, interviewed by the author, 18 September 2003.
39. Charles Denton, interviewed by the author, 18 August 2003.
40. John Jackson interview, 23 August 2003.
41. Charles Denton, interviewed by the author, 4 September 2003.
42. John Jackson interview, 23 August 2003.
43. Charles Denton interview, 4 September 2003.
44–46. John Jackson interview, 23 August 2003.
47–51. Bob Cole, interviewed by the author, 19 September 2003.
52, 53. Bob Phillis, interviewed by the author, 8 August 2003.
54. Letter from Colin Campbell to the author, 25 September 2003.
55. Anonymous former Central Independent Television board member interviewed by the author, 20 June 2003.
56. Sir Gordon Hobday, interviewed by the author, 18 and 19 August 2003.
57. Charles Denton, interviewed by the author, 19 August 2003.
58. A full account of this is contained in Lewis Chester's book *Tooth and Claw: The Inside Story of Spitting Image*, Faber and Faber, 1986.
59, 60. Letter to the author from Bob Phillis, 9 October 2003. The full text is as follows:

> I am writing further to my letter of 29th September in order to correct a number of inaccuracies in the situation that you describe relating to the *Questions of Leadership* programmes produced by Central Independent Television in 1984. As a matter of personal principle I do not comment on the detail of the deliberations of any board meeting of any public company on which I have served, let alone one of nearly 20 years ago, but I would comment as follows on the narrative included in your letter:
> 1. For the avoidance of doubt, I have at no time in my career worked for Mr Maxwell. As Chief Executive of Independent Television Publications I was responsible for overseeing new contract negotiations for the production of the *TVTimes* during 1980/81. Part of this printing business was placed with companies within the British Printing Corporation (BPC) *before* Mr Maxwell acquired BPC. After the acquisition, Mr Maxwell sought to renegotiate these contracts but Independent Television Publications would accept no change whatsoever in any of the contractual arrangements. However ITP did insist that BPC provide additional guarantees and security before final signature of the relevant agreements.
> 2. I completely reject your suggestion that I was at any time 'keen' for Mr Maxwell to join the Board of Central Independent Television. BPC did not hold an equity stake in Central at the time of the franchise award in 1981. The Independent Broadcasting Authority had required Associated Communications Corporation (ACC) to reduce its shareholding to 51 per cent of the restructured company. It proved extremely difficult to raise the required 49 per cent, and in December 1981 the then Board of Central Independent Television (of which John Jackson was not yet a member) with some reluctance decided to accept a balancing investment of 9.2 per

cent from Mr Maxwell's Pergamon Press. Mr Maxwell was not invited to join the Board at that time. A subsequent share restructuring took place during the year ended December 31 1982 and in the Annual Report and Accounts for that year Sir Gordon Hobday reported that after the share restructuring, following the entire disposal of ACC's shares:

'Just over 30 per cent of the equity has been placed with new shareholders, of which a 20 per cent holding has been acquired by Sears Investments Ltd, a subsidiary of Sears Holdings plc. The remaining 20 per cent of the ACC holding was acquired by existing major shareholders who were amongst the original subscribers in December 1981. The Ladbroke Group and D. C. Thomson have increased their holding of both classes of shares by 10 per cent and 5 per cent respectively, bringing their total holdings to 20 per cent in both cases. The BPCC/Pergamon Press Group have increased their original holdings of 9.2 per cent of the voting shares and 7.9 per cent of the non-voting shares to 13.8 per cent and 12.5 per cent. The support of these major shareholders throughout 1982 has been both constructive and consistent, and the increase in their holdings and the confidence which this reflects is welcomed.'

Further, Sir Gordon Hobday also stated in his report:

'Following the sale of the ACC shareholding in the company, to which I have referred earlier, Mr Geoffrey Maitland Smith, Chief Executive of Sears Holdings plc and Mr Robert Maxwell, Chairman of BPCC/Pergamon Group, have been invited to join the Board of your Company.'

As is normal practice in any public company, it is the role of the Chairman and non-executive directors to determine the membership of the Board. Mr Maitland Smith and Mr Maxwell joined the Board on 23 May 1983. One has to presume that the non-executive directors at the time were all agreed that Mr Maxwell should join the Board, as none of them resigned over the appointment.

3. With regards to *Questions of Leadership*, it was the Central Board who asked to see tapes of the programmes under consideration. This request came from certain of the non-executive directors. As Managing Director I did not supply the videotapes; distribution would have been via the Company Secretary's office acting on behalf of the Board.

4. Neither I nor any of the Executive Directors on the Central Board would at any time have countenanced or approved of any act of 'political censorship'. As I mentioned to you in our earlier telephone conversation, Central Television under my leadership, and thereafter, had a proud record of challenging and cutting edge programme making, which on numerous occasions required special clearance from the IBA, and sometimes the production of balancing programming.

5. Sam Silkin (later Lord Silkin), as Robert Maxwell's alternate director, would have been entitled to express his personal views and opinions as

part of a Board discussion. The Board of Central Independent Television had no interest or position in any of Mr Maxwell's other business interests. These were never discussed by the Central Board and would not have influenced the deliberations or decisions of the Board in any way. I cannot speculate on what might have been in the minds of Mr Maxwell or Mr Silkin, but Mr Silkin was only one voice amongst many on the Central Board.

6. In the statement issued by the Board on 31st July 1984 the Central Board stated:

The company is sympathetic to programmes which express controversial points of view and the board believes that Central's track record underlines this . . . But after extensive legal argument the board has reluctantly concluded that the clear risk of a successful action for defamation precludes the programme being offered to Channel 4 for transmission.

This statement would have been on behalf of the whole Board reflecting the decision that had been taken and agreed by the Board. There were no resignations from the Board then or subsequently relating to the *Questions of Leadership* programmes, and this would suggest that all members of the Board accepted that decision.

I hope that this information will assist you in basing your account on greater historical accuracy than some of your other sources have been able to recall.

61. John Jackson, interviewed by the author, 19 September 2003.
62. Ken Loach interview, 28 April 2003.
63. Richard Creasey, interviewed by the author, 12 March 2003.
64. Ken Loach interview, 28 April 2003.
65. *New Musical Express*, 24 January 1987.
66. Ken Loach interview, 28 April 2003.
67. *Guardian*, 14 January 1987.
68. Open letter from Ken Loach to the council of the Royal Court, *Guardian*, 18 February 1987.
69. Royal Court Theatre press release, 21 January 1987.
70. See Victoria Radin's account in the *New Statesman*, 27 February 1987.
71. Ken Loach interview, 28 April 2003.
72, 73. Max Stafford-Clark, interviewed by the author, 6 August 2003.
74. Letter from Ken Loach to the author, 29 September 2003.
75. Ben Hecht, *Perfidy*, Julian Messner, New York, 1961.
76. Letter from Benedict Birnberg to Jim Allen, 6 April 1987.
77. Ken Loach interview, 28 April 2003.

15. Which Side Are You On?

1. Ken Loach, interviewed by the author, 28 April 2003.
2. Melvyn Bragg, interviewed by the author, 7 May 2003.

3. Chris Menges, interviewed by the author, 2 May 2003.

4, 5. Ken Loach interview, 28 April 2003.

6. Jonathan Morris, interviewed by the author, 12 March 2003.

7. In a letter to the author, dated 22 October 2002, Nick Elliott wrote, 'My problem is I never remember anything – and I don't keep a diary. I do remember meetings with Ken over *Which Side Are You On?* but not really enough to be a credible witness.'

8. Ken Loach interview, 28 April 2003.

9, 10. Melvyn Bragg interview, 7 May 2003.

11–13. Ken Loach interview, 28 April 2003.

14. *Guardian*, 27 May 2002.

15. Ken Loach interview, 28 April 2003.

16. *Guardian*, 26 March 1987.

17, 18. Ken Loach interview, 28 April 2003.

19. Lesley Loach, interviewed by the author, 10 September 2003.

20. *Sunday Times*, 9 January 1972.

21, 22. Ken Loach interview, 18 April 2003.

23. Lesley Loach interview, 10 September 2003.

16. Troubles

1. David Puttnam, interviewed by the author, 12 May 2003.

2, 3. Ken Loach, interviewed by the author, 28 April 2003.

4, 5. Rebecca O'Brien, interviewed by the author, 12 March 2003.

6. Maurice Roëves, interviewed by the author, 4 September 2002.

7. Letter to the author from Bernard Archard, 3 August 2002.

8. Cited by Ken Loach, *Morning Star*, 11 January 1991.

9. *City Limits*, 10 January 1991.

17. A Turning Tide, Raining Stones

1. Sally Hibbin, interviewed by the author, 28 May 2003.

2–4. Ken Loach, interviewed by the author, 28 April 2003.

5, 6. Robert Carlyle, interviewed by the author, 29 October 2002.

7, 8. Ricky Tomlinson, interviewed by the author, 25 October 2002.

9. Robert Carlyle interview, 29 October 2002.

10. Emer McCourt, interviewed by the author, 20 November 2002.

11. Sally Hibbin interview, 28 May 2003.

12. Ken Loach interview, 28 April 2003.

13. Parallax Pictures press release, 1993.

14. Ken Loach interview, 28 April 2003.

15, 16. Ricky Tomlinson interview, 25 October 2002.

17. Barry Ackroyd, interviewed by the author, 9 May 2003.

18. Antony Audenshaw, interviewed by the author, 8 August 2002.

19. *What's On in London*, 6 October 1993.

20. Julie Brown, interviewed by the author, 25 June 2003.

21. Ken Loach interview, 28 April 2003.
22. Tom Hickey, interviewed by the author, 24 October 2002.
23. Ken Loach interviewed by the author, 31 October 2002.
24. *Guardian*, 12 October 1994.
25. Ken Loach interview, 28 April 2003.
26. Ricky Tomlinson interview, 25 October 2002.
27, 28. Crissy Rock, interviewed by the author, 8 May 2003.
29. Tom Keller, interviewed by the author, 30 July 2002.
30. Vladimir Vega, interviewed by the author, 14 January 2003.
31. *Sunday Times Magazine*, 14 August 1994.
32. *Sunday Times*, 18 September 1994.
33. *Observer*, 10 August 1997.

18. Last Great Causes

1. *Loach on Location – Making Land and Freedom*, BBC2, 15 May 1995.
2. Sally Hibbin, interviewed by the author, 28 May 2003.
3. Rebecca O'Brien, interviewed by the author, 12 March 2003.
4, 5. Ken Loach, interviewed by the author, 28 April 2003.
6, 7. Roger Smith, interviewed by the author, 18 December 2002.
8. Rebecca O'Brien interview, 12 March 2003.
9. Eoin McCarthy, interviewed by the author, 15 August 2002.
10, 11. *Loach on Location – Making Land and Freedom*, op. cit.
12. Barry Ackroyd, interviewed by the author, 9 May 2003.
13. Jonathan Morris, interviewed by the author, 12 March 2003.
14. *Independent on Sunday Magazine*, 24 July 1994.
15. Rebecca O'Brien interview, 12 March 2003.
16. Suzanne Maddock, interviewed by the author, 14 August 2002.
17. Cited in *The Times*, 18 September 1995.
18. Rebecca O'Brien interview, 12 March 2003.
19. *Loach on Location – Making Land and Freedom*, op. cit.
20. London *Evening Standard*, 5 October 1995.
21. Ken Loach interview, 28 April 2003.
22. Raymond Carr's Introduction to *The Spanish Civil War: A History in Pictures*, Allen & Unwin, 1986.
23. Phillip Knightley, *The First Casualty – From the Crimea to Vietnam: The War Correspondent as Hero, Propagandist and Myth Maker*, André Deutsch, 1975.
24. *Ken Loach – Un Observador Solidario*, El País/Aguilar, Madrid, 1996.
25–27. Paul Laverty, interviewed by the author, 16 December 2002.
28. Barry Ackroyd interview, 9 May 2003.
29, 30. Robert Carlyle, interviewed by the author, 29 October 2002.
31, 32. Ken Loach interview, 28 April 2003.
33. Cited *Guardian*, 21 November 1997.

19. Atlantic Crossing

1. Paul Laverty, interviewed by the author, 16 December 2002.
2–4. Ken Loach, interviewed by the author, 28 April 2003.
5, 6. Rebecca O'Brien, interviewed by the author, 12 March 2003.
7. *My Name Is Joe*, ScreenPress Books, 1998.
8. *Independent*, 29 October 1998.
9, 10. Louise Goodall, interviewed by the author, 28 October 2002.
11. *My Name Is Joe*, op. cit.
12. Simon Macallum, interviewed by the author, 27 July 2002.
13. Ken Loach interview, 28 April 2003.
14. Paul Laverty interview, 16 December 2002.
15. Rebecca O'Brien interview, 12 March 2003.
16. Ken Loach interview, 28 April 2003.
17. *Bread and Roses*, ScreenPress Books, 2001.
18. Ken Loach interview, 28 April 2003.
19. Barry Ackroyd, interviewed by the author, 9 May 2003.
20. Ken Loach interview, 28 April 2003.
21. Barry Ackroyd interview, 9 May 2003.
22–24. Ken Loach interview, 28 April 2003.
25. Tom Craig, interviewed by the author, 31 July 2002.
26. Sean Glenn, interviewed by the author, 4 September 2002.
27. Charlie Brown, interviewed by the author, 29 July 2002.
28. Tom Craig interview, 31 July 2002.
29. Steve Huison, interviewed by the author, 7 August 2002.
30. Sean Glenn interview, 4 September 2002.
31. Jonathan Morris, interviewed by the author, 12 March 2003.

20. A Changing World

1. Ken Loach, interviewed by the author, 28 April 2003.
2, 3. Paul Laverty, interviewed by the author, 16 December 2002.
4–7. Martin Compston, interviewed by the author, 15 May 2003.
8. Gary McCormack, interviewed by the author, 9 August 2002.
9, 10. Rebecca O'Brien, interviewed by the author, 12 March 2003.
11. Sally Hibbin, interviewed by the author, 28 May 2003.
12. London *Evening Standard*, 10 September 2002.
13, 14. Vladimir Vega, interviewed by the author, 14 January 2003.
15. Paul Laverty interview, 16 December 2002.
16. Eva Birthistle, interviewed by the author, 16 July 2003.
17. Atta Yaqub, interviewed by the author, 16 July 2003.
18. *Loach on Location – Making Land and Freedom*, BBC2, 15 May 1995.
19. Derek Malcolm, interviewed by the author, 24 September 2003.
20. *Independent*, 27 September 2002.
21. Lesley Loach, interviewed by the author, 10 September 2003.
22. *Loach on Loach*, ed. Graham Fuller, Faber and Faber, 1998.

GENERAL BIBLIOGRAPHY

Loach on Loach, ed. Graham Fuller, Faber and Faber, 1998.
The Cinema of Ken Loach: Art in the service of the people, Jacob Leigh, Wallflower Press, 2002.
Carla's Song, Paul Laverty, Faber and Faber, 1997.
My Name Is Joe, Paul Laverty, ScreenPress Books, 1998.
Bread and Roses, Paul Laverty, ScreenPress Books, 2001.
Sweet Sixteen, Paul Laverty, Screenpress Publishing, 2002.

Appendix I

FILMOGRAPHY

FEATURE FILMS

Poor Cow

Director (Fenchurch Films-Vic Films; UK, 1967) 101 mins, colour
Screenplay: Nell Dunn, Ken Loach (based on the novel by Nell Dunn)
Producer: Joseph Janni *Photography:* Brian Probyn *Editor:* Roy Watts *Art director:* Bernard Sarron *Music:* Donovan

Joy	Carol White
Tom	John Bindon
Dave	Terence Stamp
Beryl	Kate Williams
Aunt Emm	Queenie Watts

Kes

Director (Kestrel Films-Woodfall Films; UK, 1969) 113 mins, colour
Adaptation: Barry Hines, Ken Loach, Tony Garnett (based on the novel *A Kestrel for a Knave*, by Barry Hines) *Producer:* Tony Garnett *Photography:* Chris Menges *Editor:* Roy Watts *Art director:* William McCrow *Music:* John Cameron

Billy	David Bradley
Mr Farthing	Colin Welland
Mrs Casper	Lynne Perrie
Jud	Freddie Fletcher
Mr Sugden	Brian Glover
Mr Gryce	Bob Bowes

Family Life

Director (Kestrel Films; UK, 1971) (US title: *Wednesday's Child*) 108 mins, colour
Screenplay: David Mercer *Producer:* Tony Garnett *Photography:* Charles Stewart *Editor:* Roy Watts *Art director:* William McCrow *Music:* Marc Wilkinson

Janice Baildon	Sandy Ratcliff
Mrs Baildon	Grace Cave
Mr Baildon	Bill Dean

Black Jack

Director (Kestrel Films; UK, 1979) 110 mins, colour
Adaptation: Ken Loach (based on the novel by Leon Garfield) *Producer:*
Tony Garnett *Photography:* Chris Menges *Editor:* William Shapter *Art
director:* Martin Johnson *Music:* Bob Pegg

Tolly	Stephen Hirst
Belle	Louise Cooper
Black Jack	Jean Franval
Dr Carmody	Packie Byrne

Looks and Smiles

Director (Kestrel Films-Black Lion Films; UK, 1981) 104 mins, b/w
Screenplay: Barry Hines *Producer:* Irving Teitelbaum *Photography:* Chris
Menges *Editor:* Steve Singleton *Art director:* Martin Johnson *Music:* Marc
Wilkinson

Mick Walsh	Graham Green
Karen Lodge	Carolyn Nicholson
Alan Wright	Tony Pitts

Fatherland

Director (Kestrel II Films-Clasart Film-Mk 2 Productions; UK-West Ger-
many-France, 1986) (US title: *Singing the Blues in Red*) 107 mins, colour
Screenplay: Trevor Griffiths *Producer:* Raymond Day *Photography:* Chris
Menges *Editor:* Jonathan Morris *Designer:* Martin Johnson *Music:* Christian Kunert, Gerulf Pannach

Klaus Drittemann	Gerulf Pannach
Emma de Baen	Fabienne Babe

Hidden Agenda

Director (Initial Film and Television-Hemdale Film Corporation; UK,
1990) 108 mins, colour
Screenplay: Jim Allen *Producer:* Eric Fellner *Co-producer:* Rebecca O'Brien
Photography: Clive Tickner *Editor:* Jonathan Morris *Designer:* Martin
Johnson *Original music:* Stewart Copeland

Ingrid Jessner	Frances McDormand
Kerrigan	Brian Cox
Paul Sullivan	Brad Dourif
Moa	Mai Zetterling

Riff-Raff

Director (Parallax Pictures; UK, 1991) 96 mins, colour
Screenplay: Bill Jesse *Producer:* Sally Hibbin *Photography:* Barry Ackroyd
Editor: Jonathan Morris *Production designer:* Martin Johnson *Music:*
Stewart Copeland

Stevie	Robert Carlyle
Susan	Emer McCourt

Shem	Jimmy Coleman
Mo	George Moss
Larry	Ricky Tomlinson

Raining Stones

Director (Parallax Pictures; UK, 1993) 90 mins, colour
Screenplay: Jim Allen *Producer:* Sally Hibbin *Photography:* Barry Ackroyd
Editor: Jonathan Morris *Production designer:* Martin Johnson *Music:*
Stewart Copeland

Bob Williams	Bruce Jones
Anne Williams	Julie Brown
Tommy	Ricky Tomlinson
Father Barry	Tom Hickey

Ladybird Ladybird

Director (Parallax Pictures; UK, 1994) 102 mins, colour
Screenplay: Rona Munro *Producer:* Sally Hibbin *Photography:* Barry
Ackroyd *Editor:* Jonathan Morris *Production designer:* Martin Johnson
Music: George Fenton

Maggie	Crissy Rock
Jorge	Vladimir Vega
Mairead	Sandie Lavelle
Simon	Ray Winstone

Land and Freedom

Director (Parallax Pictures-Messidor Films-Road Movies; UK-Spain-Germany, 1995) 110 mins, colour
Screenplay: Jim Allen *Producer:* Rebecca O'Brien *Photography:* Barry
Ackroyd *Editor:* Jonathan Morris *Production designer:* Martin Johnson
Music: George Fenton

David Carr	Ian Hart
Blanca	Rosana Pastor
Maite	Icíar Bollaín
Lawrence	Tom Gilroy
Vidal	Marc Martinez
Bernard	Frédéric Pierrot

Carla's Song

Director (Parallax Pictures-Road Movies-Tornasol Films; UK-Germany-Spain, 1996) 127 mins, colour
Screenplay: Paul Laverty *Producer:* Sally Hibbin *Photography:* Barry
Ackroyd *Editor:* Jonathan Morris *Production designer:* Martin Johnson
Music: George Fenton

George	Robert Carlyle
Carla	Oyanka Cabezas
Bradley	Scott Glenn

My Name Is Joe

Director (Parallax Pictures-Road Movies-Tornasol/Alta Films; UK-Germany-Spain, 1998) 105 mins, colour
Screenplay: Paul Laverty *Producer:* Rebecca O'Brien *Photography:* Barry Ackroyd *Editor:* Jonathan Morris *Production designer:* Martin Johnson *Music:* George Fenton

Joe	Peter Mullan
Sarah	Louise Goodall
Liam	David McKay
Sabine	Annemarie Kennedy
Shanks	Gary Lewis
Maggie	Lorraine McIntosh
McGowan	David Hayman

Bread and Roses

Director (Parallax Pictures-Road Movies-Tornasol/Alta Films; UK-Germany-Spain, 2000) 110 mins, colour
Screenplay: Paul Laverty *Producer:* Rebecca O'Brien *Photography:* Barry Ackroyd *Editor:* Jonathan Morris *Production designer:* Martin Johnson *Music:* George Fenton

Maya	Pilar Padilla
Sam	Adrien Brody
Rosa	Elpidia Carrillo
Bert	Jack McGee

The Navigators

Director (Parallax Pictures-Road Movies-Tornasol/Alta Films; UK-Germany-Spain, 2001) 96 mins, colour
Screenplay: Rob Dawber *Producer:* Rebecca O'Brien *Photography:* Mike Eley, Barry Ackroyd *Editor:* Jonathan Morris *Production designer:* Martin Johnson *Music:* George Fenton

John	Dean Andrews
Mick	Tom Craig
Paul	Joe Duttine
Jim	Steve Huison
Gerry	Venn Tracey
Harpic	Sean Glenn

Sweet Sixteen

Director (Sixteen Films-Road Movies-Tornasol/Alta Films; UK-Germany-Spain, 2002) 106 mins, colour
Screenplay: Paul Laverty *Producer:* Rebecca O'Brien *Photography:* Barry Ackroyd *Editor:* Jonathan Morris *Production designer:* Martin Johnson *Music:* George Fenton

Liam	Martin Compston
Chantelle	AnnMarie Fulton

Pinball	William Ruane
Stan	Gary McCormack
Jean	Michelle Coulter

11'09"01 – September 11
Director, 'United Kingdom' segment (Sixteen Films) of Galatee Films-Studio Canal production (France, 2002) 11 mins (of 135 mins total), colour
Screenplay: Paul Laverty, Vladimir Vega, Ken Loach *Producer:* Rebecca O'Brien *Photography:* Nigel Willoughby, Peter Hellmich, Jorge Müller Silva *Editor:* Jonathan Morris *Music:* Vladimir Vega

| *Himself* | Vladimir Vega |

Ae Fond Kiss . . .
Director (Sixteen Films-Bianca Film-EMC-Tornasol Films; UK-Italy-Germany-Spain, 2004) (Alternative title: *Just A Kiss*), colour, 104 mins
Screenplay: Paul Laverty *Producer:* Rebecca O'Brien *Photography:* Barry Ackroyd *Editor:* Jonathan Morris *Production designer:* Martin Johnson *Music:* George Fenton

| *Casim* | Atta Yaqub |
| *Roisin* | Eva Birthistle |

TELEVISION

That Was the Week That Was
Actor (BBC, 1963)

Catherine
Director (BBC, 1964) 'Teletale', BBC, 24 January 1964 (30 mins, b/w)
Script: Roger Smith *Producer:* James MacTaggart

Narrator	Geoffrey Whitehead
Catherine	Kika Markham
Jack	Gilbert Wynne
Singer	Tony Selby

Z Cars
Director, three episodes (BBC, 1964)

PC Lynch	James Ellis
PC Graham	Colin Welland
Det Sgt Watt	Frank Windsor
Sgt Blackitt	Robert Keegan

Profit by Their Example BBC, 12 February 1964 (50 mins, b/w)
Script: John Hopkins *Producer:* David E. Rose

Straight Deal BBC, 11 March 1964 (50 mins, b/w)
Script: Robert Barr *Producer:* David E. Rose

| *Det Chief Insp Barlow* | Stratford Johns |

The Whole Truth. . . BBC, 8 April 1964 (50 mins, b/w)
Script: Robert Barr *Producer:* David E. Rose

Det Chief Insp Barlow	Stratford Johns
PC Smith	Brian Blessed
PC Weir	Joseph Brady

Diary of a Young Man

Director (BBC, 1964)
Script: Troy Kennedy Martin, John McGrath *Producer:* James MacTaggart
Story editor: Roger Smith *Camera:* John McGlashan *Editor:* Christopher
La Fontaine *Music:* Stanley Myers

Joe	Victor Henry
Ginger	Richard Moore
Rose	Nerys Hughes

Episode 1: *Survival or They Came to a City* BBC1, 8 August 1964 (45 mins, b/w)
Episode 3: *Marriage* BBC1, 22 August 1964 (45 mins, b/w)
Episode 5: *Life or A Girl Called Fred* BBC1, 5 September 1964 (45 mins, b/w)

Tap on the Shoulder

Director (BBC, 1965) 'The Wednesday Play', BBC1, 6 January 1965 (75 mins, b/w)
Script: James O'Connor *Producer:* James MacTaggart *Story editor:* Roger
Smith *Camera:* John McGlashan, Ken Westbury *Editor:* Geoffrey Botterill
Designer: Eileen Diss *Music:* Stanley Myers

Archibald Cooper	Lee Montague
Ronnie	Richard Shaw
Hazel	Judith Smith
Terry	Griffith Davies
Patsy	George Tovey
Tim	Tony Selby

Wear a Very Big Hat

Director (BBC, 1965) 'The Wednesday Play', BBC1, 17 February 1965 (75 mins, b/w)
Script: Eric Coltart *Producer:* James MacTaggart *Story editor:* Roger Smith
Camera: Stanley Speel *Editor:* Norman Carr *Designer:* Peter Kindred
Music: Stanley Myers

Johnny Johnson	Neville Smith
Ann Johnson	Sheila Fearn
Snapper Melia	William Holmes
Billy Mofatt	Johnny Clive

Three Clear Sundays

Director (BBC, 1965) 'The Wednesday Play', BBC1, 7 April 1965 (75 mins, b/w)
Script: James O'Connor *Producer:* James MacTaggart *Story editor:* Roger
Smith *Camera:* Tony Imi *Editor:* Pam Bosworth *Lyrics:* Nemone Lethbridge

Danny Lee	Tony Selby
Britannia Lee	Rita Webb
Prison Officer Johnson	Glynn Edwards
Johnny May	George Sewell

Up the Junction

Director (BBC, 1965) 'The Wednesday Play', BBC1, 3 November 1965 (70 mins, b/w)

Adaptation: Nell Dunn, Ken Loach (based on the book by Nell Dunn) *Producer:* James MacTaggart *Story editor:* Tony Garnett *Camera:* Tony Imi *Editor:* Roy Watts *Designer:* Eileen Diss *Title music:* Paul Jones, arranged by Mike Vickers

Sylvie	Carol White
Rube	Geraldine Sherman
Eileen	Vickery Turner
Dave	Tony Selby
The Tallyman	George Sewell

The End of Arthur's Marriage

Director (BBC, 1965) 'The Wednesday Play', BBC1, 17 November 1965 (70 mins, b/w)

Script: Christopher Logue, Stanley Myers *Producer:* James MacTaggart *Story editor:* Roger Smith *Designer:* Robert Macgowan *Music:* Stanley Myers *Title music:* Paul Jones, arranged by Mike Vickers

| *Arthur* | Ken Jones |
| *Emmy* | Maureen Ampleford |

The Coming Out Party

Director (BBC, 1965) 'The Wednesday Play', BBC1, 22 December 1965 (60 mins, b/w)

Script: James O'Connor *Producer:* James MacTaggart *Story editor:* Roger Smith *Designer:* Michael Wield *Music:* Stanley Myers *Title music:* Paul Jones, arranged by Mike Vickers *Lyrics:* Nemone Lethbridge

Rosie	Toni Palmer
Ricketts	George Sewell
Scimpy	Dennis Golding
The Princess	Carol White

Cathy Come Home

Director (BBC, 1966) 'The Wednesday Play', BBC1, 16 November 1966 (75 mins, b/w)

Story: Jeremy Sandford *Script:* Jeremy Sandford, Ken Loach *Producer:* Tony Garnett *Camera:* Tony Imi *Editor:* Roy Watts *Designer:* Sally Hulke *Music:* Paul Jones

| *Cathy* | Carol White |
| *Reg* | Ray Brooks |

In Two Minds

Director (BBC, 1967) 'The Wednesday Play', BBC1, 1 March 1967 (75 mins, b/w)

Script: David Mercer *Producer:* Tony Garnett *Camera:* Tony Imi *Editor:* Roy Watts *Designer:* John Hurst

Kate Winter	Anna Cropper
Mr Winter	George A. Cooper
Mrs Winter	Helen Booth
Mary Winter	Christine Hargreaves

The Golden Vision

Director (BBC, 1968) 'The Wednesday Play', BBC1, 17 April 1968 (75 mins, b/w)

Script: Neville Smith, Gordon Honeycombe *Producer:* Tony Garnett *Camera:* Tony Imi *Designer:* Malcolm Middleton

Joe Horrigan	Ken Jones
John Coyne	Bill Dean
Vince Coyne	Neville Smith
Brian Croft	Joey Kaye
Syd Paisley	Johnny Gee

The Big Flame

Director (BBC, 1969) 'The Wednesday Play', BBC1, 19 February 1969 (85 mins, b/w)

Script: Jim Allen *Producer:* Tony Garnett *Camera:* John McGlashan *Editor:* Roy Watts *Designer:* Geoff Patterson

Danny Fowler	Norman Rossington
Jack Regan	Godfrey Quigley
Peter Conner	Peter Kerrigan
Freddie Grierson	Ken Jones

The Rank and File

Director (BBC, 1971) 'Play for Today', BBC1, 20 May 1971 (75 mins, b/w)

Script: Jim Allen *Producer:* Graeme McDonald *Script editor:* Ann Scott *Camera:* Charles Stewart *Editor:* Roy Watts *Designer:* Roger Andrews

Eddie	Peter Kerrigan
Billy	Bill Dean
Les	Tommy Summers
Joan	Joan Flood
Johnny	Johnny Gee
Mike	Mike Hayden
Bert	Bert King
Jerry	Neville Smith

After a Lifetime
Director (Kestrel Productions, 1971) 'Sunday Night Theatre', ITV, 18 July 1971 (75 mins, colour)
Script: Neville Smith *Producer:* Tony Garnett *Camera:* Chris Menges
Editor: Ray Helm *Designer:* Andrew Drummond *Music:* John Cameron

May	Edie Brooks
Young Billy	Neville Smith
Aloysius	Jimmy Coleman
Uncle John	Peter Kerrigan
Uncle Sid	Bill Dean
Frank	Johnny Gee

A Misfortune
Director (BBC, 1973) 'Full House', BBC2, 13 January 1973 (38 mins, colour)
Adaptation: Ken Loach (based on a short story by Anton Chekhov)
Producer: Melvyn Bragg *Camera:* Chris Menges *Editor:* Roger Waugh
Designer: Martin Johnson
With Lucy Fleming, Ben Kingsley, Peter Eyre

Days of Hope
Director (BBC, 1975)
Script: Jim Allen *Producer:* Tony Garnett *Editor:* Roger Waugh *Designer:* Martin Johnson *Music:* Marc Wilkinson

1916: Joining Up BBC1, 11 September 1975 (95 mins, colour)
Camera: Tony Pierce-Roberts, John Else

Ben Matthews	Paul Copley
Sarah Hargreaves	Pamela Brighton
Philip Hargreaves	Nikolas Simmonds

1921 BBC1, 18 September 1975 (100 mins, colour)
Camera: Tony Pierce-Roberts

Ben Matthews	Paul Copley
Billy Shepherd	Alun Armstrong

1924 BBC1, 25 September 1975 (80 mins, colour)
Camera: John Else

Ben Matthews	Paul Copley
Sarah Hargreaves	Pamela Brighton
Philip Hargreaves	Nikolas Simmonds
Shep	Alun Armstrong

1926: General Strike BBC1, 2 October 1975 (135 mins, colour)
Camera: John Else

Ben Matthews	Paul Copley
Sarah Hargreaves	Pamela Brighton

Philip Hargreaves	Nikolas Simmonds
Ernest Bevin	Melvin Thomas
Ramsay MacDonald	John Young
Stanley Baldwin	Brian Hayes
Churchill	Leo Britt

The Price of Coal
Director (BBC, 1977)
Script: Barry Hines *Producer:* Tony Garnett *Camera:* Brian Tufano *Editor:*
Roger Waugh *Designer:* Martin Collins

Sid Storey	Bobby Knutt
Mr Forbes	Jackie Shinn
Geoff Carter	Duggie Brown
Albert	Stan Richards

Meet the People BBC1, 29 March 1977 (75 mins, colour)
Back to Reality BBC1, 5 April 1977 (95 mins, colour)

The Gamekeeper
Director (ATV Network, 1980) ITV, 16 December 1980 (84 mins, colour)
Script: Barry Hines (based on his novel) *Camera:* Chris Menges, Charles
Stewart *Editor:* Roger James *Designer:* Martin Johnson

Graham Purse	Phil Askham
Mary Purse	Rita May

Auditions
Producer-director (ATV Network, 1979) ITV, 23 December 1980 (52 mins,
b/w)
Camera: Chris Menges *Editor:* Jonathan Morris
With Penni Dunlop, Karen Williams, Janet Cooper

A Question of Leadership
Producer-director (ATV, 1981) ATV ITV region only, 13 August 1981 (52
mins, colour)
Compilers: Ken Loach, Barry Hines *Camera:* Chris Menges, John Davey
Editor: Roger James *Chair of studio discussion:* James Bellini

The Red and the Blue
Director (Central Independent Television, 1982) Channel Four, 1 October
1983 (78 mins, colour)
Producer: Roger James *Camera:* Chris Menges *Editor:* Jonathan Morris

Which Side Are You On?
Producer-director (LWT, 1985) Channel Four, 9 January 1985 (52 mins,
colour)
Camera: Chris Menges, James Dibling *Editor:* Jonathan Morris

End of the Battle . . . Not the End of the War
Guest programme editor (Diverse Production, 1985) 'Diverse Reports', Channel Four, 27 March 1985 (26 mins, colour)

Time To Go
Director (BBC Community Programme Unit, 1989) 'Split Screen', BBC2, 9 May 1989 (13 mins, colour)
Series producer: Gavin Dutton *Camera:* Barry Ackroyd *Editor:* Jonathan Morris

The View from the Woodpile
Producer-director (Central Independent Television, 1988) 'The Eleventh Hour', Channel Four, 12 June 1989 (50 mins, colour)
Camera: Barry Ackroyd *Editors:* Paul Jackson, Mike Burch

The Arthur Legend
Director (Clark Productions, 1991) 'Dispatches', Channel Four, 22 May 1991 (42 mins, colour)
Reporter-producer: Lorraine Heggessey *Camera*: Barry Ackroyd *Editor*: Jonathan Morris

The Flickering Flame
Director (Parallax Pictures-AMIP-Sept ARTE; UK-France, 1996) 'Modern Times', BBC2, 18 December 1996 (50 mins, colour)
Producers: Rebecca O'Brien, Xavier Carniaux *Camera:* Roger Chapman, Barry Ackroyd *Editors:* Tony Pound, Anthony Morris *Music:* George Fenton *Narrator:* Brian Cox

Another City: A Week In the Life of Bath's Football Club
Director (Parallax Pictures, 1998) 'The West Story', HTV West ITV region only, 23 April 1998 (25 mins, colour)
Producer: Rebecca O'Brien *Camera*: Steve Standen *Editor*: Jonathan Morris

Unscreened

Questions of Leadership
Director (Central Independent Television, 1983/1984) (4 × 50 mins/2 × 50 mins, colour) Commissioned by Channel Four, then edited down to two programmes, but never screened
Producer: Roger James *Camera*: James Dibling *Editor*: Jonathan Morris *Interviewer:* Keith Harper

OTHER PRODUCTIONS

In Black and White
Director (Kestrel Films, 1971) Unreleased (50 mins, colour)
Producer: Tony Garnett

Talk About Work
Director (Ronald H. Riley and Associates, 1971) Unreleased (16 mins, colour)
Producer: Michael Barden *Camera:* Chris Menges *Editor:* Alan Price

A Contemporary Case for Common Ownership
Director (Clause IV Campaign Group, 1995) (22 mins, colour)

Socialist Labour Party Election Broadcast
Director (Socialist Labour Party, 1997) BBC1 & BBC2, 26 April 1997 (5 mins, colour)

THEATRE

One Over the Eight
Actor, national tour (Shakespeare Memorial Theatre, Stratford-upon-Avon; Theatre Royal, Brighton; Royal Court Theatre, Liverpool; Streatham Hill Theatre, London; Golders Green Hippodrome, London; and Grand Theatre, Blackpool), January to February 1961, and Duke of York's Theatre, April to June 1961

Arena Theatre Company
Actor, 'Summer Play Festival' at Prince of Wales Theatre, Cardiff, June to July 1961, and Cannon Hill Park, Birmingham, July to August 1961
The Would-be Gentleman, Brer Rabbit, The Matchmaker, Roots, The Grass is Greener

Northampton Repertory Players
Assistant director with Northampton Repertory Theatre at the Theatre Royal and Opera House, Northampton, November 1961 to November 1962
The Importance of Being Earnest
The Bride Comes Back
Cinderella (Also acted one of the 'Ladies, Gentlemen, Dancers and Guests')
Salad Days (twice)
Simple Spymen
The Marquise
Murder at the Vicarage (Directed)
Tons of Money
The Irregular Verb To Love

Billy Liar
The Gazebo (Also acted Druker)
All of a Twist (Also co-devised revue, with Lionel Hamilton, and acted various roles)
Hot and Cold in All Rooms (Directed)
The Amorous Prawn (Also acted Uncle Joe)
Doctor at Sea
Guilty Party (Also acted Stanley Littlefield)
A Passage To India (Also acted Mr Burton-Fletcher)
As Long As They're Happy
The Rehearsal
Murder at Quay Cottage (Directed)

Living Theatre Company
Director, *Candida*, The Living Theatre, Leicester, 1962

Arena Theatre Company
Actor, 'Summer Play Festival' at Cannon Hill Park, Birmingham, June to July 1963
Semi-Detached, The Beaux' Stratagem, The Tulip Tree, Poor Richard

Perdition
Director, banned by the Royal Court Theatre, January 1987, performed at the Edinburgh Festival, August 1987

FILMS AND TELEVISION PROGRAMMES ABOUT KEN LOACH

The Guardian Interview (BFI, 1992) Recorded at the National Film Theatre on 28 July 1992
Talking Pictures: Ken Loach (TVF-BFI, 1993) (Edited version of *The Guardian Interview*) Channel Four, 18 April 1993
The South Bank Show (LWT, 1993) ITV, 3 October 1993
Ken Loach: Face to Face (BBC, 1994) BBC2, 19 September 1994
Loach on Location – Making Land and Freedom (ZED Production, 1995) 'The Late Show', BBC2, 15 May 1995
Citizen Ken Loach (AMIP; France, 1996) 'Cinéma de Notre Temps' French television series
Ken Loach in Nicaragua (Italy, 1996)
Ken and Rosa: The Making of Bread and Roses (Feasible Films, 2001) Channel Four, 27 April 2001
Railing Against It (BBC North, 2001) 'Homeground', BBC2 North region only, 10 May 2001

Appendix 2

AWARDS

Single Drama (Director) Award, Guild of Television Producers and Directors, 1966, 1967

Michael Balcon Award for Outstanding British Contribution to Cinema, BAFTA Awards, 1993

Special Award, *Evening Standard* British Film Awards, 1998

Lifetime Achievement Award, British Independent Film Awards, 1998

Career Golden Lion, Venice Film Festival, 1994

Lifetime Achievement Award, Dinard British Film Festival, 2002

Leopard of Honour, Locarno Film Festival, 2003

Praemium Imperiale Laureate in Theatre/Film, Japan Art Association, 2003

30th Anniversary Prize of the Ecumenical Jury, for his entire body of work, Cannes Film Festival, 2004

Cathy Come Home
Prix Italia for Television Drama (Jeremy Sandford, Ken Loach, Tony Garnett), 1968

Screenwriters' Guild of Great Britain Award (Jeremy Sandford), 1967

Kes
Crystal Globe (Ken Loach), Karlovy Vary International Film Festival, 1970

Best British Screenplay (Barry Hines, Ken Loach, Tony Garnett), Writers' Guild of Great Britain Awards, 1971

Most Promising Newcomer (David Bradley), Society of Film and Television Arts Awards, 1971

Best Supporting Actor (Colin Welland), Society of Film and Television Arts Awards, 1971

Family Life
FIPRESCI Prize, Forum of New Film (Ken Loach), Berlin International Film Festival, 1972

Interfilm Award – Recommendation, Forum of New Cinema (Ken Loach), Berlin International Film Festival, 1972

OCIC Award – Recommendation, Forum of New Film (Ken Loach), Berlin International Film Festival, 1972

Critics Award for Best Foreign Film (Ken Loach), French Syndicate of Cinema Critics, 1974

Audience Award for Best Feature-Length Fiction Film (Ken Loach), Sydney Film Festival, 2003

Black Jack
FIPRESCI Prize, Parallel Section (Ken Loach), Cannes Film Festival, 1979

Looks and Smiles
Prize of the Ecumenical Jury – Special Mention (Ken Loach), Cannes Film Festival, 1981

Young Cinema Award (Ken Loach), Cannes Film Festival, 1981

Which Side Are You On?
Gold Medal, Italian Festival dei Popoli, 1984

OCIC Award (Ken Loach), Berlin International Film Festival, 1985

Hidden Agenda
Jury Prize (Ken Loach), Cannes Film Festival, 1990

Prize of the Ecumenical Jury – Special Mention (Ken Loach), Cannes Film Festival, 1990

Riff-Raff
FIPRESCI Prize (Ken Loach), Cannes Film Festival, 1991

Best Film, European Film Awards (Ken Loach), 1991

Special Prix Italia for Fiction, Prix Italia, 1993

Raining Stones
Jury Prize (Ken Loach), Cannes Film Festival, 1993

Best Film (Ken Loach), *Evening Standard* British Film Awards, 1994

Best Screenplay (Jim Allen), *Evening Standard* British Film Awards, 1994

Critics Award for Best Foreign Film (Ken Loach), French Syndicate of Cinema Critics, 1994

ALFS Award for British Director of the Year (Ken Loach), London Critics Circle Film Awards, 1994

CEC Award for Best Foreign Film, Cinema Writers Awards, Spain, 1994

Ladybird Ladybird

Prize of the Ecumenical Jury (Ken Loach), Berlin International Film Festival, 1994

Silver Berlin Bear for Best Actress (Crissy Rock), Berlin International Film Festival, 1994

Best Actor (Vladimir Vega), Valladolid International Film Festival, 1994

ALFS Award for British Actress of the Year (Crissy Rock), London Critics Circle Film Awards, 1995

Best Foreign Actress (Chrissy Rock), Sant Jordi Awards, 1995

Land and Freedom

FIPRESCI Prize (Ken Loach), Cannes Film Festival, 1995

Prize of the Ecumenical Jury (Ken Loach), Cannes Film Festival, 1995

Best Film (Ken Loach), European Film Awards, 1995

Best Foreign Film (Ken Loach), César Awards, 1996

Critics Award for Best Foreign Film (Ken Loach), French Syndicate of Cinema Critics, 1996

Best New Actress (Rosana Pastor), Goya Awards, 1996

Best Film (Ken Loach), Sant Jordi Awards, 1996

Carla's Song

The President of the Italian Senate's Gold Medal (Ken Loach), Venice Film Festival, 1996

Coral for Best Work of a Non-Latin American Director on a Latin America Subject (Ken Loach), Havana Film Festival, 1996

Best Actor (Robert Carlyle), *Evening Standard* British Film Awards, 1998

ALFS Award for British Actor of the Year (Robert Carlyle), London Critics Circle Film Awards, 1998

The Flickering Flame

Special Mention (Ken Loach), Marseille Festival of Documentary Film, 1997

Prize of the Trade Union IG Medien (Ken Loach), Leipzig DOK Festival, 1997

My Name Is Joe

Best Actor (Peter Mullan), Cannes Film Festival, 1998

Golden Spike (Ken Loach), Valladolid International Film Festival, 1998

Audience Award (Ken Loach), Valladolid International Film Festival, 1998

Best Actor (Peter Mullan), Valladolid International Film Festival, 1998

Best British Independent Film, British Independent Film Awards, 1998

Best British Director of a British Independent Film (Ken Loach), British Independent Film Awards, 1998

Best Original Screenplay by a British Writer of a Produced Independent Film (Paul Laverty), British Independent Film Awards, 1998

ALFS Award for British Newcomer of the Year (Peter Mullan), London Critics Circle Film Awards, 1999

Best Non-American Film (Ken Loach), Bodil Awards, 1999

Audience Award for Best Film (Ken Loach), Portland International Film Festival, 1999

Best Non-American Film (Ken Loach), Robert Festival, 1999

Best British Actor (Peter Mullan), *Empire* Awards, UK, 1999

Bread and Roses

Best Foreign Film, Rio de Janeiro Film Festival, 2000

Phoenix Prize (Ken Loach), Santa Barbara International Film Festival, 2001

Outstanding Supporting Actress in a Motion Picture (Elpidia Carrillo), ALMA Awards, 2002

Best Theatrical Feature Film, Imagen Foundation Awards, 2002

Jury Award for Best Feature Film (Ken Loach), Temecula Valley International Film Festival, 2000

The Navigators

Children and Cinema Award (Ken Loach), Venice Film Festival, 2001

Rota Soundtrack Award (George Fenton), Venice Film Festival, 2001

Best New Writer (Rob Dawber), BAFTA TV Awards, 2002

Sweet Sixteen

Best Screenplay (Paul Laverty), Cannes Film Festival, 2002

FIPRESCI Prize (Ken Loach), European Film Awards, 2002

Golden Spike (Ken Loach), Valladolid International Film Festival, 2002

Best Director of Photography (Barry Ackroyd), Valladolid International Film Festival, 2002

Best British Independent Film, British Independent Film Awards, 2002

Most Promising Newcomer (Martin Compston), British Independent Film Awards, 2002

Best Actor in a Feature Film (Martin Compston), BAFTA Scotland New Talent Awards, 2002

ALFS Award, British Newcomer of the Year (Martin Compston), London Critics Circle Film Awards, 2003

Golden Camera 300 (Barry Ackroyd), Brothers Manaki International Film Festival, 2003

II'09"01 – September II

FIPRESCI Prize for Best Short Film (for the segment directed by Ken Loach), Venice Film Festival, 2002

UNESCO Award (Youssef Chahine, Amos Gitai, Alejandro González Iñárritu, Shohei Imamura, Claude Lelouch, Ken Loach, Samira Makhmalbaf, Mira Nair, Idrissa Ouedraogo, Sean Penn, Danis Tanovic), Venice Film Festival, 2002

Ae Fond Kiss . . .

Prize of the Ecumenical Jury (Ken Loach), Berlin International Film Festival, 2004

Prize of the Guild of German Art House Cinemas (Ken Loach), Berlin International Film Festival, 2004

INDEX